Schooling the Poorer Child

SCHOOLING
the Poorer Child

Elementary Education in Sheffield 1560–1902

MALCOLM MERCER

Sheffield
Academic Press

Copyright © 1996 Sheffield Academic Press

Published by Sheffield Academic Press Ltd
Mansion House
19 Kingfield Road
Sheffield S11 9AS
England

Printed on acid-free paper in Great Britain
by The Cromwell Press
Melksham, Wiltshire

British Library Cataloguing in Publication Data

A catalogue record for this book is available
from the British Library

ISBN 1-85075-534-5

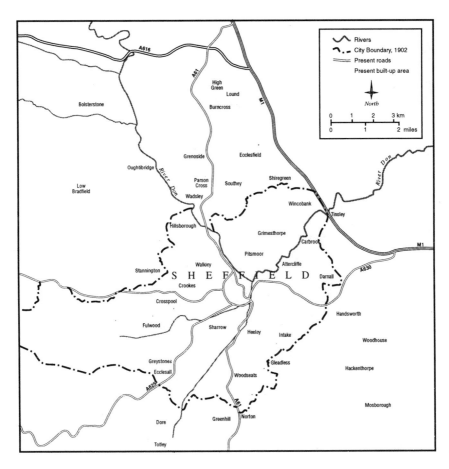

Map of the city of Sheffield, 1902

Contents

Preface

In this study I have set the development of elementary education and the growth of basic literacy within the cultural experiences of the people of Sheffield from 1560 to 1902 in relation to many social, economic, religious and to some extent political factors. I have examined the importance parents placed on setting the child to work and how far the change from voluntary to compulsory schooling impinged on their offspring's lives.

In an attempt to unravel the strands of elementary education I have drawn attention to factors peculiar to this region. The enormous diversity in the advance of formal and informal educational practices has led to some elements being neglected and the existence of others being misconstrued. Consequently, misconceptions have arisen and generalizations have been assimilated without critical inquiry. Primarily an exercise in local history, it is a contribution to the historical understanding of how popular education evolved in a provincial city.

Part One stems from an investigation into the evolution of formal schooling in the Sheffield region from 1480 to 1833 presented as an MA thesis to Sheffield University in 1978. The accessibility of mid-nineteenth-century newspapers and official reports on the lives of children at work and at school facilitated my examination of the years outlined in Part Two.

In Part Three I have concentrated on aspects of schooling beyond the scope of John Bingham's admirable assessment of the Sheffield School Board, though inevitably there is some overlapping. Combining the re-examination of school board minutes, school logbooks and other contemporary sources I have undertaken to provide a broader perspective of the expansion of elementary education in the years following the introduction of compulsory schooling to the creation of the Sheffield Education Committee in 1903.

I am indebted to the Sheffield City Library and Archive Service for their consideration and forbearance over a period of thirty years. In particular my thanks are due to Doug Hindmarch, Senior Local Studies

Librarian for his invaluable assistance in locating most of the illustrations included in the book. I would like to thank the Trustees of the Church Burgesses Educational Foundation for their generous financial support and I am especially grateful for the encouragement and helpful suggestions of Professor John Roach who by his criticism preserved me from significant errors and kindly undertook the tedious task of reading the proofs. To the editor, Andrew Kirk, I wish to express my thanks for his perceptive comments and painstaking correction of my mistakes. Finally I owe an especial debt to my wife Jean who has listened patiently to my monologues over many years on the subject of schooling the poorer child.

Acknowledgments

The author and publishers wish to thank the following for permission to reproduce illlustrations:

Sheffield City Libraries:	1, 2, 3, 6, 8, 10, 11, 12, 14, 15, 16, 17, 18, 19, 20, 22, 23, 24, 27, 28, 29, 31, 32, 33, 35, 36, 37, 38, 39, 40, 41, 42
Sheffield Newspapers Ltd:	5, 21
Mrs P. Harrison, Headteacher, St John's C.E. School:	59
Mr B. Starr & Mrs I. Hill:	25

We are grateful also for the assistance of Graham J. Allsopp, Chief Cartographer, Sheffield University, in creating the introductory map of Sheffield.

List of Tables

List of Illustrations

List of Abbreviations

CEC	Children's Employment Commission
CCE	Committee in Council for Education
HMI	Her/His Majesty's Inspector/ate
NEL	National Education League
PCC	Parochial Church Council
PP	*Parliamentary Papers*
SCA	Sheffield City Archives
SCL	Sheffield City Library
SI	*Sheffield Independent*
SPCK	Society for Promoting Christian Knowledge
SSB	Sheffield School Board
THAS	*Transactions of the Hunter Archaeological Society*

Part I

Evolution and Endowments 1560–1839

Chapter 1

Vocational Training and Godly Learning 1560–1660

> For a great part of the beggary that is among the poor, can be
> imputed to nothing so much as to idleness and the negligence of
> parents, which do not bring up their children either in godly
> learning, honest labour, or some commendable occupation or trade
> whereby when they come of age, they might get their living.
>
> *Homily against Idleness* (1563)

Sheffield today is Britain's fifth largest city with a population of over
half a million. Since it became a city in 1893 it has absorbed the West
Riding parishes of Handsworth and Ecclesfield including its extensive
chapelry of Bradfield, the Derbyshire parish of Norton and several
North Derbyshire villages, hamlets and townships. In this study of
elementary education I have focused on the enlarged city before the
boundary changes of 1974 but even so, the edges are a little blurred.

Sheffield in the sixteenth century was essentially a small market
town with a population of less than a thousand in the urban township.
Most of the more wealthy burgesses lived in the scattered hamlets of the
sprawling parish. Whilst the town was dominated by smiths and cutlers,
the more substantial inhabitants combined their agrarian wealth with
edge tool making, thus providing a dual occupation and a dual
economy.[1]

Stimulated by the rising affluence of the upper half of the nation's
population, the cutlery and edge tool trades, in common with the
building and clothing industries, reaped the harvest. When Elizabeth's
government revived the Act forbidding imports of foreign cutlery, the
Hallamshire cutlers pressed George Talbot, Lord of the Manors of
Sheffield and Hallamshire, to sanction their own constitution and
trading regulations.

The national system of apprenticeship devised in 1563 as the Statute
of Artificers was adapted by the cutlers for their 'Ordinances for the

Mayntenance of the Commonwealth of the Cutler's craft and Cuttelars Occupacion'. What had hitherto been common practice became the rule. Although a minimum of seven years' apprenticeship was imposed, craft apprenticeship in the cutlery trade varied from seven to eleven years and many boys were indentured from the tender age of eight years upwards. Robert Rollinson, son of a prosperous corviser, was apprenticed at the age of eight and a half years in 1624. William Warter, master cutler in 1645, was apprenticed at the age of ten. Not until 1728 did the Cutlers' Company fix twelve years as the minimum age.[2] The Statute effectively favoured the offspring of the middling sort—gentlemen, husbandmen, merchants and skilled craftsmen. The Cutlers' code also restricted entry to the craft so that 'gentlemen and others of living might have some means to place their younger sons in reasonable continuance and calling'.

Being set to work was the common experience of most children and the primary source of education. Informal apprenticeship and the farming out of youngsters had been practised for generations amongst all classes of society. In 1497 a Venetian diplomat at the court of Henry VII observed:

> The want of affection in the English is strongly manifested towards their children, for having kept them at home till they arrive at the age of seven or nine at the utmost, they put them out, both males and females, to hard service in the houses of other people, binding them generally for another seven or nine years, and these are called apprentices, and during that time they perform all the most menial offices and few are born who are exempted from this fate, for everyone however rich he may be, sends away his children into the houses of others, whilst he in return, receives those of strangers into his own.[3]

The argument that the English had little affection for their children is seriously flawed[4] but preparing them for 'some honest occupation' was the good parent's responsibility and girls were no more exempt than boys. Their vocational training was governed by the demands of the household. Domestic service was seen as the perfect preparation for marriage and the art of household management. When John Staniforth of Darnall prepared his daughter to enter service in London he contacted his clerical brother-in-law Stanley Gower, curate of Attercliffe (1630–35) and member of the Westminster Assembly. In 1648 Gower advised him:

> I hope you let hir not lose hir tyme with you especiall hir reading
> and hir wryting; this with a little cookery will render hir acceptable
> in very good places when you think hir fit for the City none shalbe
> more forward to settle hir than we.

> My wife, my corrector, tells me I say not well in putting cookery,
> though my simplicity thought it best, instead of w[ch] you must read
> sewing and starching.[5]

In post-Reformation England, poverty and idleness were regarded as
crippling diseases best treated whilst young. National concern over
social order, vagrancy, and the general condition of the poor led to the
codifying of the Poor Law legislation in 1597 and 1601. Writing in
1600 Sir Thomas Wilson commented:

> They are not suffered to be idle in their cities as they be in other
> parts of Christendom but every child of six or seven years old is
> forced to some art whereby he gaineth his own living and some-
> thing besides to help enrich his parents or his master.[6]

Where children were abandoned, impoverished, or not gainfully
employed, the legislation empowered churchwardens and Overseers of
the Poor to bind them apprentice to households irrespective of class or
occupation. The householder was expected to keep his parish apprentice 'under his rule, government, instruction and correction within his
own home and among his own family'. Whereas craft apprentices
acquired vocational skill, pauper apprentices provided a pool of unpaid
servile labour, bound to little more than 'husbandry and housewifery'.

When the Hallamshire gentry complained that they had no trade to
teach their apprentices and ought to be immune from the legislation
their pleas were rejected. The Justices reiterated that:

> the meaning of ye statute was not for the education of boys in arts
> but for charity to keep ym and relieve ym from turning to roguery
> and idleness, so a man's house was as it were a Hospital in yt case,
> rather than a shop or trade for they might be brought up to
> husbandry, cookery, dayery and the like service in an house.[7]

There were some safeguards against child abuse and neglect, but
there was no injunction on the master to provide either craft skills or
technical instruction. Nevertheless, many boys did pick up skills and
some were fortunate enough to be taught a trade when older, such as
Abraham Abdy, a pauper apprentice at eight and indentured to a cutler
at 13, 'for the better enabling him to get his livelihood hereafter'.

Fortune rarely smiled so sweetly on poor girls, many of whom were condemned to a life of drudgery and despair. Eight-year-old Mary Ragg was 'bound to serve faithfully and obediently...to make things for herself and to act faithfully and honestly' as a servant and apprentice. When nine-year-old Sarah Bower was indentured to William Bullos she was obliged 'to dwell, serve and abide with him until she was twenty one unless she married earlier...to well and faithfully serve according to her power and capacity and abilities and honestly and obediently in all things shall demean herself towards all ye rest of the family'. Her master proved considerate, however, and Sarah was later assigned to a Bolsterstone clothier as a craft apprentice.[8]

The religious and social changes that were to affect education took place in the second half of the sixteenth century. Religious orthodoxy, secured by the Augustinian Canons of Worksop since 1308, was defended in the fifteenth and sixteenth centuries by the noble house of Talbots until the death of Earl Francis in 1560. Succeeded by his son, George, sixth Earl of Shrewsbury, there was a gradual recognition of the Protestant Settlement as the trappings of conservative Catholicism were swept away. Seven days after the funeral of Earl Francis, the *Roman Missal* gave way to the *Book of Common Prayer*, the Scriptures were read in English, Bible reading was encouraged and lay patronage initiated the introduction of preaching pastors.

It is perhaps difficult today to appreciate the impact of a godly preacher on post-Reformation Sheffield but religion penetrated all secular affairs and conformist Calvinism 'supplied a creed to the classes which was to dominate the future'.[9] *The Books of Homilies*, introduced into the Parish Church in 1564, explored a wide spectrum of social issues relevant not only to commercial undertakings but also to domestic and social life including the nurture of children. Insistence on personal responsibility and discipline, the sanctity of work and the sinfulness of poverty and idleness combined to elevate the vocational training of the young.

Calvinist theology, embraced widely in Sheffield in the wake of the induction of Robert Holland as Vicar of Sheffield in 1569, stimulated individualism and self-sufficiency. It also heightened concern for the poor and stressed the need for charity. The early years of the seventeenth century were years of exceptional hardship caused by poor harvests and high prices.[10] Imbued with religious zeal, the principal inhabitants were prompted to survey the extent of deprivation in 1615. Their findings revealed that wealth was distributed very unevenly in the parish. Out of a total population of 2,207 only one hundred families had any surplus and no more than ten had land of their own. Of the 160 householders unable to relieve others, sickness could reduce them to extreme poverty and a third of the population were begging poor. When the Cutlers achieved independence in 1624 they ensured assistance for their more vulnerable members and set aside fines 'for the relief of the poorest sort of the said occupation'.

Four years later it was resolved to erect a workhouse to meet the rising tide of unemployment and vagrancy. Land was leased at West Bar in 1628 and a convenient stock of flax, wool, thread and stuff to set the poor to work was assembled. To contend with the growing number of young paupers, a school of industry for 20 children was set up. The youngsters were instructed in spinning wool and coarse flax, how to knit stockings and the craft of the cobbler.[11] No attempt was made to teach literacy and the school should not be confused with nineteenth-century industrial and workhouse schools but the inculcation of moral and ethical conduct plus elements of religious instruction was inescapable in a Puritan poorhouse. The school was allowed to lapse after the Restoration and the parish officers reverted to apprenticing all the parish poor as soon as they were old enough. Ratepayers were thus relieved of the cost of maintenance as illustrated by Ralph Carr's indenture of 1703:

> and he (Thomas Handley) shall provide for the said apprentice that he be not anyway a charge to the said parish or parishioners of the same; but of and from all charge shall and will serve the said parish and parishioners harmless and indemnified during the said term.[12]

The *Homily against Idleness*, first preached in Sheffield by Richard Haward, Vicar of Sheffield (1559–67) focused on the upbringing of children and the negligence of parents as the root cause of idleness. Alongside its insistence on the social duty of labour it emphasized the significance of 'godly learning'. Straightaway the Church Burgesses located suitable premises for a grammar school. Temporary arrangements were made for seating the scholars in the parish church in 1565, the schoolmaster was elected and in accordance with Elizabeth's Injunctions of 1559, was licensed 'to kepe the school' in 1568.[13]

Incorporated in 1554 by Mary Tudor as a strengthening measure to restore Catholic orthodoxy, the Twelve Capital Burgesses of the Town and Parish of Sheffield, hereafter called the Church Burgesses, were invested with impropriated revenues confiscated in 1548. Charged with maintaining the fabric of the Parish Church of Sheffield, supporting the clergy team of three assistant ministers and applying the surplus to approved secular purposes, they were enabled to establish a school and fund the education of the deserving poor by augmenting the school-master's stipend.

The school at Town Head set in a large house of '3 baies and a coal house all slated within a croft, garden, and orchard, and surrounding court occupying three roods' attracted sons of the industrious sort and the middling classes—yeomen, husbandmen, substantial tradesmen and the more prosperous edge tool makers—and a few of the professional classes—clergy, scriveners and apothecaries. The aim of the school was to prepare for university entrance by concentrating on a classical curriculum of Latin and Greek and 'all that profits to the knowledge of Christ and godlynesse'. Church worship was obligatory and loose benches were provided for the boys in the parish church from the outset.

Admission to the Grammar School was normally between the ages of seven and eight. As it was desirable that the boys could read English and write legibly, ushers were employed to teach the elementary stages and give special attention to the poor scholars. Residual Catholicism in the Church Burgesses ensured a succession of masters and assistants who were at least conservative and many retained their pre-Reformation title until Sir William Sampson, usher and assistant minister, was accused of recusancy in 1604 together with five other Sheffield schoolmasters.[14]

At the turn of the seventeenth century the school was re-established as 'The Free Grammar School of James, King of England within the town of Sheffield in the County of York'. The change of status to a free grammar school was due entirely to the bequest of a wealthy native of the town, Thomas Smith, who in 1604 bequeathed thirty pounds annually for the 'finding of two sufficient and learned men to teache and bring up the young children there in godlinesse and learning'. Instruments and Articles of Management were drawn up and agreed by a newly elected body of school governors who demanded religious conformity from both staff and scholars.

> No Schoolmaster or Usher shall be chosen and being chosen shall not continue in his place who shall not ffrequent and usually repair to divine service preaching and sacraments and shall not be a favourer of the truth and of ye religion by law established and that

no scholler shall be admitted or continued in the said school who
shall obstinately refuse to come to divine service sacraments preach-
ings and catechizing.[15]

The chairmanship of governors rotated annually but the superintendence of the school was the responsibility of the *ex officio* Vicar of
Sheffield. He was to examine the pupils twice yearly and 'give testimony to the rest of the Governors of their fitting in learning or back-
wardness and to deliver his opinion whether the fault be in the maister
or schollers and whether of negligence of the one or absence of the
other or want of dexterity in the maister or capacity of the schollers'.

The legal costs of re-founding the town Grammar School were met
by the whole parish. A rate was levied on all 473 householders
according to their ability to pay. Sums ranged from 2d to 40 shillings.
When the school needed rebuilding in 1645–48 the capital expenditure
was the governors' responsibility. As their income was insufficient to
meet the cost of rebuilding on the same site, it was necessary to raise a
loan and appeal for gifts. The stone was quarried in Crookesmoor and
the partly demolished Sheffield Castle was also plundered.

Admissions fluctuated but rarely numbered more than fifty. Yet
throughout the seventeenth century at least one boy from the Grammar
School was admitted each year to the Universities of Oxford or
Cambridge.[16] Pupils were largely drawn from the neighbourhood and
those living within the parish were taught gratis. Boarding accommodation for about eight boys was provided by the master in the house
adjoining the school. For those who lived beyond daily walking
distance it meant lodging with kinsfolk or friends. School days were
long. The morning session extended from 7.0 a.m. to 11.0 a.m. and
the afternoons were equally drawn out, 1.0 p.m. to 5.0 p.m. The
'narrow, arid, linguistic grind' was alleviated only by holy days and 'no
more than twelve play days in the year on any account whatsoever'.

Shortly after the founding of Sheffield Grammar School, the
Ecclesfield Feoffees established a parish school (1573) in the village.
The seventeenth century witnessed the opening of more parish schools.
Some foundations were due entirely to local initiative such as Low
Bradfield (1604), Parson Cross (c. 1630), Attercliffe (1658) and Sharrow
Moor (1668). Elsewhere, private philanthropy ensured elementary
schooling was available. By his will, Ralph Ellis provided for the main-
tenance of a schoolmaster at Bolsterstone in 1622. Richard Spoone
endowed the school at Stannington in 1652 and two years later

Figure 1a. Two seventeenth-century parish schools. Norton School in School Lane where Sir Francis Chantrey attended as a boy was provided by private philanthropy in 1654.

Figure 1b. Sharrow Moor School, Bagshot Street was erected by public subscription in 1668 and extended in 1769.

Leonard Gill created a school in the neighbouring parish of Norton.[17] Towards the south-east of the town Joseph Stones endowed Mosborough School in 1680 and John Newbould assigned funds for the education of poor boys in Hackenthorpe (1699).

The existence of this network of parish (petty) schools in the Sheffield region by the end of the seventeenth century demonstrates clearly the need, not only for godly learning but also for basic literacy. It points to thriving communities of rural metal workers in the outlying hamlets and villages who could afford school fees and were able to forgo their children's labour. Where schools were endowed the financial provision was almost entirely for 'the care and relief of the poorer sort'.

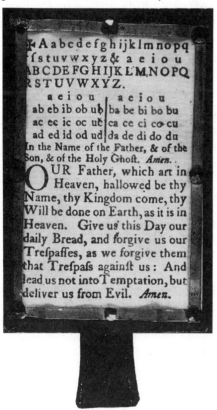

The teaching of reading and spelling was the essential task of these parish schools, sometimes called ABC schools, for the ABC primers and catechisms were normally the first books to be mastered. Children were usually taught their letters from the hornbook (reading sheets mounted on a wooden tablet and covered by a translucent covering of horn). They were made to follow the 'Christ cross code' backwards and forwards until all the letters were thoroughly committed to memory. Groups of syllables were gradually introduced before the primer was tackled. When the child's vocabulary was sufficiently extended, a start was made on the creation stories of Genesis. Learning the catechism by rote ran parallel to basic reading instruction. Poorer children would leave school at this stage to start work. Others would learn to write and count prior

Figure 2. A typical hornbook (actual size). Hornbooks were in common usage until the turn of the nineteenth century. The alphabet preceded by the sign of the cross + was commonly known as the 'Christ cross (criss cross) row.

to apprenticeship or as a preparation for grammar school entrance.

The irregular nature of schooling during this period is well summed up by John Shaw of Bradfield, born 1608. In his journal he wrote, 'through the great want of good schoolmasters in that country at those times I was tossed from one school to another without that benefit which (otherwise) I might have obtained'.[18] He was eventually admitted to Christ's College, Cambridge, and studied alongside John Milton. A contemporary of John Shaw, William, son of Ulysses Fox of Fulwood, was sent to Bradfield for part of his schooling. Over a period of seven years he was taught by Roger Atty, John Bateson and Matthew Booth before entering Sheffield Grammar School for a final year under Thomas Rawson. Fox was admitted to Sidney Sussex College, Cambridge in 1632 at the age of 18.

Where children of 'the poorer sort' were given a taste of school they were inevitably withdrawn, unless exceptional, before they could read 'any whit well'. Charles Hoole, the distinguished Master of Rotherham Grammar School (1634–37) claimed they were 'permitted to run wilding up and down without any control adventuring to commit all manner of lewdness'.[19] Schooling for the poorest in Sheffield's inner township, however, was altogether beyond their experience. The incentive to set the child to work was far more vital than godly learning.

Notes

1.   D. Postles, 'An Early Modern Town: Sheffield in the Sixteenth Century', *Transactions of the Hunter Archaeological Society* 12 (1983), pp. 61-67.

2.   R.E. Leader, *History of the Company of Cutlers in Hallamshire* 1 (1905), p. 46.

3.   Quoted in P. Hughes-Hallett (ed.), *Childhood* (1988), p. 384.

4.   Hughes-Hallett, *Childhood*, pp. 41-51, 287-304. See also R.A. Houlbrook, *The English Family 1450–1700* (1984), and L. Pollock, *A Lasting Relationship: Parents and Children over Three Centuries* (1987).

5.   J. Hunter, *Hallamshire: The History and Topography of the Parish of Sheffield* (ed. A. Gatty, 1869), p. 412, n. 2.

6.   Quoted in A. Hughes, *Seventeenth Century England: A Changing Culture. I. Primary Sources* (1980), p. 3.

7.   Leader, *History*, pp. 76 and 57 n.

8.   Leader, *History*, p. 47. See also V.M. Mercer, 'The Contrasting Patterns of School Provision in Three South Yorkshire Parishes—Ecclesfield, Rotherham and Sheffield 1480–1833' (unpublished MA thesis, Sheffield University 1978); Parish Apprentices, Tibbetts Collection TC 434, 1-13, SCA.

9. R.H. Tawney, *Religion and the Rise of Capitalism* (1926, 1938 edn), p. 103.

10. C. Hill, *Reformation to Industrial Revolution* (1967, 1969 edn), p. 84.

11. J.D. Leader, *Records of the Burgery of Sheffield* (1897), pp. 121f.

12. Parish Apprenticeship Indenturies, Brightside Bierlow, CA1-5 (1703), SCA.

13. Church Burgess Accounts 1553–1573. CB 159, 160, SCA; Hunter, *Hallamshire*, p. 247.

14. A.C.F. Beales, *Education under Penalty* (1962), p. 197 and n.

15. Orders and Articles Agreed upon by Sheffield Grammar School Governors *c.* 1610, SCA.

16. G.C. Moore Smith, 'Sheffield Grammar School', *Transactions of the Hunter Archaeological Society*, 4 (1937), pp. 145f.

17. See Mercer, 'School Provision', pp. 83f.

18. *Surtees Society*, 'Yorkshire Diaries: Memoirs of John Shaw', 65, p. 123.

19. C. Hoole, *A New Discovery of the Old Art of Teaching School* (1660, 1913 edn), p. 25.

Chapter 2

Educational Expansion 1660–1780

> Going to school in comparison to working is idleness, and the
> longer boys continue in this easy sort of life, the more unfit they
> will be when grown up for downright labour, both as to strength
> and inclination.
>
> Bernard Mandeville, *Essay on Charity and Charity Schools* (1724)

At the turn of the eighteenth century the industrious sort in Sheffield
were still motivated by residual Calvinism but its theology and discipline had almost lost its grip. The relaxation of repressive Tory legislation targeted at Nonconformity in the wake of the Stuart Restoration
allowed sectarian divisions to become permanent. Religious toleration
was cemented by the economic necessity of co-operation. Relieved of
the depressing effects of the Hearth Tax, the Hallamshire cutlers
concentrated on diversification and the commercial complexities
demanded by their allied crafts. Sheffield had entered a period of social,
political and religious stability that enabled it to emerge as a bustling
energetic town. Considered populous and large by contemporary
observers, they noted its considerable expansion with 'an abundance of
new erections upon new foundations'.[1] In 1672 rural households in the
parish still outnumbered those in the central township. Sixty years later
the urban population had grown from an estimated 2,300 to 10,121—
more than double the rural inhabitants.

Throughout the whole period craft apprenticeships remained an
essential part of technical and vocational training. Apprentices no
longer came from the middle social groups, however, and the Cutlers
recognized the need to supplement their training by furthering their
education. In 1697 a 'release' clause was added to many indentures and
henceforward it became common for apprentices to be released in
order to attend writing schools.[2]

Joshua Stork, an Ecclesfield cobbler's son, was permitted to go home
for a month in the summer time of his first two years' apprenticeship

'to learn to write'. In 1698 Malcolm Stacy agreed that his apprentice should have one month yearly to learn at the writing school. John Dale was released from two months of his first year in 1700. When Jacob Roberts, son of Samuel Roberts of Stubbin House (Birley Edge), was apprenticed to William Warburton of Neepsend for $9^1/_4$ years he was allowed 'one months time of the first two years to go to the writing school—a month each year—and in the third and fourth year a fortnight in each year'. In contrast, Hugh Fenton and Thomas Broadhead undertook to teach their apprentices to read and write themselves.

Stimulated by this pressure for writing schools, scrivenors, surveyors and private schoolmasters opened their homes or adapted rented accommodation to satisfy the demand. The proliferation of writing masters for older pupils and adults is impossible to quantify but their contribution to basic literacy should not be underestimated.

The second significant contribution to the growth of elementary education at this time was the religious promotion of charity schools. An upsurge in devotional activity combined with an increasingly nationwide concern for the enforcement of law and order, moral reformation, and the general profligacy of the age generated many religious societies. The evolution of the Society for Promoting Christian Knowledge (SPCK) was to have a noticeable impact on Sheffield and its neighbours. In 1699 the Society circularized its clergy correspondents.

> The visible decay of religion in this Kingdom with the monstrous increase of Deism, profaneness and vice, has excited the Zeal of several persons of the best character in the cities of London and Westminster and other parts of the nation, to associate themselves in order to consult together how to put a stop to so fatal an inundation.[3]

Godly learning was seen to be the antidote to 'the barborous ignorance observable among the common people, especially those of the poorer sort'. The remedy prescribed was to encourage generous and well-disposed persons to contribute towards the erection of subscription schools;

> for the instrucion of such poor children in Reading, Writing, and in the Catechism whose parents are not able to afford them the ordinary means of Education; and as they look upon this to be the most effectual method to train up the poorer sort in sobriety and ye knowledge of Christian principles, so they assure themselves that the

good effects which may be wrought thereby will prove a powerfull argument to engage others in better circumstances to make so necessary a provision for their children.[4]

SPCK's aim was a distinctly practical one—to disseminate proposals for financing schools and libraries and to encourage missionary activity at home and abroad. In 1705, Nathan Drake, Vicar of Sheffield (1695–1713), asked the parish clerk, William Ellis, to make enquiries. SPCK responded by sending 50 copies of the Dean of Lincoln's sermon preached at the first annual charity school assembly in St Andrew's, Holborn, in 1704; 50 sheet accounts of the Society's progress, and a digest of the charity schools established. In his sermon Richard Willis summarized a three-fold plan for the Christian nurture of the urban poor.

> First, and especially, to have the children instructed in the principles of the Christian Religion as it is professed in the Church of England.
> Second, to instruct them in such other things which may qualify them for Honest Employment.
> Third, actually to place them out to some trade or other way of getting a living as they shall be enabled to do it by charitable contributions.[5]

Copies of the complete sermon and SPCK's report were distributed widely within the parish and neighbourhood. By mid-December 1705, Ellis was able to confirm that Vicar Drake had preached a charity sermon, £50 was subscribed and more was anticipated.[6] The subscription principle was welcomed by both Anglicans and Dissenters. A temporary school was located in the Earl of Shrewsbury's Hospital. Galleries were erected in the Parish Church specifically for the pupils, and plans were formulated for the erection of a purpose-built Charity School at the north-eastern corner of the churchyard. Drake, his curate at Ecclesall, Robert Turie, and William Ellis the parish clerk were the most active in canvassing the project which attracted substantial donations from the Duke of Norfolk, the attorney Robert Banks, George Ellis of Brampton and Thomas Watson Wentworth, heir of the first Earl of Strafford. The school was opened in 1710 at a cost of £275.[7]

The school was designed to accommodate orphans, the fatherless and destitute. Initially 12 boys were boarded, clothed and schooled under the direction of schoolmaster James Creswick (1706–44). The

Figure 3a. The Boys' Charity School in East Parade opened in 1710 and was rebuilt in 1825–26.

Schooling the Poorer Child

A VIEW

Of the Children's present State of Improvement,

Taken March 10, 1811.

NAMES.	Baptised.	Admitted.	Can Read. Alphabet	Guide	Testament	Bible	Dictionary	Can Read. Wrote. Slate	Paper	Re. Catechism	Accompts.
1 William Watts	April 1798	Aug. 5, 1806									Subtraction. Comp.
40 Thomas Turnediff.	April 29, 1798	Sept. 23, 1803									Subtraction.
23 John Fowler	May 15, 1798	Jan. 20, 1803									Division.
33 David Pratt	May 21, 1798	Jan. 8, 1806									Comp. Division
15 George Hooper	July 10, 1798	Dec. 23, 1806									Reduction.
54 Samuel Broadhead	July 22, 1798	Nov 17, 1807									Division.
43 John Hall	Sept. 5, 1798	June 14, 1808									
11 John Ward	Sept. 9, 1798	June 14, 1808									
30 Robert Cooper	Nov. 4, 1798	July 14, 1807									
35 George Staniforth	Jan 21, 1799	June 12, 1810									Comp. Division
16 William Brooks	Feb. 10, 1799	Oct. 2, 1806									
29 George Parker	Feb. 17, 1799	June 20, 1809									
32 John Smith	May 5, 1799	Nov. 30, 1808									Subtraction.
30 John Hurst	May 5, 1799	May 26, 1807									
34 William Lovett	June 23, 1799	July 1806									Division.
33 Benjamin Holmes	June 23, 1799	April 1, 1807									Division.
6 William Mellor	Aug. 16, 1799	July 9, 1810									
1 James Saxton	Aug. 18, 1799	Sept. 23, 1807									
45 John Corbidge	Aug. 25, 1799	May 26, 1807									
23 John Jackson	Oct. 27, 1799	Oct. 16, 1807									
2 George Heathcoat	Dec. 23, 1799	Dec. 6, 1808									
17 John Jennings	Nov. 10, 1799	May 2, 1811									
12 James White	Dec. 29, 1799	Nov. 2, 1809									
7 Charles Downes	Jan. 11, 1800	Nov. 2, 1809									
32 John Nelson	Feb. 2, 1800	Sept. 25, 1807									
19 Samuel Shirt	Mar. 1, 1800	Jan. 1, 1811									
11 Abraham Hardy	Mar. 23, 1800	Jan. 22, 1810									

17

NAMES.	Baptised.	Admitted.	Can Read. Alphabet	Guide	Testament	Bible	Dictionary	Wrote. Slate	Paper	Re. Catechism	Accompts.
29 John Torr	Mar. 30, 1800	Nov. 30, 1807									
5 Thomas Whiteley	Mar. 31, 1800	Oct. 11, 1803									
20 Jonas Gillatt	Mar. 31, 1800	Nov. 12, 1805									
39 William Shaw	April 13, 1800	Dec. 29, 1807									
47 John Bownes	April 15, 1810	Aug. 30, 1808									
43 John Greaves	April 20, 1800	Dec. 20, 1809									
4 George Sellors	May 12, 1800	Jan. 24, 1805									
9 James Walker	May 23, 1800	Mar. 17, 1810									
49 Thomas Crofts	June 3, 1800	Oct. 11, 1808									
18 John Sheldon	July 13, 1800	May 20, 1808									
48 W. Cartledge	Aug. 29, 1800	Mar. 28, 1809									
27 John Wright	Oct. 12, 1800	April 12, 1808									
44 William Ward	Oct. 26, 1800	Mar. 12, 1808									
37 John Brownell	Nov. 30, 1800	Mar. 17, 1809									
21 William Batersby	Dec. 23, 1800	Aug. 26, 1809									
24 Thomas Bolsover	Dec. 23, 1800	Aug. 26, 1810									
22 Horatio Nelson	Feb. 6, 1801	Mar. 12, 1810									
25 Benjamin White	Feb. 22, 1801	Jan. 15, 1810									
3 Samuel Smith	Mar. 27, 1801	Jan. 30, 1810									
31 John Goodlad	April 5, 1801	Nov. 9, 1809									
46 William Powell	April 5, 1801	June 15, 1809									
13 Alfred Webster	Sept. 27, 1801	Feb. 14, 1811									
11 George Carter	Nov. 30, 1801	Feb. 7, 1811									
10 William Stanford	Jan. 10, 1802	Feb. 14, 1811									
36 Isaac Nelson	May 9, 1802	Dec. 20, 1810									
35 John Rodwell	Dec. 15, 1802	Aug. 28, 1810									
51 John Aspenwell	Dec. 26, 1802	Dec. 20, 1810									

Children upon the late Mr. Hanbey's Establishment.

NAMES.	Baptised.	Admitted.									
60 William Pickering	Aug. 26, 1798	June 29, 1806									Mensuration.
59 William Parkin	Feb. 16, 1801	Jan. 17, 1809									
56 William Middleton	Aug. 7, 1801	Jan. 15, 1810									
58 James Hall	Nov. 28, 1801	Nov. 25, 1809									
55 Francis Ward	Oct. 31, 1802	April 1810									
57 Charles Turner	Oct. 1803	Mar. 12, 1811									

N. B. *b* signifies "born" inserted in such cases only where the date of baptism cannot be ascertained from the Register.

Figure 3b. Achievement records of the boys were published in the annual reports from 1789 onwards.

number of day scholars fluctuated but rarely exceeded 25. The curriculum of reading, spelling, writing and accounts was that considered appropriate to their condition. Religious and moral instruction was moulded to their social subordination reinforced by the prayers they recited. Their blue coat uniform constantly reminded them of their low estate as charity scholars and the duty and respect owed to their betters. 'Confined to the poor and maintained by the relatively rich' is how Joan Simon defined such foundations 'designed to rescue from idleness and irreligion the unemployed poor aged from seven to twelve and set them on a path to a useful working life'.[8] The importance of the Charity School lies in the fact that it was the only institution providing full-time education for Sheffield's urban poor in the first quarter of the eighteenth century.

As a focus for charitable subscriptions, supporting the school became fashionable. Merchants, tradesmen, and cutlers, the gentry and their ladies, Dissenters and Anglicans subscribed annually. Additional income was generated from charity sermons, the town trustees, legacies and profits from life insurance policies, school lettings for dancing and card-playing, and—the most imaginative—the sale of nitrous earth from the closets to gunpowder makers.

The outpouring of private philanthropy for education stemming from SPCK's initiative stimulated a fresh spate of educational charity in the Sheffield region. The Grammar School was an immediate beneficiary. By his will in 1709 James Hill, Usher (1655–98), gave his estate in Kimberworth for the benefit of the schoolmaster.[9] The receipt of his gift coincided with the erection of a house for the recently appointed Revd William Humpton who was expected to concentrate solely on the school and not augment his stipend by surplice duties except 'on Sundays and on extraordinary occasions'.

Six years later William Birley, a native of Sheffield and a London merchant in the Sheffield trade, left £900 and his Neepsend estate for the benefit of the poor of the town. A third of the investment income was apportioned 'for the encouragement of writing and arithmetic to be taught at the free school or such proper place by a fit person and the said income to be allowed him for it'. In common with many of his generation he was critical of the classical bias of the Grammar School and conscious of the need to extend the curriculum in accordance with the demands of commerce and industry.[10]

The trustees resolved to lease the schoolhouse adjacent to the Grammar School and employ a master competent to introduce more 'useful' non-classical studies. The impact of this Free Writing School was considerably to strengthen the appeal of the Grammar School when similar establishments were declining. On average, 60 boys were admitted, 40 of whom were nominated as free scholars and taught writing and arithmetic. Fees were required for 'extra' subjects and for pupils not on the charity list.

One master of merit was the Sheffield schoolmaster and antiquarian, Ralph Gosling (1732–55), who surveyed the town between 1732 and 1736. A successor, John Eadon (1760–1810), advertised his ability 'to teach writing in all its usual hands, arithmetic in all its branches, book-keeping and the mathematics'. In 1764 Edward Goodwin reported that Eadon was on a salary of £16 per annum plus a house and that the 60 boys were 'taught writing and accompts free'. Eadon published a practical manual, *The Arithmetician's Guide*, in 1766 and in the 1790s he prepared a four-volume tome on mathematics though only the first volume was printed. Although the school was regarded as a preparatory stage to the Grammar School, the inclusion of mathematics was recognized as a fundamental component of an education in a town where technical progress and economic expansion was vital.

Robert Turie's educational legacy owed much to SPCK guidelines for rural districts where residential charity schools were beyond their means. The Scotsman, Revd Robert Turie, Curate of Ecclesall and Assistant Minister in Sheffield (1695–1720), co-operated closely with his friend, Vicar Nathan Drake, and acted as consultant and chaplain to the Cutlers' Company. Inspired by the Scottish parochial school system, Turie became an enthusiast for the catechetical schools promoted by SPCK. Prior to his death in 1720 he put £80 into the hands of William Steer, Vicar of Ecclesfield, to be invested for the schools at Parson Cross and Shiregreen because 'they had nothing for encouraging a master to stay with em'. In each school the trustees were to nominate six poor children to be taught 'to read English and write' and Turie directed that they should be 'taught the Church Catechism and particularly cautioned against lying, swearing, and breaking the Sabbath'.[11]

In like manner Turie divided £80 between the Ecclesall School at Sharrow Moor[12] and the Brightside School at Grimesthorpe. As no body of trustees was elected in Ecclesall the endowment was vested in parish stock and subsequently became the responsibility of the Overseers of the Poor. Turie handed the gift to Thomas Handley of Hall Carr for the Brightside School. Handley, a Church Burgess with

Presbyterian sympathies, neglected his responsibilities and the Curate of Attercliffe, Benjamin Ferrand, complained to the Archdeacon in 1723.

> Attercliffe Chapelry: Thomas Handley of Hall Carr Parish of Sheffield one of the trustees of the school in Brightside Byerley for refusing to act in conjunction with the other trustees and not accompting for the endowment of the said school nor taking care to provide a sufficient master.[13]

Eventually the trust was managed 'agreeably' but in 1753 the endowment was applied to the erection of the Brightside workhouse. A memorial tablet recited that the income should be paid to the schoolmaster 'for teaching and instructing six poor children either boys or girls of the said township to read till they should have been taught and perfected to read the Bible and instructed in the Church Catechism and should have learnt the same by heart'.

Sheffield Charity School benefited from Turie's will in the shape of profits from life insurance policies taken out on himself and his wife and the lives of Nathan Drake and his wife. Turie added £10 to the endowments on Fulwood School established by the Dissenter, John Fox of Fulwood Hall (1714). He also endowed schools over the Derbyshire border in Dore, Bamford, Derwent, Stony Middleton, Edale and Killamarsh plus the Yorkshire villages of Wales and Riccall.[14] In 1729 Thomas Marshall added to the parish schools in Ecclesall by endowing the one at Broad Oak Green.

Whereas Robert Turie ensured the continuation of many parochial schools created by local initiative, William Ronksley's contribution stimulated new school building. Son

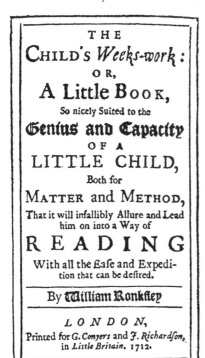

THE

CHILD's *Weeks-work :*

OR,

A Little Book,

So nicely Suited to the

Genius and Capacity

OF A

LITTLE CHILD,

Both for

MATTER and METHOD,

That it will infallibly Allure and Lead him on into a Way of

READING

With all the Ease and Expedition that can be desired.

By William Ronksley

LONDON,

Printed for G. Conyers and J. Richardson, in Little Britain. 1712.

Figure 4. The title page of William Ronksley's *The Child's Weeks-work* published in 1712.

of George and Ellen Ronksley of Fulwood, born in 1650, he was educated at Sheffield Grammar School, matriculated at Magdalene College, Cambridge, but did not graduate. He set himself up as a conformist schoolmaster in Bakewell and concentrated on writing grammar text books in English and Latin. In 1683 he accepted the invitation to become secretary to Francis Jessop FRS at Broomhall. There he met Jessop's scientific friends and was no doubt involved in their controversies over rational religion. On the death of his patron Ronksley became tutor to one of Jessop's relatives. In 1712 he published his most notable composition, *The Child's Weeks-work*, arguably the first graded English reader for children and used widely throughout the country and the American colonies. To Ronksley, reading was an experience to be enjoyed and in contrast to the Puritan authors of his day, Bunyan, Janeway and Isaac Watts, there was a complete absence of religious fervour in his writing.[15]

Ronksley's concern was to ease the grind in learning to read but not to deny the vice of idleness and mischief. Amongst the precepts he devised he included the following school rules:

> At no time talk or quarrel in the school, but be quiet, peaceable and silent, much less mayest thou deceive thyself by trifling thy time away in play.

> Bawl not aloud in making complaints; A boys tongue should never be heard in school but in answering a question and repeating his lesson.

> Divulge not to any person whatsoever elsewhere anything that hath passed in school, either spoken or done.

Evidence of Ronksley's ambivalent attitude towards religion is revealed in the distribution of his estate on his death in 1724. His major benefaction was for the erection of a Dissenting chapel in Fulwood. Coupled with that he spurred the householders of his native village to erect a schoolhouse and left sufficient for four children of the poorer sort to be educated free. Fulwood School in that 'wild and populous country' opened its doors in 1730. John Dossie, Vicar of Sheffield, William Humpton, curate of Ecclesall, and Ronksley's nephew Humphrey Wardle applied for a Bishop's Licence for Thomas Hague and certified him to be 'a man of good life and conversation conformable to the Doctrine and Discipline of the Church of England as by law established'.[16]

Ronksley supplemented the endowments at Stannington and

Figure 5. Fulwood Endowed School, School Green Lane, was built by the inhabitants of Fulwood in 1730, extended in 1793 and closed in 1875.

Sheffield Charity School and indicated that the largest portion of his bequest for education should facilitate the purchase of a school in Crookes where there was neither church nor school. His lifelong friend Judge William Jessop and his heirs were nominated as executors with the power of admitting and displacing the schoolmaster and the 12 poor scholars on the foundation. Towards the end of the century the school attracted further endowments and a new school was built by public subscription in 1791.

Schooling for the poorest children in the town's urban centre was confined to the Charity School until the Hollis Charity School was established in 1726.[17] Born in Rotherham and apprenticed in Sheffield, Thomas Hollis prospered as a London merchant and was 'numbered amongst the most prominent of Nonconformist laymen'.[18] Hollis and his family were instrumental in founding the Dissenters' meeting houses in Sheffield and Rotherham, almshouses in Sheffield and charity schools in both towns. When the Dissenters vacated New Hall in Mill Sands, for their newly built Upper Chapel, Hollis converted New Hall to a hospital for the elderly in 1703 and by his will created a school in the same premises.

> To a schoolmaster and schoolmistress for teaching fifty poor artificers
> and tradesmen's children, boys and girls to read knit and sew
> £16.00 per annum.
>
> To a master to teach them to write and find the paper, pens and ink.
> £5.00 per annum.

Educational endowments interwoven with hospital charities were not uncommon but the Hollis Charity was unique in South Yorkshire. The management of the trust was divided between Nonconformist nominees in Sheffield and the Hollis family in London. Children were admitted between the ages of five and six years and were allowed to remain in the reading school for a maximum of three years. The writing master was employed only during the summer months. The school rarely averaged more than 45 children, 60 per cent of whom entered the writing classes. Prayers were an integral part of the school day but the Hollis passion for civil and religious liberty forbade any catechism or religious formulary. Not until the school and hospital were rebuilt in 1776 were salaries upgraded to permit writing throughout the year and 'some arithmetic taught'.

Unlike the subscription schools promoted by SPCK and established in a climate of non-sectarian co-operation, the Hollis School depended solely on trust income. Isaac Watts, the eminent Dissenter who lived with the Hollis family between 1702 and 1710, was prompted to encourage the creation of charity schools on this model in his essay, *Towards the Encouragement of Charity Schools Particularly Those Supported by Protestant Dissenters* (1728), because they had found

> that the children were brought up in too many of these schools (SPCK sponsored) in principles of disaffection to the present government in bigoted zeal for the word Church, and with a violent enmity and malicious spirit of persecution, against all whom they were taught to call Presbyterians though from many of their hands they received their bread and clothing.[19]

Whilst the school promoted by Thomas Hollis was the only charity school totally independent of SPCK influence, it emanated from the same religious source. The intrinsic importance of SPCK in the development of elementary education lies in its stimulation of the subscription method for financing schools and inspiring the endeavours of those anxious to benefit the education of the poorest children.

In the absence of 'staunch Jacobites and furious high Churchmen' Sheffield settled for a predominantly Whig complexion and accepted the Hanoverian Succession. The preponderance of Christian moderates ensured sectarian differences were not inflamed. As a consequence, open hostility to educating the poorer sort as politically subversive did not surface on the streets. Nor was there much support for Mandeville's contention that:

> Charity schools and everything else that promotes idleness and keeps the poor from working are more accessory to the growth of villainy than the want of reading and writing or even the grossest ignorance or stupidity.[20]

The reality was that the increased provision was secured by the industrious sort for the deserving poor. The greater proportion of the urban poor still found little time to spare for schooling.

Educational expansion was not confined to the parish of Sheffield. Throughout the neighbourhood, village and parish schools were established, endowed and maintained. Most influential was William Steer, Vicar of Ecclesfield (1708–45). Son of a Darnall yeoman, Steer formed a close liaison with Drake and Turie in Sheffield, and his marriage to Ann Banks, sister of the Sheffield attorney and daughter of SPCK correspondent Revd Robert Banks of Hull, kept him in contact with educational development.

Steer's first priority was to upgrade the Ecclesfield Free School. He contrived to lift the status of the foundation from a petty school by encouraging his curates to teach English and Latin. He furthered the erection of Lound (1716) and Grenoside schools (1735) and superintended the schools at Parson Cross (c. 1630), Shiregreen (1706) and Wadsley (pre-1709). In addition, the schools at Bradfield, Stannington and Bolsterstone attracted further endowments. In the pottery making village of Midhope, on the fringe of Bradfield Chapelry, a school opened in 1732.

Maintenance of these endowed parish schools was a charge upon the parish rate. In Sheffield the parish or township vestry accepted a general responsibility for structural repairs, hiring and firing of schoolmasters and the nomination of poor scholars. In Ecclesfield the parish rate was supplemented by a portion of the land tax and occasional contributions from the Feoffees.[21]

School building and furnishing costs were relatively small at the turn of the eighteenth century but rose steadily. In 1706 the cost of erecting Shiregreen School was £11 6s 10d, whereas Holmesfield School over the Derbyshire border cost £18 6s 8d in 1725. The freeholders of Totley were unable to raise sufficient money for a school in 1753. When the Free School in Ecclesfield required rebuilding in 1763, £57 4s 8d was raised. Towards the end of the period building costs spiralled. Attercliffe township had to raise £197 1s 4d in 1779 and Crookes Endowed School cost £264 in 1791. Individual subscriptions varied enormously from the labourer's pence to the gentleman's guinea. When rebuilding Ecclesfield School, two guineas was the largest individual contribution. Fifteen years later Attercliffe township school attracted donations of five guineas.

By 1730 much of the enthusiasm engendered by SPCK's initiative was spent. This expanding network of schools did, however, provide security of tenure for many schoolmasters, enable a rising number of poor children to receive a free basic education, and afforded a nucleus around which fee paying pupils accumulated.

Private Schools

The 'ordinary means of education' available in the urban township was provided by private enterprise. Private venture schools offered a wide range of instruction from the indigenous common dame school to the middle-class academy. In almost every community there was someone prepared to 'mind' the children. For a few coppers the dame would teach them their letters and prevent them from straying. The parson poet George Crabbe depicts such a dame.

> A deaf poor patient widow sits
> And awes some thirty infants as she knits;
> Infants of humble, busy wives, who pay
> Some trifling price for freedom through the day.
> At this good matron's hut the children meet,
> Who thus becomes the mother of the street.
> Her room is small, they cannot widely stray—
> Her threshold high, they cannot run away;
> With band of yarn she keeps offenders in,
> And to her gown the sturdiest rogue can pin.[22]

The common day school was a male-dominated sphere. In his auto-biography Samuel Roberts, born in 1763, tells how he was first sent 'together with twenty or thirty urchins of both sexes to a school taught by a teacher of the old style of poor gentlemen' called Mr Quin.[23] He was then moved to a reading school run by Nicholas Hick. Hick was something of an educational entrepreneur. On the strength of his novel method of teaching reading and spelling he was appointed master of the Hollis School (1755–75). Prior to his appointment, Hick had opened a complex of rooms in West Bar near the workhouse and engaged his wife, his son, son-in-law and daughters to teach in the separate rooms. He introduced a graded series of syllabaries until the child was capable of mastering the tenth chapter of Nehemiah. Children were then considered able to read the Bible and recommended to tackle the next stage of their education elsewhere. The Hollis trustees waxed enthusias-tically about Hick's methods. His private school proved so popular that, in 1756, 160 children were on roll. Twelve years later the school was oversubscribed with five hundred scholars in attendance. Fees were 2d per week—the average for teaching reading locally—plus 3d or 6d fire money and 6d per year to cover the cost of the printed sheets of syllables.

As soon as young Roberts could read, his parents sent him to William Thompson's school at Darnall before completing his schooling at the Milk St. Academy run by 'a little lame man' called Schofield. We know few eighteenth-century elementary scholars apart from those on the charity lists but Jonathan Parkin, born 1737, son of a Southey cutler, started his schooling at the endowed school at Parson Cross, moved to the school of a Mrs Greaves before attending Mr Bradley's writing school in Sheffield.

William Ellis, the parish clerk of Sheffield (1703–43), taught a school in his home in East Parade, as did his neighbour William Timm who leased a cottage in Church Lane. Sarah Moore and her mother ran a school in Fargate—the first quarterly meeting place of the Methodist Society. Nonconformist clergy frequently augmented their stipends by teaching. When Jonathan Shuttleworth wanted to upgrade Attercliffe township school by teaching grammar in 1690 he was frustrated by the existence of the Dissenting Academy. The curate of Attercliffe complained to the Archbishop that Dissenting clergy—Richard Frankland and Timothy Jollie—prejudiced the township school:[24]

> besides which some of the Dissenters have brought in another to teach school thowe in a place which is fitted for a meeting house which is no little prejudice to that which was wont to be the public school.

Frankland was drawn to Attercliffe by his nephew, Robert Banks. He established his Academy in Attercliffe Hall, the home of William Spencer, in 1686. Inspired by the relaxation of the Conformist legislation and the strength of the local Nonconformist congregations, Frankland, a former Cambridge don and ejected minister, migrated to Sheffield to attract high calibre students excluded from the universities. On his return to Rathmell three years later, Jollie reconstituted the Academy as a theological college for the Dissenting ministry. This brief reference to the institution points to a demand for higher education locally but is outside the scope of this discussion.

Classical education was confined to the Grammar School for much of the eighteenth century but the Quaker schoolmasters, William Fairbank—father and son—attracted many boarding pupils—boys and girls—to their commercial school (1723–74). Patronized by many of the leading families, instruction was given in writing, mathematics and mensuration, French and Latin. Fees were 6d per week plus one shilling entrance fee. Evening scholars paid $7^1/_2$d weekly.[25]

Documented private schools invariably attracted a rising middle class. As the eighteenth century progressed, trade expanded and diversified, the birth rate steadily increased, the demand for education became more constant and the opportunities for teaching 'extra' subjects more varied. In 1787 there were nine private schoolmasters listed in the *Sheffield Directory*. Teachers in the common day schools endured a much more uncertain living with very meagre rewards.

Popular Literacy

In order to evaluate the growth of elementary education it is necessary to examine the development of popular literacy—commonly defined as the ability to read and write. Before the nineteenth century, reading was invariably taught before writing and partial literates were more likely to be able to read than write.

The basis of our measurement of literacy is derived from a variety of sources showing the ability of adults to sign their names. As almost all of the local evidence before 1754 relates to industrial agreements, it is confined to the ability of men to sign the relative documents. With the passing of Lord Hardwicke's Marriage Act of 1753, all brides and grooms were required to sign the marriage registers or make their mark. From that date it is possible to provide a common yardstick for both sexes. The ability to sign one's name does not indicate that much more could be written but it is now widely accepted that 'signature literacy was a good indicator of the ability to write'.[26]

For the early modern period all conclusions on literacy are necessarily tentative. According to recent calculations, literacy levels for men measured by signature evidence rose generally from 10 per cent at the end of the fifteenth century to some 20 per cent in the sixteenth, 30 per cent midway through the seventeenth century rising to 45 per cent by 1714. On the other hand, few women could sign their names before the sixteenth century but by 1641–42 about 10 per cent could do so and by 1714 almost 25 per cent did.

When we turn to the local scene, it is clear that a significant proportion of workmen could read in the seventeenth century. At the Doncaster Sessions of 1637, out of a batch of 15 offenders committed for stealing, five South Yorkshire labourers—two from Ecclesfield—claimed the privilege of 'benefit of clergy'. Saved from the death penalty by their ability to read prescribed verses—usually Ps. 51.1—they were branded on the left hand. In 1680 the Scissorsmiths of Hallamshire endorsed their covenant. Out of the 141 covenanters, 49 were able to sign their name, suggesting a male literacy rate of almost 35 per cent, and by implication at least 50 per cent would be able to read.[27]

The Nailmakers of South Yorkshire assembled in Ecclesfield in 1733 to confirm their 'agreement' to the reordering of their craft regulations. Of the 221 nailmakers, 94 signed the document. Considering that nailmaking was pretty low in the hierarchy of craft skills, a 42.5 per cent literacy rate for the rural metal workers is a reasonable assumption. The

Sheffield Filesmiths initiated a grievance procedure in 1749. Of the 21 masters, 19 signed the deed which stipulated that 'any workman or journeyman shall first bring and produce a note in writing from under the hand of his master signifying his consent that such journeyman may depart and leave his service'.

Literacy did not prove much of a problem either for the elected parish officers of Brightside Bierlow. Between 1697 and 1770 only one Chapel Warden and six Overseers of the Poor were unable to sign the indentures of 76 parish apprentices. In contrast, when the Governors of Sheffield Charity School required the approval of parents and guardians to a resolution in 1777 'that such of our children shall at a proper age be put out at apprentice at the option of the trustees of the said charity', 20 out of 44 males signed the agreement compared with 9 out of 38 females able to do so. Thus, out of a sample of 82 indigent poor, 45.4 per cent of males and 23.7 per cent of females were basically literate.

Evidence quarried from local parish registers confirms the ability of brides and grooms to sign the registers (see Table 2.1) and compares favourably with national statistics. Continuous progress is revealed for much of the century. In the 1760s half the brides and grooms could sign but male superiority is clear. Only one third of the women possessed some degree of literacy compared with two thirds of the men (see Table 2.1).

Table 2.1

The literacy rate of brides and grooms in the neighbourhood of Sheffield,
1766–70

Parish		Number	Percentage	
Bradfield Chapelry	men	79	65.4	
	women	40	35.3	
	Total	119	Average 52.6	Sample size 226
Ecclesfield	men	107	66	
	women	55	33.9	
	Total	162	Average 50	Sample size 324
Handsworth	men	32	71.1	
	women	19	42.2	
	Total	51	Average 56.7	Sample size 90

Norton	men	32	80	
	women	20	50	
	Total	52	Average 65.6	Sample size 80
Sheffield	men	809	64.9	
	women	421	33.8	
	Total	1,230	Average 49.3	Sample size 2,492

Incidentally, the percentage of adults able to sign the marriage registers in the rural parishes abutting Sheffield discloses a superior level of literacy to the urban township. Nevertheless, it would be foolish to make generalizations about rural communities on such limited evidence. Their social and economic structure, population density, outlook on life and attitude to education defy simple classification. Moreover, W.B. Stephens reveals a very wide variation between the towns and cities of England at this time; for example, Bristol 51 per cent, Exeter 56, Lincoln 36, Nottingham 54, Oxford 67, Halifax 42, Leeds 32, York 93, Stockport 50, Blackburn 33, and Manchester 48. What does emerge is that industrial towns with expanding populations appear to be 'somewhat less literate' than commercial centres and county towns.[28]

Sustaining the movement of literacy was dependent not only on the widespread network of schools but also on the availability of reading matter. Neville Simmons capitalized on the religious controversies and theological divisions of the 1680s when he set up his publishing and bookselling business. His family pursued the trade of booksellers and newsagents for much of the eighteenth century. In 1692, Simmons held a 'very sizeable' auction of books in the town. At the same time Thomas Spooner left 'bookes mapps lanshipps and pamphlets' valued at £6. Amongst the possessions of the Sheffield cutler, George Harrison, were 44 books. When Church Burgess John Waterhouse died in 1720 his library was worth £20.[29]

Inspired by SPCK, Nathan Drake introduced a parochial library in the Parish Church in 1709. Cavendish Neville, Vicar of Norton, assembled a similar library in his parish.[30] Robert Turie left his books to Bradfield Chapelry. In 1753 a circulating library was opened in the town. The following year Lister established the *Sheffield Weekly Journal* and four booksellers subscribed to the prestigious *Harleian Miscellany*. Six years later a second circulating library was started and William Ward launched the *Sheffield Public Advertiser*. The Sheffield Book Society created a subscription library in 1771. Clearly a wide variety of books, journals and pamphlets were accessible but the libraries were exclusive and used mainly by the merchants, manufacturers and professional classes. Not until Joseph Gales founded the *Sheffield Register* in 1787 and set new standards in provincial journalism was popular literacy really stimulated.

Notes

1. D. Hey, 'Sheffield on the Eve of the Industrial Revolution', *THAS*, 14 (1987), pp. 1-10.

2. Leader, *History*, pp. 46f.

3. W.E. Lowther Clarke, *A History of the SPCK* (1959), p. 14.

4. W.O.B. Allen and E. McClure, *Two Hundred Years: The History of SPCK 1698–1898* (1898), pp. 136f.

5. SPCK Minute Book 1-330 (17 May 1705).

6. SPCK GM 358 (20 December 1705).

7. Account Book of Sheffield Charity School MD 2079, SCA.

8. J. Simon, 'Was there a Charity School Movement?'; B. Simon (ed.), *Education in Leicestershire 1540–1940* (1968), p. 62.

9. *Endowed Charities* (City of Sheffield 1897) p. 63; Sheffield Grammar School Accounts 1604–1724. Microfilm N 570. SCA.

10. *Endowed Charities* (Sheffield), pp. 13f., 71f. King Edward School, Birmingham, diverted income for a writing school in 1751. Bedford School took similar action in 1764.

11. V.M. Mercer, *The School at Parson Crosse 1630–1980* (1980).

12. Sir John Bright of Badsworth leased land at Sharrow Moor to trustee members of the Bright family. W.W.M. Box 46 Ecclesall School Counterpart Lease (23 June 1668), SCA.

13. York, Borthwick Insitute of Historical Research, Court Book 1723.

14. See Mercer, 'School Provision', pp. 88, 92, 94, 106-108, 196-98, 218-19 and plaque in Sheffield Cathedral for further references to the life of Robert Turie.

15. See M. Mercer, 'William Ronksley (1650–1724): Schoolmaster, Writer and Philanthropist', *THAS*, 14 (1987), pp. 11-18.

16. York, Borthwick Insitute. SM Nom. 1729.

17. See M. Mercer, 'The Hollis Educational Trust: A Nonconformist Contribution to Elementary Education', *THAS*, 12 (1983), pp. 68-81.

18. C. Robbins, *The Eighteenth Century Commonwealth Man* (Harvard 1950), p. 26.

19. Quoted in W.H.G. Armytage, *Four Hundred Years of Education* (1970), p. 45.

20. Armytage, *Four Hundred Years*, p. 47.

21. J. Eastwood, *History of the Parish of Ecclesfield* (1862), pp. 338-39; and Miscellaneous Documents, Ecclesfield Parish Church (1709, 1723–24).

22. G. Crabbe, *The Borough*, Letter XXIV (1810).

23. S. Roberts, *Autobiography* (1849), p. 25.

24. York, Borthwick Insitute. SM R *IV* N 462 (1690).

25. W.T. Hall, *Incunabula of Sheffield History* (1937), p. 209; W. Fairbank, Account Book AB1 (1753–74), SCA.

26. W.B. Stephens, *Education, Literacy and Society 1830–70* (1987), pp. 3-4.

27. See Mercer, 'School Provision', pp. 467-68.

28. Stephens, *Education, Literacy and Society*, pp. 6-7.

29. Hey, 'Sheffield on the Eve of the Industrial Revolution', p. 5.

30. Norton Parochial Library is lodged in the Sheffield City Library. See R.C. Norris, 'A Catalogue of the Parochial Library of Norton, Derbyshire' (Typescript), SCL.

Chapter 3

Popular Education and Useful Learning 1780–1839

> Surely it cannot be advisable in Britain to keep up the tyrannical
> spirit of the feudal times, to confine people to casts as in the East
> Indies and shut up the book of knowledge from the Poor. If they
> can avail themselves of useful learning for improving their circum-
> stances and if they can honestly procure it they have as much right
> to it as the greatest man in the kingdom.
>   Revd Edward Goodwin, Curate of Attercliffe, *Gentleman's
>   Magazine*, 67 (1797)

Towards the end of the eighteenth century Sheffield was losing its
image as a bustling market town and taking on the mantle of a
thrusting industrial centre. Water power was giving way to steam.
Conical cementation furnaces and rectangular chimney stacks were
escalating. Craftsmanship and the discovery of a way of making fused
plate were projecting the silver and hollowware trades into the luxury
market. As the town's industrial base broadened, its attraction to migratory labour intensified. Coupled with a considerable natural increase
the population of the parish trebled between 1736 and 1801 from an
estimated 14,531 to 45,755, and expanded to 110,891 by 1841.

During this period of sustained population growth, the mass of the
people became politically aware but not yet conscious of the class
struggle emerging in the more labour-intensive heartlands. The
concentration of urban poor in the central township accentuated the
challenge to established values and disturbed the social order, yet
Robert Leader writing in 1831 observed that 'drunkenness and
debauchery are not rife in our streets nor is the Sunday generally
devoted to low riot and dissipation. Sheffield is the most sober, orderly
and best governed manufacturing town in the whole kingdom'.[1]
Nevertheless, it was the combination of social and religious issues that
were to create and dominate the demand for useful learning and subsequently popular education.

Sunday Schools

The Wesleyan evangelical revival, largely ignored by the Established Church in the eighteenth century, roused the old Dissenters into a flurry of new building. Christian sensitivities of all denominations were ruffled, however, by the gross violation of the Sabbath by youngsters free from daily toil. When news of the Gloucester experiment of school on Sundays initiated by Robert Raikes percolated into Sheffield in 1783 religious instruction on Sunday was perceived as a viable solution. Non-sectarian in its appeal, plans for the creation of Sunday schools were canvassed, subscriptions raised, private teachers sought and accommodation located. Mrs Rebecca Loftus was the first to open her home at Westfield in January 1785 but, inundated by children, the school moved first to a private school in West Street and shortly afterwards to premises in Backfields. Over a hundred children were taught by two private school teachers and supervised by Daniel Hinchcliffe, a scissor manufacturer of Nursery Street. Teaching the children to read the Bible and inculcating the Christian faith were the most important objectives of the school. Church attendance occupied much of the morning session. The youngsters were taken down to St Paul's 'where they assembled in front of the communion table. Their orderly procession from school to church week by week was the subject of keen interest and surprise'.[2]

The coordinator of the Sunday school movement in the beginning was the Revd Edward Goodwin, Curate of Attercliffe (1774–1817). He opened a Sunday school in the recently rebuilt Attercliffe township school in February 1785, addressed a pamphlet *To Parents, Masters and Poor Children* in 1786, defended the movement nationally in the *Gentleman's Magazine* in 1797, and acted as Secretary to the Sheffield Sunday schools throughout his lifetime. In his pamphlet he argued that 'few would deny that some degree of learning may be useful even to the poor'. He recognised the value of the charity and endowed schools yet 'there are abundantly more who through poverty of their parents or some other cause remain uninstructed'. He stressed the need for masters to encourage their apprentices to grasp the opportunities of instruction 'for by your conduct you will make them more faithful and honest, sober and steady, diligent and industrious'.

In response to the criticism of Joseph Gales, the radical editor of the *Sheffield Register*, who claimed that in 1790 Manchester and Salford had almost 5,000 scholars in attendance compared with a paltry 750 in Sheffield, a correspondent asserted that the Committee was not

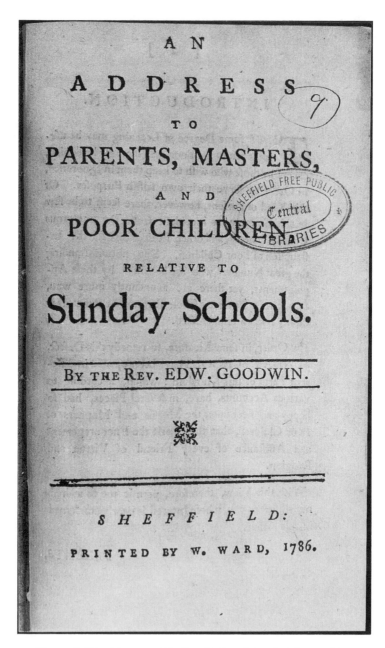

Figure 6. The title page of the Revd Edward Goodwin's pamphlet
To Parents, Masters and Poor Children advocating the benefits of Sunday schools in 1786.

prepared to pay 'insufficient teachers and the useless instruction of irregular and disorderly scholars'. The schools were evaluated quarterly and unsatisfactory schools were discontinued.

Table 3.1

Sunday schools and teachers in Sheffield, 1791[3]

Instructed by		Number of Scholars	Visited by
Mrs Long	Pond Lane	40	Messrs Levick and Newton
Mrs Smith	Queen St.	60	Messrs Creswick and R. Wilson
Mr Lee	Hollis Hospital	70	Messrs Love, Palfreyman, Nanson, Brook, Lucas, Hutchinson and Martin
Mr Fox and Mrs Quixall	Backfield	100	Messrs D. Hinchcliffe and Brockenbrow
Messrs Haywood and Fox	Broad Lane	140	Messrs Vickers, J. Jarvis and T. Wild
Mrs Levick	Broad Lane	50	
Mr Hurst	Spring Croft	80	Mr Sykes
Mrs Ramsden	Park	70	Mr Ashforth
Mr Richardson	Park	80	Mr Machon
Mr Haslehurst	Park	80	Mr Hague
		770	

Instructed gratis every Sunday by	Scholars
Messrs Haywood and Fox	30
Mr Richardson	13
Mr Haslehurst	10
Mr Fox and Mrs Quixall	8
Mrs Smith	7
Mrs Levick	6
Mrs Ramsden	6
Mr Hurst	2
Total by the benevolence of the teachers	82

General visitors superintending all schools:
Messrs C. Procter, J. Eyre, and A. Hufton

The first purpose-built Sunday school was erected in Garden Street in 1789 by the Methodist manufacturers of Britannia Metal, James Vickers and Francis Hawke. As in all the schools, day-school teachers were employed at a rate of 1d per pupil or 4s 6d per annum. It is clear that in most schools the teachers offered to squeeze in a few extra pupils at their own expense. When John Richardson, Master of Park Free School, advertised his evening classes, he 'took the opportunity to acquaint poor widows who have children that his Sunday School is open for their reception and that at the present time there are five vacant seats'. Gathering children together on Sundays made an immediate impact on the town centre as one observer remarked in 1792:

> The effects on morals and manners in the town may not perhaps be so visible in this as in towns less populous but in situations where there is a fair opportunity of seeing them, they are obvious to every man's observations. Witness the Park, now distinguished for order and regularity on the Lord's Day and which a few years ago was equally remarkable on a contrary account.[4]

In 1797 the first voluntary teachers were recruited, the sectarian Sunday school was inaugurated, and a broader curriculum developed. The radical Independent Methodists of Scotland Street invited the Revd Alexander Kilham, leader of the 'Tom Paine' Methodists and recently expelled from the Wesleyan Conference, to be their minister. The Methodist New Connexion evolved out of the Kilhamite secession and immediately embarked on a programme of evangelism and proselytization. The active canvas of voluntary teachers was a priority and Kilham's wife Hannah wrote in August 1797: 'Since returning from Nottingham a Sunday School plan has been in progress. We spent part of the day in calling on friends to ask them to teach.'[5]

The school opened in September in a large room above a wagon carriers in Sycamore Street. Four years later five hundred children attended regularly and were instructed in reading, writing and casting accounts. Writing was encouraged in most Nonconformist sponsored schools in Sheffield but arithmetic was less common. The success of the Kilhamite Sunday school spurred the orthodox Wesleyans to open their Pea Croft school six months later. Henry Longden entered in his diary on 11 February 1798: 'This morning we have begun a Sunday School. Many brethren and sisters offered their services as teachers and many children were admitted.'[6]

The thrust for denominational schools was entirely from within the Nonconformist churches. In 1811 the attention of the Established Church was drawn to the fact that there was an imbalance of schools in favour of Nonconformity at the ratio of 10:1. The following year the

Wesleyans rationalized their provision and opened a large central Sunday school at Red Hill for 1,300 pupils. In an attempt to make all schools more effective George Bennett and James Montgomery stimulated the formation of the Sheffield Sunday School Union. Meanwhile the Anglicans, now alive to the competition, set about erecting their own school in Carver Street large enough to admit a thousand.

Over the first 25 years of the movement the Anglicans had been content to rely on the established pattern of non-sectarian schools taught by professional teachers. Stirred by the newly formed National Society (1811) the Anglican Church in Sheffield embarked upon its own programme of creating identifiable Church Sunday schools and attracting voluntary teachers—an exercise outside the experience of most Anglican laity.

> Let not the lower ranks of life be discouraged from joining their superiors in this divine occupation and let not those in the upper ranks of life think too little in this respect of that assistance which they may desire from their inferiors.[7]

When the Anglicans entered into union with the National Society, the rules precluded them from joining the Sunday School Union. In consequence they formed their own Sheffield and District National Society. In 1814 the Society recorded six Sunday Schools with 730 pupils. Eight years later 40 schools were registered with 3,200 children attending.[8] The Nonconformist Sunday School Union made even more dramatic progress. In 1816 1,300 voluntary teachers instructed 6,500 children in 29 affiliated schools—a pupil–teacher ratio of 5:1.[9]

At the outset, Sunday schools attracted the respectable poor. With the introduction of the denominational schools the appeal was widened and a renewed effort was made to interest the poorest children: 'the children of all those parents who have it not in their power, or have no opportunity to give them instruction any other way are admitted without any distinction of party whatsoever.'[10]

Few children escaped the net completely but the schools failed to retain the necessitous for any length of time. In 1824 the Sunday School Union trawled the town only to discover that 'at least 1500 of the lowest classes of society do not avail themselves of the advantages of Sunday School education'.[11] A similar investigation in 1831 revealed a widening gap—3,500 were outside the net.[12] Awareness of their own ragged condition and the insistence on *cleanliness* proved insurmountable barriers for urchins and street children—arguably a class of children most in need of rescue: 'I am always to come to school with my hands and face clean washed and my hair combed.'[13]

Table 3.2

Sunday schools in Sheffield and neighbourhood, 1833[14]

Parish	No. of Sunday Schools	No. of children	Percentage of whole population
Sheffield	55	9,964	11
Ecclesfield	7	998	12.5
Bradfield Chapelry	11	836	15
Handsworth	4	380	16
Norton	2	70	4
Dore and Totley Chapelry	1	140	16

One effect of the injection of voluntary teachers into the movement was to question traditional modes of discipline. Initially, corporal punishment was sanctioned as a means of preserving good order and reinforcing moral values.

> Children who are found guilty of immorality as lying, swearing, sabbath breaking or improper talk or conduct after having been properly reproved shall be publickly chastised and disgraced, and if no marks of reformation appear shall be expelled. That the teachers shall at all times reward or punish as circumstances require.[15]

The Methodist Sunday school at Red Hill purchased four dozen canes in 1802 and Park Wesleyans spent 4d on canes in 1820. Assisted by a generous pupil/teacher ratio, the Wesleyan management at Red Hill resolved to forbid the use of the cane in 1812: 'No corporal punishment shall be used but the incorrigible shall be expelled.' Some schools formed 'reprobate classes' and Chapeltown Sunday school experimented with handcuffs until advised by their Sheffield colleagues that such treatment was degrading and 'puts them on a level with a common felon'. It is clear that the voluntary teachers rejected the stern disciplinary measures approved by John Wesley's generation. They preferred to emphasize perfect silence and continual occupation plus 'private and affectionate reproof' before expelling the most aggravating cases.

As an influence of good on thousands of children, Sunday schools were of great importance. In terms of educational achievement the outcome was disappointing. Reading and spelling were taught in all schools but the standards reached were invariably mechanical and dismally low. Bibles, Testaments and general readers containing spelling lessons and easy scriptural passages were all used but, with few exceptions, little emphasis was placed on comprehension. Reading habits were substantially extended and reinforced when the larger schools created libraries from 1814 onwards.

The teaching of writing was rarely performed in the Church Sunday schools and discouraged by orthodox Wesleyans as 'an abuse of the Sabbath'. Nevertheless, inspired by James Montgomery, the central Methodist Red Hill Sunday school retained writing in the curriculum well into the 1860s, as did all the New Connexion and some of the Dissenting Sunday schools.[16] Denominational differences about writing did, however, lead to the growth of evening classes run by Sunday school teachers.

Religious instruction was confined to the catechism, the collects and proofs of doctrine in Church Sunday schools. The Nonconformists focused on piety and the way of salvation. Annual reports of the Sunday School Union were packed with instances of children 'dying in the Lord', and examples of happy deaths. Scribbled on the back of a library ticket only days before one child died was the little verse:

> All you who come my grave to see
> Prepare yourselves to follow me.
> Repent in time make no delay
> For youth and age will soon decay.
> Life is uncertain, death is sure,
> Sin is the wound but Christ the cure.[17]

The Unitarian Sunday school for boys successfully mixed secular and scriptural knowledge, but in general, teaching secular knowledge on Sundays was frowned upon. The schools that insisted on teaching writing had little time for general knowledge or even scriptural geography. The Wesleyan Revd J. Henley summed up the situation in 1841 when he observed:

> It is absurd to suppose that a few hours on one day in seven should
> be sufficient for even the moral and religious training of children
> who are for the most part exposed to the influences of corrupt
> examples all the week besides.[18]

The Children's Employment Commissioner J.C. Symons visited many Sunday schools and concluded that they were 'of great utility as

Figure 7. Parson Cross School opened c. 1630 and was rebuilt in 1793. The adjoining schoolhouse built in 1829 was intended to be a school for girls but the master requisitioned it for himself.

Figure 8a. The plaque on the wall of Crookes Endowed School reveals various local initiatives to re-build and extend the school.

Figure 8b. The Handsworth Church School plaque indicates the nature of the charity.

preventers of evil. They do little to impart knowledge but much to prevent vice'.[19]

When assessing the value of Sunday schools we must not lose sight of the social consequences and total commitment of a host of enthusiastic amateur teachers. The movement integrated a wide social mix of clergy, gentlemen, attorneys, shopkeepers, tradesmen, skilled artisans and metal workers. As the years progressed, clerks, cashiers and labourers replaced the professional classes in this predominantly male activity. In the remarkably homogeneous society of Sheffield where a master was hardly distinguishable from his workers, the democratization of the social classes fostered the ethic of respectability and enhanced the job prospects of many 'promising young people'. As the relatively affluent came into contact with real poverty they emerged more responsive to the plight of the poor and the inadequacy of their educational opportunities.

Parish Schools Restored

The periodic groundswell of concern over social order and moral degeneration, aggravated by surfacing cells of revolutionary radicalism, not only led to the foundation of Sunday schools from 1785 onwards but also stimulated another spate of school building and educational philanthropy. In the Sheffield parish and outlying townships between 1778 and 1815 the educational infrastructure was revitalized almost entirely by local initiative and public subscription.[20] Twelve schools were rebuilt, four attracted significant endowments and five new schools were opened. The schools rebuilt and enlarged include Attercliffe (1779), Norton (1787), Crookes (1791), Fulwood, Tinsley and Parson Cross (1793), Oughtibridge/Onesacre (1797), Wadsley, Bolsterstone, and Handsworth (1800), Grimesthorpe (1802), and Grenoside (1807). The Boys' Charity School, together with Sharrow Moor, High Green and Heeley, benefited from additional gifts, and the new schools created were Woodhouse (1778), the Girls' Charity School (1787), Park Free School (1789), the Girls Industrial School (1797) and Gleadless (1815).

The purpose of new school creation is best described by looking at Park Free School which was established in the mould of earlier township schools. Revd John Downes, Chaplain to the Shrewsbury Hospital, called a public meeting at the Sign of the Harrow in 1787. The announcement ran:

The District of the Parish of Sheffield, called Sheffield Park, being very large and populous and principally inhabited by poor persons, many of whom being unable to send their children to school, to receive the first Rudiments of Education; and others who may be better able, having it not in their power without very great Inconvenience, the said District not being furnished with any Master properly qualified to undertake the Instruction of Children; by which means the said Children are denied the blessed Advantages of a decent Education; and, brought up in ignorance, become an easy prey to vice.[21]

The school opened in 1789 with John and Mary Richardson of Paradise Square the appointed teachers. Richardson specialized in mathematics and geography in his evening classes and was author of the text book *Key to the Globes*.

Schooling for girls was available in every parish and township school but single sex girls' schools were non-existent until the end of the eighteenth century, except in the private sector. In 1776 Adam Smith affirmed 'There are no public institutions for the education of women, and there is accordingly nothing useless, absurd or fantastical in the common course of their education'.[22] So when Edward Goodwin arranged a public meeting in August 1785 to discuss the feasibility of a Girls' Charity School whereby poor girls could be rescued from vice and immorality, there was considerable enthusiasm. The latitudinarian Vicar of Sheffield, James Wilkinson, chaired the meeting and the ubiquitous subscriptions were promptly set in motion. Built in 1786 at the north-west corner of the churchyard to accommodate fifty girls, the school opened in 1787. The Girls' Charity School conformed to the religious principles of the Established Church yet had the support of all sections of the community. Charity sermons were not only preached in the Parish Church and St Paul's but the Wesleyan and Independent pulpits supported the venture by sermon and collections—particularly in the 1790s when times were hard and the cost of living was abnormally high.

The cost of the building was in the region of £1,500 and the generation of income became a particular feature of its creation. Inspired by Goodwin, a series of promotions were held in St Paul's and the Parish Church including a Feast of Harmony, a presentation of Handel's *Messiah* and other oratorios and festivals. The school attracted gifts, legacies and annual subscriptions from a variety of sources remarkably free from sectarian bias. Unfortunately, the Napoleonic Wars created many inflationary pressures and the financial control was strained for many years.

The emphasis of the school was unquestionably on religious and useful learning. All appearances of vice were suppressed; piety and virtue were promoted. The curriculum included English, religious instruction and the Church catechism. Spinning, sewing, knitting and

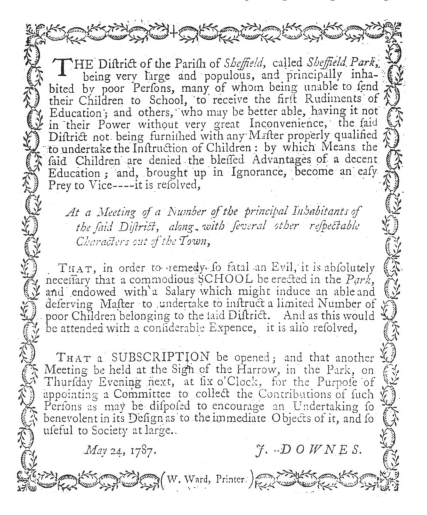

THE District of the Parish of *Sheffield*, called *Sheffield Park*, being very large and populous, and principally inhabited by poor Persons, many of whom being unable to send their Children to School, to receive the first Rudiments of Education; and others, who may be better able, having it not in their Power without very great Inconvenience, the said District not being furnished with any Master properly qualified to undertake the Instruction of Children : by which Means the said Children are denied the blessed Advantages of a decent Education ; and, brought up in Ignorance, become an easy Prey to Vice----it is resolved,

At a Meeting of a Number of the principal Inhabitants of the said District, along with several other respectable Characters out of the Town,

THAT, in order to remedy so fatal an Evil, it is absolutely necessary that a commodious SCHOOL be erected in the *Park*, and endowed with a Salary which might induce an able and deserving Master to undertake to instruct a limited Number of poor Children belonging to the said District. And as this would be attended with a considerable Expence, it is also resolved,

THAT a SUBSCRIPTION be opened; and that another Meeting be held at the Sign of the Harrow, in the Park, on Thursday Evening next, at six o'Clock, for the Purpose of appointing a Committee to collect the Contributions of such Persons as may be disposed to encourage an Undertaking so benevolent in its Design as to the immediate Objects of it, and so useful to Society at large.

May 24, 1787.   *J. DOWNES.*

(W. Ward, Printer.)

Figure 9. A public notice advertising the vital necessity of a school for the poor in Sheffield Park. Initiated by Revd John Downes, Chaplain of the Shrewsbury Hospital in 1787, Park Free School opened in 1789 and was one of the earliest day schools affiliated to the National Society in Sheffield.

domestic management were the key secular elements. The girls were employed 'in rotation according to their age, strength, and understanding in the business of the house such as cleaning the rooms, making and repairing and washing their cloathes etc.' Goodwin, who served as secretary until his death in 1817, also produced a primer for daily use. Two examples of his subject matter illustrate the moral and utilitarian content.[23]

Lesson V

Learn to spin wool and linen.
Learn to sew shifts and shirts and caps.
Learn to knit hose.
Learn to bake and brew and wash.
Learn to clean rooms and pots and pans

Lesson VI

Do no wrong.
It is a sin to steal a pin.
Swear not at all, nor make a bawl.
Use no bad words.
Live in peace with all as much as you can.

Goodwin inserted prayers for daily use which reinforced the two-dimensional view of society whereby those of inferior status were regularly reminded of their subordinate role.

Give me Grace I beseech thee O God,
to live this day as in thy sight
and to do always such things as please thee.
Make me dutiful and obedient to my Benefactors
and Charitable to my Enemies. Make me temperate
and chaste, meek and patient, just and true in all
my dealings, content and industrious in my station.

It is clear that charitable duty was a strong motivator of patronage. The growth of fashionable properties around Paradise Square, Hartshead and to the west of the town proved an equally important factor for there was an insatiable demand for domestic servants and the institution was recognized as a vital source. Girls were admitted at the age of seven who were certified 'free from all imperfections in their eyes, from scrophulous and other diseases and were not deformed'. Dressed in their distinctive plain blue uniforms—leghorn hats, printed linen tippets,

THE

POOR GIRLS

PRIMER.

B E Good.
  Be a good Girl.
Be a good Girl, and God will love you.
  Be a good Girl, and God will love, and
blefs you.

LESSON 2.

Learn to pray.
  Pray to God, and he will give you what
is good.
  Strive to pleafe him, and he will be your
friend.
Love his Law, and do what he bids you.

LESSON 3.

Speak the Truth, and do not lye.
Truth needs no fine Words.
Let thy Lips fpeak right Things.
Lye not to gain the World.

LESSON 4.

Keep your Cloaths clean.
Wafh your Hands, and Face.
Comb your Head.
Tye your Shoes.
       A 2   LESSON

Figure 10a. Introductory exercises for the Charity School Girls set by the Revd
Edward Goodwin in the *Poor Girls' Primer* 1787.

1811.

HYMN

TO BE SUNG BY

THE CHARITY GIRLS.

Set to Music by Mr. Mather.

GUARDIAN Guides of Innocence!
    Almoners of Providence!
Hither turn your eyes, and view
Infant-hands upheld for you.

Friendlefs, helplefs did we ftray
No one mark'd to Heav'n our way:
Now in you we friends poffefs ;
Now a Saviour's name confefs.

Bleffings, bleffings then receive ;
We have nothing elfe to give ;
Yet beyond the ampleft ftore
Are the bleffings of the poor.

Hear then HEAV'N! our earneft pray'rs
Make each bleffing tenfold theirs :
May they never be diftrefs'd ;
But for bleffing ever bleft.

GOD of LOVE! to thee belong
Higheft ftrains of grateful fong :
Tho' from men this bounty came
Thou didft raife the gen'rous flame.

Let each voice with ours combine
To adore the fource divine :
Great eternal Three above !
GOD of LIFE and GOD of LOVE !

Figure 10b. A *Hymn* sung by the Charity School girls on October 27th 1811.

checked aprons for weekdays and plain white for Sundays—the 60 charity girls were boarded, clothed and lodged until they reached the age of 13 or 14 before being placed out to service.[24]

The success of the Girls' Charity School prompted a non-denominational attempt to rescue an even lower strata of deprived girls ten years later. In 1797 a group of ladies—mainly Quakers—resolved to open a day School of Industry for girls on the model promoted by Mrs Trimmer in Brentford.

> Seeing that the tender minds of poor children trained up in indolence and destitute of instruction and lamentably subject to be corrupted by ill habits, it is proposed that a fund shall be raised by annual subscription and donations for the purpose of procuring a schoolroom and hiring a mistress to teach about fifty girls reading, knitting and sewing, one half to be taught in the forenoon and the rest in the afternoon.

> The most neglected children will be preferred for this charity, so that it will not be confined to any particular sect and as the subscribers may be of different persuasion, to avoid dissension it is not intended that any form of prayer or catechism shall be introduced into the school but that the scriptures shall be frequently read them, discouraging vice, promoting morality and industry are the principal objects.[25]

Various venues and mistresses were tried until satisfactory premises were located in the Hartshead. The management of the school was eventually vested in the ladies' committee of the Society for Bettering the Condition of the Poor formed in 1803. The Society was founded initially by Sir Thomas Bernard in 1796 together with Shute Barrington, Bishop of Durham, William Wilberforce and others. Bernard, son of Sir Francis Bernard (last Royal Governor of Massachusetts) and Amelia Offley of Norton is remembered largely for his promotion of the Royal Institution. He retained his ancestral links with the Shores of Norton and visited Sheffield regularly.

The overwhelming demand for admission to the Industrial School, plus the recognition by the patrons of the need of the most necessitous for daytime employment, led to the commencement of evening classes in 1803, and extended to working boys in 1805. Eventually this girls' school was incorporated into the Lancasterian School in 1815.

Monitorial Schools

A totally new dimension in elementary education was achieved by the introduction of monitorial schools. Enthusiasts for the Sunday school movement were amongst the first to recognize that schooling on one day per week was inadequate if education was socially to discipline the masses. Joseph Lancaster's solution of 'factory' schooling, whereby one master with the aid of monitors and machinery could supervise 'the instruction of a thousand children', appealed enormously to the professional and emerging middle classes.

James Montgomery, the Moravian editor of the *Sheffield Iris*, publicized Lancaster's system in November 1807 when an enterprising schoolmaster opened a school in Watson Walk on the Lancasterian plan—offering to teach reading, writing and arithmetic for only 4d per week including the cost of books. Led by Dr John Browne, founding father of the General Infirmary (1797), the Society for the Promotion of Useful Knowledge invited Joseph Lancaster, the Quaker schoolmaster, to lecture on his plan. Within three months of Lancaster's presentation in 1809, a disused rolling mill in Gibraltar Street was refurbished to accommodate the education of a thousand boys. With the exception of the Anglican clergy the proposals were greeted with widespread enthusiasm.

The huge schoolroom, paved with brick, rose gradually from the master's desk like a theatre floor, enabling him to have 'a bird's eye view'. The space was filled with rows of benches for written exercises, allowing one central aisle. Lessons on boards were fixed to the walls so that 'drafts' of children could stand around and receive instruction from the monitors. The master exercised his control via the telegraph that transmitted the signals to the monitors who were drilled in the various chains of command.

Reading was at the heart of the curriculum. As the child graduated from the alphabet and monosyllables to simple sentences, the Bible and other religious texts were introduced but no reading matter of a sectarian nature was admitted. Reading, spelling and writing went hand in hand. Drill in cyphering was approached in a similar manner before the four rules of arithmetic were attempted. The value of the institution 'where too many children have hitherto been suffered to grow up in idleness, ignorance and civility' was obvious to its supporters who welcomed its regulations by the prescribed system of rewards and punishments.

Admission to the school initially was by nomination of the subscribers. By the end of the first year 620 boys had been admitted. Subscribers found it increasingly difficult to find more boys when allowed four places for every guinea subscribed. Poor boys whose parents received parish assistance were recommended by the Overseers of the Poor. The Female Friendly Society, the Bettering Society and the house surgeons of the General Infirmary were also invited to propose pupils but all efforts were met by acute truancy. The management committee envisaged all instruction would be free but reluctantly decided to charge one shilling per quarter for non-nominated pupils, arguing that little value was placed 'on that which costs nothing to attain'.

By 1814 the school was recognized as a teacher-training establishment. The management, which consisted of 35 gentlemen plus treasurer and secretaries elected annually, were justly praised by Sir Thomas Bernard, Joseph Lancaster and James Montgomery. Nevertheless, subscriptions proved inadequate for the maintenance of the school. One major factor was the rival creation of the National School (1813).[26]

Anxiety about the success of the Lancasterian schools was expressed nationally by Churchmen in 1810 and 1811. Inspired by Joshua Watson and the Hackney Phalanx, the National Society for the Education of the Poor in the Principles of the Established Church was founded to secure, for the Church, the fundamental principle that the national religion should be the foundation of a national education. The National Society was to replace SPCK as the Church's supervisory body for elementary schools.

The Church in Sheffield was divided on the proposal to establish another large day school when the Lancasterian School was little over half full. Moreover, prominent laymen were involved in its superintendence and 40 per cent of the scholars were connected with the Established Church. Most of the clergy, however, were anxious that an identifiable church school should become available.

Under the pretext of setting up a large Church Sunday school and a day school for girls to meet a recognized deficiency, a public meeting was called to outline the scheme. Montgomery welcomed the plan 'as most desirable in this populous town when the peace of society depends so much upon the morals of the lower class of females'. A pamphlet war erupted briefly but the influence of Montgomery,

Rowland Hodgson (Churchman, treasurer and first chairman of the Lancasterian School) and a few of Hodgson's friends steered the proposals through—ensuring co-operation rather than competition, Asline Ward, a Dissenting ally was aggravated by the presumption of the Church 'to call their system National' but assisted in preventing any real clash.

The first National School organized in accordance with Dr Bell's Madras System was built in Carver Street. Designed to cater for 500 boys and 500 girls on two levels it cost in the region of £2,200. Bell's arrangements differed marginally from Lancaster's—the desks invariably faced the wall and the central space was occupied by the classes under monitorial instruction standing in squares. The application to be united with the National Society qualified the school for grant aid but restricted the school to using only those books that were listed in the Society's catalogue.

The girls' school opened in May 1813 under Sarah Watson at a salary of £50 per annum with 479 girls present. By the end of the year 536 girls were on roll. In total 749 were admitted but some left for work and others were dismissed for 'irregular behaviour'. The curriculum included religious instruction and the three Rs and for two hours every day sewing, knitting and marking. Within twelve months the school was so overcrowded that a search began for an overflow annexe. Garden Street Sunday School was transferred to the trustees in 1815 and a sixteen-year-old ex-monitor was placed in charge of the little ones.

The opening of the boys' school was delayed until October 1813 because Robert Brierley, the appointed schoolmaster who was offered one hundred guineas per year, would not adapt to the rigorous training schedule practised in the Barrington Training School in Durham. Eventually an organizing schoolmaster, Mr Proud, opened the school.

Pupils were first taught their alphabet in sand and then proceeded through a series of monosyllabic cards before being challenged by the sentences in the National Society's *Reading Book 2*. The next step was the Society's *Reading Book 3* which related the story of Joseph and his brothers. Abridged versions of the Bible and Mrs Trimmer's Scripture lessons were then introduced. Memory was exercised by the rote learning of prayers, psalms and portions of the Church catechism which reinforced pupils' duty to God and neighbour. 'Habits of subordination,

of diligence and of veneration for the establishments of their country'
were repeatedly instilled.[27]

Fears that the National School would undermine the stability of the
Lancasterian School were rapidly dispelled. The demand for girls'
places outstripped the provision. Consequently, the Lancasterian
Committee decided to convert their Gibraltar Street premises to
accommodate a girls' school and expand their overall provision by
opening an annexe for 200 girls in Allen Street Sunday School. The
pressure for admission to both monitorial schools and the necessity to
liquidate debts contributed to the agreement in 1817 to charge every
child 6d per quarter to cover the cost of books and assist the funds of
the institutions.

Evidence of the goodwill that existed between the two educational
bodies is substantiated in the ninth Annual Report of the Lancasterian
School in 1818.

> We esteem the facilities which are now afforded to the children of
> the poor of acquiring the ability to read the word of God by the
> Lancasterian and Bellian modes of education as the peculiar blessings
> of heaven and the forerunner of that glorious day...We would bear
> a testimony of goodwill to those [schools] supported by our friends
> of the Establishment denominated Sheffield National Schools. We
> do not account these respectable Institutions as opponents but as
> fellow helpers in the same great cause of humanity and kindness.
> Hence we may consider our respective schools as saying one to the
> other in the language of Abraham to Lot; Let there be no strife I
> pray thee, between thee and me, and between my herdsmen and thy
> herdsmen for we are brethren.

In 1818 Lord Brougham promoted an Inquiry by a Select
Committee into the Education of the Lower Orders. The returns for
the parish of Sheffield were concerned only with the poor and revealed
the numbers receiving free education or paying no more than $1/2$d per
week.

Table 3.3

Provision of school places for the poor, 1818[28]

Parish of Sheffield		Boys	Girls	Total
Lancasterian Schools		630	640	1,270
National Schools:	Carver Street	463	550	1,013
	Garden Street		140	140
	Aux. Park	139	84	223
	Brightside	68	40	108
	Attercliffe	100		100
		1,400	1,454	2,854
Grammar School		20		20
Charity School for Boys		60		60
Charity School for Girls			60	60
Heeley (Endowed)				18
Sharrow Moor (Endowed)				14
Broad Oak Green (Endowed)				6
Crookesmoor (Endowed)				30
Heeley (Unendowed)				50
				3,112

The conclusion reached by the Select Committee was that in Sheffield 'The Poor have in general nearly sufficient means of education'. In contrast neighbouring Rotherham and Ecclesfield corresponded with the broad generalization that

> There is the most unquestionable evidence that the anxiety of the poor for education continues not only unabated but daily increasing; that it extends to every part of the country, and is to be found equally prevalent in those smaller towns and country districts where no means of gratifying it are provided by the charitable efforts of the richer classes.

The growing demand for educational opportunities for girls in the outer townships continued to create concern. In 1824 the Curate of Attercliffe, Revd John Blackburn, opened a girls' school in the township as did Thomas Sutton, Vicar of Sheffield, at Greystones. In 1829 the Misses Harrison established another school for girls at Crookesmoor and Hannah Rawson of Wardsend built one at Parson Cross but seven years later the headteacher appropriated it for his personal use as a schoolhouse. More National Schools were opened in the 1830s for both boys and girls: St Mary's, Hermitage Street (1830),

St Philip's (1832), Ecclesall (1834), Pitsmoor (1836) and Wadsley (1837). The initiative held by the Nonconformists at the turn of the century was now with the Established Church. Not until 1833 did the Methodist Society open their first day school at Red Hill and the first Roman Catholic day school opened in 1834.

Infant Schools

Infant schooling was largely disregarded in the pursuit of popular education for the masses. Dame schools always admitted toddlers. Sunday schools refused admission under the age of seven and the monitorial schools made six years their age of entry. In 1824, however, attention was drawn to the value of infant schools by a correspondent in the *Sheffield Iris*. Two years later John Holland revived interest by publicizing the work of Samuel Wilderspin in the columns of the *Iris*.[29] Encouraged by Henry Brougham and the philosopher James Mill, Wilderspin inspired a national movement in favour of infant education based on ideas practised by Robert Owen in his New Lanark Mills. 'The schools or asylums for poor youngsters between the ages of two and six hopefully replace inefficient dame schools and release older children from acting as nursemaids.'

Churchmen, preoccupied with church extension in the 1820s—St George's (1825), Attercliffe (1826), St Philip's (1828) and St Mary's (1830)—were reluctant to tax new congregations for school subscriptions. Not until 1829 was an Infant Society formed and the first schools built—created largely by private philanthropy: the Misses Harrison in the Park and Weston Hall, James Wilson at Sharrow, Revd John Blackburn at Attercliffe, Revd W.H. Vale at Ecclesall Parsonage and Rowland Hodgson at Hermitage Street. In 1831 an infant school was incorporated into the Lancasterian School. The parliamentary survey of 1833 furnished the information summarized in Table 3.4 about infant schools supported by subscriptions and weekly pence.

Table 3.4

Infant school places in Sheffield, 1833[30]

Parish	Year established	Boys	Girls	Total	Salary
Sheffield	1829	40	40	80	£30
Sheffield	1830	75	75	150	£85 Master and Mistress

Sheffield	1831	150	130	280	£95 Master and Mistress
Lancasterian					
Sheffield	1832	80	80	160	
Ecclesall	1830			160	
Ecclesall	1833	29	35	64	
Attercliffe	1823			120	

Also three Private Infant Schools in Sheffield Township—118 children

The injection of evangelical clergy by Vicar Sutton, prompted and encouraged by the local press, accounts for the initial surge in infant school provision. The religious and educational virtues of the schools and the pitfalls of illiteracy were strenuously emphasized. The economic advantages to mothers free to pursue employment or alternatively relieved of parental duties were duly advertised. School fees of $1^1/_2$d per week were not considered excessive given the opportunities for early learning. Promoters went to great pains, however, to reassure parents that they had no intention of usurping parental responsibilities.

Reviewing the merits of infant schools, White's *Sheffield Directory* for 1833 reported that:

> they are conducted on the ingenious system of Wilderspin and Wilson by which infants between the ages of two and six under a pleasing interchange of exercises, amusement and instruction, experience a gradual development of the bodily and mental powers. Thus the children are kept from that danger and neglect to which many young children of the poor are exposed whilst their parents are engaged in their private avocations.

State Involvement in the Public Sector

Education and its relation to poverty exercised the minds of reformers from the turn of the century, but not until the Reformed Parliament of 1832—when Sheffield was first enfranchised—was radical change a possibility. In 1833 the first effective Factory Act endorsing the principle of inspection was passed and although John Arthur Roebuck—later to become MP for Sheffield—failed in his bid for an Education Bill, he was compensated by the approval of the first parliamentary grant of £20,000 for school provision. Whilst acknowledging the efforts of the British and National School Societies, it signalled the introduction of state involvement in education. 5 per cent of the first parliamentary grant was received in South Yorkshire. The proposed Roman Catholic school in Surrey Street was an immediate beneficiary and the two National schools at Ecclesall and St George's were also awarded grants. The new Wesleyan schools at Brunswick and Park became grant-aided and Pitsmoor National School benefited in 1836.

The parliamentary debates of 1833 also sparked off the first full investigation into the state of education nationally. The survey, published in 1835 and referred to as the Kerry Returns, afford a somewhat suspect guide to the extent of school provision and the number of children at school. According to the national summary almost 9 per cent of the population were under daily instruction and 11 per cent attended Sunday schools. There was, however, a serious shortfall in the number of schools and scholars recorded locally. The underestimate nationally varied between a third and a tenth. If we abide by the figures presented, Sheffield was well below the national average whilst Sunday school attendance at 11.6 per cent was marginally above.

Table 3.5

Day school provision in the neighbourhood of Sheffield, 1833[31]

Parish		No. of Schools	Boys	Girls	Total	Percentage of population
Sheffield						
population	Public	18	1,597	1,337	2,934	
91,692	Private	78	1,745	1,359	3,104	
	Infant	10	578	554	1,132	
		106	3,920	3,250	7,170	7.8
Ecclesfield						
population	Public	5	183	145	328	
7,911	Private	12	139	135	274	
		17	322	280	602	7.6
Bradfield Chapelry						
population	Public	6	152	108	260	
5,504	Private	5	104	119	223	
		11	256	227	483	8.8
Handsworth						
population	Public	3	158	76	226	
2,338	Private	3	18	49	67	
		6	176	125	293	12.5

Norton						
population	Public	1	56	42	98	
1,747	Private	3	46	41	87	
	Infant	1	15	15	30	
		5	117	98	215	12.3
Dore and Totley Chapelry						
(Dronfield Parish)						
population	Public	2	41	49	90	
878	Private	1	13	12	25	
		3	54	61	115	13.0

Private Sector

The dramatic expansion of public schooling to meet the needs of the rapidly growing urban population in the half century beginning 1780 was matched by the exceptional growth of the private sector. *White's Directory* of 1833 listed 96 private academies in the Sheffield region compared with nine in 1787. However cautiously we treat the Kerry Returns, 47 per cent of children under instruction were attending private schools. Considering the fact that fees were required in every school—with the exception of the free places—there was clearly an increasing willingness on the part of parents to purchase some degree of education.

Thomas Sutton's analysis of private schools in 1838 shown in Table 3.6 gives us a clearer picture of the scale of private school provision and considerably broadens our perspective of the educational alternatives. He calculated that the total number of children attending day school within the parish of Sheffield had risen to 10.396, almost 10 per cent of the population—with 40 per cent in private schools. Unlike the Overseers of the Poor who discounted dame schools in their 1833 Inquiry, Sutton included them and demonstrated that only 25 per cent of the private sector were actually attending such schools.

Table 3.6

Private schools in the Parish of Sheffield, 1838[32]

No. of schools	Under 5		5 to 15		Upwards of 15		Total
	Boys	Girls	Boys	Girls	Boys	Girls	
31 Superior Day	17	18	536	655	13	34	1,273
22 Middling Day	30	12	599	325	5	—	971
27 Common Day	35	42	524	418	—	—	1,019
46 Dame Schools	215	171	184	456	4	7	1,037
	297	243	1,843	1,854	22	41	4,300

The proliferation of middle-class private schools competing with the Grammar School was a significant development during this period. The superior and classical schools provided a real alternative with their totally different ethos and purpose to the once popular Grammar School which declined in popularity after the death of Revd Edward Chadwick even though it was relocated in 1825. Abraham's Milk Street Academy specialized in the sciences and modern languages. Arguably

Figure 11. J.H. Abraham's middle-class Milk Street Academy c. 1830. His systematic time-table extended from 7 am to 5 pm six days a week.

Figure 12. Built in 1837 the Sheffield Wesleyan Proprietary School was re-established as King Edward VII Secondary School for Boys in 1906.

'the most innovative private schoolmaster teaching in Sheffield',[33] J.H. Abraham was a Fellow of the Linnean Society and represented the Sheffield Literary and Philosophical Society at the first meeting of the British Association in 1832.

Nonconformist clergy educated in the Dissenting academies, such as Hunt Piper at Norton and Peter Wright at Glossop Road, were not only well equipped to teach the classical languages and the humanities but were also skilful in the art of instruction. During the 1820s when there was talk of 'the flourishing state of trade' there was an upsurge in the demand for classical studies and modern languages in the pursuit of social status and university entrance. University College, London, supported by Dissenters and reformers opposed to the religious tests imposed by Oxford and Cambridge, emerged in 1828. James Guion at Red Hill taught French, Latin, Greek, Hebrew and English grammar with classical analysis. George West in his school opposite the Friends' Meeting House offered French, Hebrew and Italian in addition to the classics and William Wright, undermaster at the Grammar School for twelve years, branched out in Bank Street before moving to Steel Bank, Commonside, specializing in the classics and mathematics. Boarding schools for the upwardly mobile escalated in pre-industrial Attercliffe, Ecclesfield and Bradfield Chapelry. Such demand for a superior level of schooling eventually gave birth to the proprietory school movement that established the Collegiate School in 1835 and Wesley College in 1837.[34]

Excluded from the grammar and proprietory schools, girls outnumbered boys in the superior schools investigated by Sutton. Although most of the day schools accepted both sexes, the distribution of girls' private schools was extremely widespread and ranged from the superior finishing school, to the common day variety. In the Kerry Returns of 1833 only four girls' schools were identified yet in White's *Directory of Sheffield* for the same year 16 ladies' boarding schools were listed. Generally speaking, the curriculum for girls was less substantial than that offered to boys and tended to emphasize literary skills, needlework, and 'provide the opportunity for forwarding and perfecting a polite and Christian education'.

The majority of schools advertising during this half century were geared towards the commercial needs of Sheffield's trade and industry. In addition to the three Rs, accounts, bookkeeping, geometry, mensuration, geography, drawing and European languages were offered. As the demand for clerks, cashiers and warehousemen increased, commercial wings were added to the middling schools.

Middling and commercial schools served the children of shop-keepers and tradesmen, lawyers' clerks and skilled artisans. Some measure of their effectivness can be gauged from the length of service and expansion by some proprietors. The Mycock Academy conducted by J. and E. Mycock opened in 1786 and moved to Burgess Street in 1790. In July 1807 they had a much larger school built in Holy Street. When Mrs Mycock retired in 1827 the commercial wing still continued to function. West Street Academy, the home of the first Sheffield Sunday school in 1785, had a number of worthy schoolmasters including Mr Ingle, the first master, J. Youle, one-time master of the Boys' Charity School and J. Downend, advocate on behalf of the 'suffering negro' and superintendent of the Wesleyan Red Hill Sunday School before his premature death. It was immediately let to the Misses E. and H. Mather in 1826 who had recently vacated the Vicarage School.

The cross-fertilization of teachers between the private and public sector can be illustrated by the changes at Queen Street Academy which maintained a strong mathematical bias. When Job Cawood opened in 1808 he engaged his brother to teach Latin and French. Cawood extended the premises in 1812 to accommodate girls, only to be elected to succeed John Eadon at the Free Writing School shortly afterwards. He was succeeded at Queen Street by John Eadon's nephew who had learned his trade at the Free Writing School before branching out into the more 'genteel' world of the private school. John Eadon Jnr remained in Queen Street from 1812 to 1829 before moving to even more spacious accommodation in the Red Hill School.

In contrast to the superior and middling schools where the location was significant, the common day schools were much more ephemeral, known only by the teacher's name and almost impossible to quantify. They rarely advertised, were far more difficult to trace, yet instantly recognizable by their comparatively low fees of between 4d and 6d per week for teaching reading. When Mr B. Stacey opened in Burgess Street in 1788 his aim was 'to qualify such as are intended for trade in a short time' by offering to teach reading at 3 shillings per quarter, writing 5 shillings per quarter and 7 shillings for writing and arithmetic. Mr Roome of Brocco Bank, who experimented with the Lancasterian system in his school at Watson's Walk, was in this category as was Robert Brierley, the rejected master from the National School who reopened his school in the Assembly Rooms in Norfolk Street 'for the poorer classes'. He charged 4d per week for reading, 6d for writing and 8d for accounts.

Dame schools were largely run by women but it was not unknown for men to teach them, just as some common day schools were taught by women. In general only basic reading, spelling, sewing and knitting were taught in the dame schools. When the curriculum was expanded it encroached on the province of the common day school. In many respects the dame school was little more than the extension of the parent–child relationship, kept by persons in the same walk of life in a house remarkably similar to their own. Responsive to the demands of the locality, dame schools represented acceptable values. In contrast to the public schools they tolerated the most spasmodic attendance and simply accommodated the daily routine of working-class family life. Excluded from serious consideration by 'expert witnesses' who invariably admitted that a wide gap existed between the quality of some dame schools compared with others, their traditional presence in the heart of every community as portrayed by such poets as Shenstone, Goldsmith and Crabbe points to their prevalence. In fact, many rural endowed schools at this time achieved little more as non-superannuated teachers degenerated in the service of the school.

Essentially small, averaging little more than 20 pupils, dame schools rarely charged more than 2d per week. Owing to the nature of vernacular housing in the Sheffield area, the children were gathered together in the dame's kitchen or living-room in contrast to the cellars and garrets of Manchester or Liverpool. Whilst the proportion of children under five in dame schools was not large (37 per cent) it is reasonable to suggest that Thomas Sutton was unable to unearth them all and that more children were in their care than actually stated. In an age when the majority of children began school at the age of six, dame schools clearly fulfilled a useful service and were of 'considerable economic importance'. In the light of current theories on preschool education, dame schools should not be dismissed solely because they were child-minding establishments.

In a rare and lengthy obituary in the *Sheffield Iris* on 5 September 1809, James Montgomery recalled an untold number of the poorest children taught by one revered dame.

> At last this place on Friday aged 74 Mrs Hardy who for the last 27 years kept a school in Copper St. where she had instructed many thousands of little children in the mysteries of reading and spelling

Figure 13. *The Dames School* by Alfred Rankley (1819–1872).

by a method of her own, peculiarly easy and expeditious. Among her pupils she went by the name of Giant Grumbo, her real name being unknown to most of her nearest neighbours till it appeared on her coffin plate. Her school was numerously attended and from a humane consideration that when she was gone they might never get so good a mistress again. She preferred taking the children of the poorest people whom she taught at the rate of two pence a week and would never raise her terms under any hardship of circumstances. Her integrity and independence of spirit were equal to her fidelity and skill in her humble profession. She lived alone and in almost entire seclusion, generally locking her door as soon as she had dismissed her pupils.

Private infant schools for the more well-to-do were stimulated by the initial success of the public infant schools between 1829 and 1833. When Mrs Rhodes opened her school at Westfield Terrace in 1833 she invited the master of the Lancasterian Infant School to examine her pupils publicly. Spelling, reading, figures, geography and natural history featured in the examination together with displays of marching exercises, recitation and choral items. In Surrey Street Miss Piper conducted a similar school and charged 10s 6d per quarter.

The statistical evidence assembled in the 1830s reinforces the view that a considerable proportion of pupils attended private schools— schools run for profit and maintained solely by parental contributions— and that such schools were preferred, not only by the middle classes but also by a significant proportion of the labouring classes. A Parliamentary Select Committee return of 1838 recorded that 3,359 working-class children in Sheffield attended 'very indifferent' common day schools. 5,905 working-class children attended 'other better schools'.[35] J.C. Symons, the Children's Employment Commissioner, confirmed in 1842 that 'as many children not belonging to the working class will be found in common schools as there are working class children in the middling schools'.[36]

The reasons are not difficult to find. There was an implicit rejection of the publicly regulated schools by many working-class families. The mechanistic and regimented nature of the monitorial schools was patently disliked, especially when parents were expected to pay for their offspring to be taught by someone else's children. Other parents objected to the religious character of the denominational schools. Parents unused to the new techniques adopted in public schools clung to the traditional individual methods used in the more homely surroundings of the teacher's hearth or even local Sunday school rooms where numbers were small. And for some, the rigid rules of time-keeping, cleanliness, the regular collection of school pence and the instilling of subordination ensured the public schools were effectively shunned.

Early Learning

Dominated by the need to earn a living, the great mass of working people, estimated by Symons to be two-thirds of the population, were still preoccupied in setting their children to work. A ten-year span of schooling advanced by middle-class reformers was totally unrealistic for the working classes. The majority of children were regularly employed by the age of ten or eleven. In 1816 the Lancasterian School reported that 400 out of the 531 on roll were ten years old or younger. Twenty years later the Bettering Society complained:

> The children are not sent to school so generally or so regularly as they ought to be...thinking the little they can learn at the Sabbath School sufficient or being heedless whether they learn anything but to work at some business by which at the early age of nine or ten years upwards they may earn something if it be but a shilling or eighteen pence a week towards the maintenance of a family. For this profit boys or girls who were making good progress in useful knowledge at the National, Lancasterian and other excellent schools have been removed to shops and warehouses to the injury of their health and morals.[37]

In 1842 Symons declared that it was 'very rare for children to commence work before they were eight years of age. Many are found at work particularly at the houses of their parents at nine or ten; but the great majority do not begin until they are eleven'. The Children's Employment Commission discovered only 652 boys and 102 girls under thirteen regularly employed in the Sheffield Trades. The casual nature of child employment in the town was more difficult for observers to assess, and accounts in no small measure for spasmodic school attendance and to some extent for the frequent changes of address and schools. Few working-class children enjoyed a continuous span in any one school—twelve months was the average in the Church schools. There is evidence, however, of the persistent interchange between the public and private sector and from school to school. Many children learned to read before being admitted to National Schools.

This created something of an organizational problem because throughout the public sector the three Rs were tackled simultaneously whereas in the private schools writing and number were not normally introduced until the elements of reading had been mastered.

Clearly, far more children were at school in pre-Victorian Sheffield than has been popularly supposed. Children on the outskirts of the parish fared better than those in the urban centre where four years of intermittent learning sandwiched between infancy and premature employment was all that could be afforded. Nevertheless, with the growth of alternative sources of education, the movement of basic literacy was once again on an upward plane.

Literacy
Before the turn of the nineteenth century, almost every educational facility provided in the Sheffield region was from below. The 'public' schools were the outcome of local endeavour and public subscription. Schools were repaired and maintained out of local taxation and school-masters were almost entirely dependent on school fees. Financial assistance from Church and State was non-existent. Charitable endowments spurred many local communities into educational activity but were essentially for the education of the poorest. Private schools multiplied as the town expanded and the local demand for literacy grew. The innovation of Sunday schools afforded a substitute to day schools for a few but overall was only a supplement to the formal and informal instruction available.

Despite all the attempts to boost the number of public school places between 1779 and 1815 the provision was totally inadequate to meet the needs of the growing population. Mounting concern over revolutionary tendencies permeating the larger towns and cities gave rise to new initiatives that would offer basic literacy for the masses and embrace a measure of social control. Monitorial schools, National schools, infant schools and evening classes all emerged in the first quarter of the nineteenth century—places where religious values could be instilled and behaviour moulded. Subsidized schooling, initially by local benevolence and later by Church and State, markedly increased school enrolment but the impact on basic literary measured by the ability to sign the marriage register was not appreciably improved until the early Victorian period. It is important to remember, however, that formal schooling was not the only criterion for assessing educational standards. Informal learning at home or at the workbench, and the

Schooling the Poorer Child

development of popular reading habits all combined to reinforce the prevailing degree of literacy.

The statistical evidence that we have indicates that the majority of Sheffield workmen could read and about half of them could write. Male literacy sustained its superiority over female literacy but a perceptible increase in the number of literate brides is discernible. However, the initial rise in literacy noted in the 1760s declined towards the end of the century and shows little sign of recovery before the 1840s. The deterioration in the movement of literacy was parallelled in most of the expanding industrial centres of the Midlands and the North.[38]

Table 3.7

The literacy rate of brides and grooms in the neighbourhood of Sheffield, 1796–1830

Parish	1796–1800		1826–1830	
	Number	Percentage	Number	Percentage
Bradfield Chapelry				
men	59	56.2	57	65.4
women	28	26.6	44	50.0
Total	87	41.4	101	57.4
Sample size	210		176	
Ecclesfield				
men	130	56.5	190	70.4
women	94	39.6	129	47.8
Total	224	48.7	319	59.1
Sample size	460		540	
Handsworth				
men	29	67.4	126	65.6
women	21	48.8	77	40.0
Total	50	58.1	203	52.9
Sample size	86		384	
Norton				
men	34	83.0	45	85.0
women	23	56.0	38	71.7
Total	57	69.5	83	78.3
Sample size	82		106	

Sheffield

men	1,304	62.5	2,396	62.9
women	678	32.5	1,416	35.8
Total	1,982	47.6	3,812	48.2
Sample size	4,168		7,902	

In 1791 the Freemen of the Cutlers' Company petitioned against a Bill before parliament to amend the Incorporation Act of 1624. The petition was signed by 1,493 out of a total of 2,476, suggesting a literacy rate of 65.8 per cent which is well above the marriage signature index and compares well with national estimates.[39] In a petition to the House of Lords in 1815, 126 Catholic inhabitants of Sheffield opposed to the numerous and degrading penal laws signed the document.[40] At the 'climbing boys' annual dinner in April 1824, when 24 lads were invited, 'only one was found who didnt learn to read, of the rest many could both read and write'.[41]

Between 1833 and 1842, 1,900 apprentices attended the Mechanics' Institute of whom it was estimated that only one in 200 could not read and 40 (20 per cent) were incapable of writing.[42] In contrast, Symons interviewed 53 boys and girls aged between seven and $17\frac{1}{2}$ years who worked in local industries (metal, iron, potteries and coal). Of these, 34 could read (64 per cent); 20 could both read and write (37 per cent).[43]

Evidence from a totally different source is derived from the wealth of statistical data accumulated in the 1830s by Dr G.C. Holland during his investigations into the health and physical condition of Sheffield workmen.[44] The staple trades demanded a complex variety of skills and dexterity in some branches whilst a considerable degree of muscular energy was required for others. The benefits of literacy in the workplace more often than not reflected the degree of craftsmanship and design involved in the occupation.[45] It is patently clear that the silver plate and edge tool manufacturers expected a higher degree of literacy in their workforce and the majority of cutlers and tradesmen had required literate apprentices since the seventeenth century. Whereas 83 per cent of saw grinders and 66 per cent of saw handle makers could read, 95 per cent of sawsmiths (or makers) could both read and write. Similarly, there were not above half a dozen silversmiths and platers— 'numbered amongst the most intelligent and best paid men in the light trades'—who could not read and write. At the other end of the scale, out of 197 men and boys employed in fork grinding—the occupation most injurious to health—only 109 could read (55.3 per cent) and 69 could write (35 per cent).

The wide discrepancy of male literacy between one branch of the Sheffield trades and another complicates the interpretation of the data in Table 3.8. Such averages include experienced and younger workers—many of whom left school in the difficult Napoleonic War years. Nevertheless, it is a representative sample of Sheffield workmen and affirms that almost two-thirds could read and nearly half could write.

Table 3.8

Occupational literacy of Sheffield workmen, 1830s

	Total	Able to read	Able to write
Penblade grinders	319	244	223
Razor blade grinders	275	135	84
Scissor grinders	213	115	98
Fork grinders	97	54	34
Sawsmiths	208	197	191
Silversmiths	400	394	394
Spring knife cutlers	2,250	1,125	450
File cutters	1,420	1,136	994
	5,182	3,400 (65.6%)	2,468 (47.6%)

Significantly, their apprentices (excluding the silver plating aristocracy) aged between 10 and 21 who had more recently left school show a marked improvement both in reading and overall literacy.

Table 3.9

Occupational literacy of Sheffield apprentices, 1830s

	Total	Able to read	Able to write
Penblade grinders	215	182	168
Razor blade grinders	191	76	50
Scissor grinders	117	75	60
Fork grinders	100	55	35
Sawsmiths	130	130	130
Spring knife cutlers	600	360	125
File cutters	700	595	525
	2,053	1,473 (71.7%)	1,093 (53.2%)

Female literacy appears to be well below the national average which according to Laqueur rose from 36 per cent in the 1750s to 43 per cent by 1810. Even so a more cheerful picture is presented when compared with Manchester and industrial Lancashire.[46]

Table 3.10

Female literacy in Sheffield and industrial Lancashire, 1760–1820

	1760s	1790s	1820s
	Percentage	*Percentage*	*Percentage*
Industrial Lancashire	24	26.4	21
Manchester	28	30.3	21
Sheffield	33.8	32.5	35.8
Ecclesfield and Bradfield	34.5	36.4	48.3

In the light of the evidence in Tables 3.8 to 3.10 we must treat with caution the conclusions reached by the Poor Law Officers in 1838 on the state of literacy in the neighbourhood of Sheffield, particularly in the densely packed centre. In the returns submitted to the Secretary of State it was represented that only 20 per cent of the whole population of the Ecclesall Poor Law Union—comprising Ecclesall Bierlow, Upper and Nether Hallam, the Parish of Norton and the Chapelries of Dore and Totley—could neither read nor write. Additional data was supplied to Symons by the registrar in 1842.[47]

Table 3.11

Literacy of informants of death in Ecclesall Poor Law Union, 1842

	Ecclesall Bierlow	Nether Hallam	Upper Hallam and Dore	Norton
Number who signed their name	364	88	30	39
Number who made their mark	185	74	30	15
	549	162	60	54
Percentage of literacy	66.3%	54.3%	50%	72.2%

In the Sheffield Union—which included Attercliffe and Darnall, Brightside, the Parish of Handsworth and the Township of Sheffield—the outcome was even more optimistic. Six per cent were said to be unable to read and 33 per cent unable to write. The clerks presented their findings following a house-to-house survey of every adult in the Attercliffe township.

Such evidence supports the conclusion that there was a fluctuating growth in the number of people who were literate and is counter to the pessimistic impression frequently conveyed. In general we can confirm that by 1840 two thirds of the male population were basically literate and approaching fifty per cent of females—in line with national estimates.[48] It is certainly clear that 'the younger generation possessed a higher degree of literacy than did their parents'.

In the search for clues in the movement of literacy, many of those who could sign their names could probably write little else before the drive for mass education. Unlike reading, which was taught universally, writing was not considered an essential component of the school curriculum until midway through the nineteenth century. With the introduction of libraries in the town centre, Sunday schools and the large monitorial schools, many more children and adults acquired reading habits. It was claimed that 'admission to and exclusion from the privilege of having a book from the (school) library supercedes the necessity for any other reward or punishment'. In 1824 the Mechanics' Library opened. It was intended for the labouring and artisan class but was monopolized by 'subscribers in good circumstances'. Restricted to the acquisition of sound information, all novels, plays and works 'subversive of the Church' were prohibited. Increasingly, however, books were becoming accessible to the working classes.

Newspaper reading escalated during the French Revolutionary period and was not entirely confined to the middle classes. In 1792 the Sheffield Society for Constitutional Information reported 1,400 subscribers for a pamphlet edition (at 6d) of the first part of Paine's *Rights of Man* which was read 'with avidity in many parts of the workshops of Sheffield'.[49] At the same time, Joseph Gale's radical opinion expanded the circulation of the *Sheffield Register* to 2,000 copies weekly—a considerable feat for the provincial press in the eighteenth century. James Montgomery retained a fair circulation when he revamped the paper as the *Sheffield Iris* but could not maintain the figures achieved by his predecessor. In a letter to Samuel Taylor Coleridge referring to the wretchedness of the people, Montgomery wrote: 'as for the poor in the town, who were formerly great readers, they are reduced to ashes by the war'.[50]

In the 1830s the combined circulation of the four weekly newspapers published in the town topped 4,000. Taxation had driven the price up to 6d in 1800, and 7d in 1815, thus preventing the artisan from purchasing his own copy.[51] Nevertheless, informal channels of distribution were widespread and copies were available in libraries and news rooms, coffee shops and ale houses. Arguably the most significant factor in reinforcing working-class literacy was the phenomenal output of Sunday school tracts which ran into millions. The Religious Tract Society, the British and Foreign Bible Society, SPCK and the Sunday School Union all had depots in the town and were the major agencies in the distribution of religious literature. The promotion of literacy was a prerequisite of the moral reformer and the religious educator. Clearly the contribution of the Sunday school movement and its allied press was an essential element in sustaining the development of literacy throughout the first half of the nineteenth century.

Notes

1. *SI* (6 August 1831).
2. J.J. Graham, *Wesleyan Methodism in Sheffield Park* (1914), p. 16.
3. *Sheffield Times* (6 June 1846).
4. *Sheffield Register* (24 February 1792).
5. H. Kilham, *Memoir of Hannah Kilham* (1837), p. 22.
6. H. Longden, *The Life of Henry Longden* (1813), pp. 138-39.
7. *Sheffield Iris* (9 August 1814).
8. Sheffield District National Society, *Annual Report* (1822), SCL.
9. Sheffield Sunday School Union, *4th Annual Report* (1816), SCL.
10. Sycamore Street Sunday School Rules 1810. MP 904, SCL.
11. *Sheffield Iris* (8 June 1824).
12. *Sheffield Iris* (24 May 1831).
13. Red Hill Sunday School Rules. MD 2710-3, SCL.
14. *Abstract of Education Returns*, 1835, 3, pp. 1160-61, 1188, 1191-93.
15. *Newspaper Cuttings Relating to Sheffield*, 12, SCL.
16. See Trust Deed, Red Hill Sunday School (20 September 1816), MD 2710, SCA; Red Hill Sunday School Committee Book, NR 561, SCA. The success of the pro-writing faction in Sheffield was contrary to the conclusions drawn by E.P. Thompson, *The Making of the English Working Class* (1968), p. 389, and T.W. Lacqueur, *Religion and Respectability* (1976), p. 83.
17. Red Hill Sunday School, Miscellaneous Papers. MD 2710-4, SCA.
18. *Children's Employment Commission, Second Report*, Trades and Manufactures, 1843, J.C. Symons' *Report on the Trades of Sheffield and on the Moral and Physical Condition of the Young Persons Employed in Them.* Henley Evidence. Appendix, e6.
19. CEC *Second Report*, Trades and Manufactures, 1843, *Symons' Report*. Appendix, E26.
20. Mercer, 'School Provision', pp. 376-95, 397-403.

21.   Park Free School Tablet 1787. St John's C. of E. School, Manor Oaks Road, Sheffield.

22.   A. Smith, *Wealth of Nations*, 2 (1904 edn), p. 302.

23.   *Poor Girl's Primer: For the Use of the Charity School in Sheffield* (1789).

24.   See Sheffield Girls' Charity School *Annual Reports* (1788, 1789); *Sheffield Iris* (18 March 1796; 29 August 1800; 3 October 1800).

25.   *Newspaper Cuttings Relating to Sheffield*, 2, p. 35.

26.   Lancasterian School *Annual Reports*, SCL; G.J. Eltringham, 'The Lancasterian Schools in Sheffield', *THAS*, 5 (1943), pp. 147-52; Mercer, 'School Provision', pp. 303-306.

27.   Sheffield District National Society *Annual Reports* (1815–26), SCA.

28.   *Digest of Returns to Circulars on the Means of Parochial Instruction*, 1819, pt II, p. 1156.

29.   *Sheffield Iris* (5 October 1824, 21 February 1826).

30.   *Abstract of Education Returns*, 1835, 3, pp. 1191-93.

31.   *Abstract of Education Returns*, 1835, 3, pp. 1160-61, 1188, 1191-93.

32.   CEC *Second Report*, Trades and Manufactures, 1843, Appendix E20.

33.   I. Inkster, 'Culture, Institution and Urbanity: The Itinerant Science Lecturer in Sheffield 1790–1850', in S. Pollard and C. Holmes (eds.), *Essays in the Economic and Social History of South Yorkshire* (1977), p. 223.

34.   See Mercer, 'School Provision', pp. 419-57 for more detailed discussion of private schools.

35.   *Report of Select Committee on the Education of the Poorer Classes*, 1838, p. viii.

36.   CEC *Second Report*, Trades and Manufactures, 1843, Appendix E19.

37.   Quoted in G.C. Holland, *Inquiry into the Moral, Social and Intellectual Condition of the Industrious Classes* (1839), p. 35. In 1851 Horace Mann calculated that 'upon average the labouring classes may perhaps have $4^2/_3$ years of schooling. A very considerable part of their instruction is imparted during what may be described as the infant period'. *Census of Great Britain 1851*, 1852–1853, vol. XC, p. 41.

38.   Compare M. Sanderson, *Education, Economic Change and Society in England 1780–1870* (1983), pp. 14-15; 'Literacy and Social Mobility in the Industrial Revolution', *Past and Present*, 56 (1972); W.T. Lacqueur, 'Literacy in the Industrial Revolution', *Past and Present*, 64 (1974); W.B. Stephens, *Education Literacy and Society*, pp. 6-7; D.F. Mitch, *The Rise of Popular Literacy in Victorian England* (Philadelphia 1992), pp. 1-2.

39.   Petition of Cutlers' Company (1791), MD 571-74, SCA.

40.   Petition to the House of Lords (1815), MD 249, SCA.

41.   *Sheffield Iris* (20 April 1824).

42.   G.C. Holland, *Vital Statistics of Sheffield* (1843), p. 233.

43.   CEC *First Report*, Mines, 1842, pp. 226-29. CEC *Second Report*, Trades and Manufactures, 1843, Appendix, e1-35, e54-58.

44. G.C. Holland, *The Mortality, Sufferings and Diseases of Grinders*, 1, p. 21, 2, p. 17, 3, p. 25 (1841–42), and Holland, *Vital Statistics*, pp. 156f.

45. See Mitch, *Rise of Popular Literacy*, pp. 5-78 for a fuller discussion of this.

46. W.T. Lacqueur, 'Literacy in the Industrial Revolution', *Past and Present*, 64 (1974); Sanderson, *Education, Economic Change and Society*, Table 2, p. 15.

47. *SI* (1 December 1838); *Sheffield Mercury* (1 December 1838); Symons, Report, CEC Trades, p. 13.

48. See *Registrar General's Annual Report* (1840). Percentage of marriage marks for England and Wales: male 33.6 per cent, female 50 per cent.

49. Quoted in Thompson, *English Working Classes*, p. 164.

50. Quoted in F.K. Donnelly and J.L. Baxter, 'Sheffield and the English Revolutionary Tradition', Pollard and Holmes, *Economic and Social History*, p. 101.

51. D. Read, *Press and People 1790–1850* (1961), p. 170.

Part II

Voluntary Effort and State Support 1839–1870

Chapter 4

Political Opinion and Popular Education 1839–1870

Education is an instrument of good or evil
According to the power that wields it.
                    Red Hill School Banner (1841)

Midway through the 1830s, the vision of educating all the common
people was superimposed on the contemporary philosophy of
educating the poor. The concept of 'popular education', a term widely
used in the twentieth century, surfaced as 'National Education' when
one of Sheffield's most popular figures, Dr Arnold Knight, canvassed
the idea in 1836. Knighted for his services to the community in 1841,
co-founder of the Sheffield Literary and Philosophical Society (1822)
and Medical School (1829), the Roman Catholic physician at the
General Infirmary advocated an effective universal system of elementary education embracing the social and moral as well as the intellectual
improvement of the rising generation. Supported by Dissenters and
Radicals, the phrenologist James Simpson, a founder of secular schools
in Scotland and admirer of the Liverpool 'mixed' schools, was invited
to give a series of lectures in the town.

    In the ensuing debates, the Revd Robert Slater Bayley, voiced the
cry of aggrieved Dissenters excluded from the universities and their
'spawning grounds' the grammar schools. He railed against the incompetence of the teachers in the ineffectual National schools as 'a bed of
sectarian education under the spiritual police of the state clergy' and
argued that civil liberty and popular education were unlikely to be
furthered by 'the ingrowth of Methodism through the walls of the
Established Church'. He called for a national system that extended
beyond religion, morality and the basic subjects to an all-embracing
liberal education.[1] Ebenezer Elliott, the Corn Law rhymer, visualized
the time 'when the have nothings will be educated if the have some-
things will let them, aye and whether they will or not'.

Conservative evangelicals within the Church and Methodism sought the education of every child but were not prepared to leave 'the means to the wisdom of Parliament'. Suspicious of Catholic intervention and the secular emphasis of protagonists they were opposed to an education reduced to a vague knowledge of children's duty to God, their neighbours and themselves. They maintained that 'the reading of the Holy Scriptures and instruction in the faith and duty of a Christian' was an essential and integral part of any adopted system.

The outcome was a petition of 12,000 signatures to the House of Commons in favour of popular education on the Irish model as developed in the interdenominational 'mixed' schools of Liverpool.[2] Sheffield was congratulated by the champion of education reform in parliament, the Catholic Sir Thomas Wyse,[3] but the movement for a state system of education failed. However, a committee of the Privy Council was created in 1839 to supervise the distribution of parliamentary grants to schools associated with inspection.

As the scale of grant aid increased, the arm of the Established Church was effectively strengthened to the unconcealed dismay of Dissenters and secularists alike. Four fifths of the annual budget went to Church-aided schools and concessions allowed the archbishops to approve the Inspectorate of the burgeoning network of National schools. Whilst the Committee could not accept the claim of the Church that education was essentially an ecclesiastical concern, for historic reasons and economic considerations, parliament was not prepared to impose its civil authority.

With the change of government in 1841, the Tory Home Secretary attempted to strengthen the education clauses of the proposed Factory Act in 1843. He advocated compulsory education for all factory and pauper children and affirmed that religious instruction was the vehicle for subjugating the tendencies to violence, insurrection and crime. Consequently he was prepared to defer to the Church if necessary. This antagonized the Nonconformists and disturbed the Roman Catholics. Eighteen petitions from Wesleyan congregations and schools throughout the Sheffield region opposed to the teaching of the Anglican catechism and liturgy were presented to John Stuart Wortley, Earl of Wharncliffe and Lord President of the Council (1841–45).

R.S. Bayley argued that the country could not afford the increased taxation 'even for education'. The Roman Catholics were opposed to the notion of inspection, fearing that the Inspectors would compare their 'Poor Schools with the fine Protestant schools and compel them to shut'. Robert Leader, editor of the *Sheffield Independent,* voiced local Dissenting opinion when he wrote:

> The Bill did not provide equally or justly to all the religious sects. They had long urged the duty of the state to provide for the working classes but they objected to schools maintained by the public yet having no influence on their management or conduct.[4]

In the event, the educational clauses of the Factory Act of 1844 were withdrawn and the hope of establishing universal elementary education was postponed for almost thirty years. One outcome of the controversy, however, was the increasing influence of a body of Dissenters whose declared object was to resist all state intervention in educational issues. Inspired by Edward Baines of Leeds, they became known as the Voluntaryist party who embraced 'the doctrine of educational free trade and the immorality of state action'.

Militant Nonconformity in Sheffield had the ear of Lord Wharncliffe, a Peelite politician who favoured the development of educational measures undertaken by the previous Whig Ministry and supported the rights of Nonconformists and Roman Catholics to an equal share of state aid. He was congratulated by the *Sheffield Independent* for his liberal stance but vilified by *The Times* for promoting a system of secular education on which the Church did not dominate. Although he lacked weight in Cabinet to extend his plan he increased the education budget from £40,000 to £70,000, he vigorously encouraged the promotion of voluntary schools and before his untimely death in 1845 he created a climate conducive to the publication of the Committee of Council Minutes of December 1846.

When the Minutes were presented to parliament in 1847, however, the hostile reaction in the town was unprecedented. Commentators declared 'it surpassed almost anything of the kind usually seen at the time of a general election'. Walls were plastered with bills, and posters and placards opposing the measures appeared on every conceivable hoarding. The fury was directed at the scheme to develop teacher training. Kay-Shuttleworth, the energetic Secretary of the Committee, proposed to improve the discredited monitorial schools by inaugurating a pupil-teacher system. The programme contemplated financial rewards for more effective teaching, increasing the education estimates to £100,000 and the introduction of the Queen's Scholarship whereby selected students could attend a training college. The whole package was seen by many as a ploy to intensify the powers of the state.

Whereas the *Sheffield Iris* welcomed the proposals and believed they 'would immensely assist the labouring poor to obtain an education much superior to the imperfect and barren one which has heretofore been given them', articulate working men objected to the notion of teachers being paid by the state and one trenchant placard read 'When government begins by paying my schoolmaster it will probably end by compelling the attendance of my children'. The *Sheffield Independent* regarded the whole scheme as 'a prodigal expense' and totally unnecessary.[5]

A public meeting scheduled for the Town Hall had to adjourn to Paradise Square where almost 4,000 were assembled. The Town Council, incorporated in 1843, voted overwhelmingly in favour, as did most of the influential churchmen and townsfolk. Isaac Ironside, President of the Workers' Educational Institute, together with Richard Otley and Michael Beal, all Town Councillors, voiced their Chartist support. They scorned the sectarian differences and begrudgingly voted for the government and Church.[6] Whilst opposing the use of the catechism as a class book Bayley pressed for the separation of the secular from the religious but acknowledged that 'the Dissenters cannot meet the educational wants of the country nor have they shown how it can be done'.

Nevertheless, public opinion sided with political dissent and voted three to one against the measures and further state interference; 17,570 were persuaded that the policy was unjust and centralizing. The concentration of power in the government and the Church would only create 'servility in the people'. A petition showed 5,732 in favour. The Sheffield vote failed to obstruct government policy, however, and once the co-operation of the National Society and the Wesleyan supervisory body was confirmed, a safe passage for the Minutes was assured.

The political after-effects in Sheffield were quite far-reaching. Militant Nonconformity resolved to support the Voluntaryist position and form a district committee of the Congregational Board of Education which refused all education grants, parted from the British and Foreign School Society and stiffened denominationalism. On the other hand the Chartist and Owenite Hall of Science members backed the radical, secularist approach of the Lancashire Public School Society. Their sponsored MP for Oldham, the Unitarian W.J. Fox urged that a liberal, comprehensive, unsectarian education for all should be funded by a special rate. The Town Council petitioned in support of the Fox

Bill in 1850 and twelve months later passed a motion advocating a general system of secular instruction supported by local rates. There was a general agreement that 'a good education would diminish intemperance, misery and crime, promote morality and was conducive to the best interests of all classes'.

Active campaigns to mould public opinion and a sequence of abortive Bills in the 1850s failed either to give town councils the local representation they sought or to meet denominational expectations. Eventually Sir John Pakington secured the appointment of a Royal Commission in 1857 'to inquire into the present state of education in England and to consider what measures if any are required for the extension of sound and cheap elementary instruction to all classes of people'. Samuel Ellis discerned an 'armed truce' between the educational adversaries locally but R.S. Gainsford of Darnall Hall was convinced that some form of coercion was necessary to get more children to school and keep them there longer.[7]

As the clamour for education to combat moral degeneration and social disorder declined, the fear of democracy emerged as a central issue in the promotion of educational extension. Early in 1858, the popular evangelical Canon Sale, Vicar of Sheffield (1851–73), expressed the views troubling the middle classes. 'We are gradually approaching the time when the government of the country will be more in the hands of the working classes. It is important therefore that the people should be so educated as not only to enable them to use that power wisely and properly but to fit them for all the duties of life'. His son-in-law Revd James Moorhouse, agreed. 'With democracy staring us in the face unless we choose to allow the people to be led by mere windbags we must educate them and enable them to judge as to the character of the men that presented themselves for election.' John Brown, Industrialist and Churchman, concurred, 'We cannot educate the working classes too well'.[8]

Scrutiny of the civil estimates in the wake of the costly expedition to the Crimea (1854–56) fuelled criticism of the total budget. The inquiry into the state of popular education, subsequently known as the Newcastle Commission (1858–61) set about finding a more cost-effective instrument for securing elementary school efficiency. The report in 1861 confirmed that the government grant for public education had quadrupled over the past ten years, was rising at around £100,000 per year and was now in the region of £800,000. There was a significant rise in the number of pupils taught, yet less than half were in grant-aided schools. To bring the whole child population within the orbit of state assistance would create an insuperable financial burden. In consequence the Commissioners pragmatically resigned themselves to proposals for tackling the irregularity of attendance, the chronic brevity of school life, ineffective teaching and a simplification of the grant system.

In general, the press in Sheffield welcomed the Report and its proposals. They accepted Vice-President Lowe's forecast that 'if it did not promote efficiency it would at least be cheap'. Leader in the *Sheffield Independent* subscribed to the maxim that 'when the state pays for education it must have proof that children actually received the education'. He believed that under the old system of inspection teachers were being paid independently of the success of their own exertions and secured their salaries with the connivance of managers whether they taught efficiently or not. He charged the teachers with a sense of unmerited arrogance as they had assumed 'a rather lofty status as servants of the government' and foresaw that the proportion of grant would be seen as a test of merit by which the relative efficiency of the schools could be compared.[9]

Sheffield schoolmasters protested at the retrograde steps which would curtail the developing curriculum of 'extra subjects' and check the progress of popular education because the attendance of children over the age of eleven would be discouraged. They forecast a significant withdrawal of certificated teachers and a diminution in the quality of the teaching force when less competent assistants could be acquired more cheaply. Teacher opposition was anticipated but the sympathetic support of the clergy was not.[10]

Canon Sale acknowledged the progress made since the turn of the century when one in seventeen of the population was under instruction compared with the current one in seven. He reiterated his call to elevate the masses and fit them to enjoy the franchise by having them educated properly. But he feared the effects of the Revised Code. 'At present the children are not only receiving instruction but are being trained to habits of cleanliness, discipline and order. Under the new code things are to be entirely changed.'

Whereas the teachers did not welcome the prospect of being 'at the mercy of the discretion and capricious acts' of school managers, the clergy were not convinced that the Code provided any inducement for pupil teachers to work or behave well which affected the discipline of the whole school. In response to their complaint that there was no financial incentive to teach religious instruction the legislators responded by saying it was never their intention to provide religious instruction 'but only to assist those by whom it was offered requiring in return for their assistance a certain amount of secular education'.

The Revised Code of 1862 was sanctioned after considerable parliamentary debate and compromise. School inspections were to give way to individual pupil examination. Subjective evaluation was replaced by objective assessment and in the words of the Commission 'it made the prospects and position of the teacher dependent to a considerable degree on the results of these examinations'. The system of 'payment by results' was born. National performance targets were set in the three Rs for all children from seven years of age upwards. The curriculum was restricted to the basic subjects plus religious instruction and needlework for the girls. Regulations regarding the general condition of the schools—that is, lighting, drainage, ventilation, space per child, competence of the head teacher and adequate staffing—were all prescribed.

When the Revised Code become operative in August 1863 modifications to the grant structure were tabulated. Each child over the age of six who attended over two hundred meetings per year earned the school a grant of four shillings and a possible further eight shillings subject to examination. Failure to satisfy the Inspector in the required standard of any of the basic subjects involved the forfeiture of 2s. 8d per subject. Providing the instruction of children under six years was appropriate and did not interfere with the education of older children, a grant of 6s. 6d per child could be earned. Payments direct to certificated teachers were abolished and paid instead to school managers. A lower class of certificate was instituted but uncertificated teachers were denied the benefits of grant-aided status. The school logbook now became mandatory. The effects of the Revised Code have reverberated through the corridors of primary education ever since.

Purely by chance, Sheffield became the focus of national attention midway through the 1860s. The National Association for the Promotion of Social Sciences (NAPSS) arranged its annual congress in the town in 1865. In the same year the *Report of the Children's Employment Commission on the Metal Manufactures of the Sheffield District* was published. The quality of the conference and the ensuing report and discussions induced the Town Council to survey all the neglected and labouring children within its borders. Well before the investigations were finalized, the town was rocked by press disclosures of violence, intimidation and 'the abominable practice of rattening' in the cutlery trade. The scandal of the Sheffield Outrages led to an inquiry by Her Majesty's Inspectors into the state of elementary education in the town.[11]

The Town Council's inquiry into school attendance in 1866 revealed a school population of 19,000 (10,363 boys, 8,669 girls) under the age of 12 in 265 schools. These statistics, which Isaac Ironside, Chairman of the Committee, found encouraging confirm Her Majesty's Inspector (HMI) Buckley's view that '49 per cent of children neither work nor attend schools but spend their time in idleness or something worse'.[12]

The outcome of HMI Watkins' investigation into the quality of Sheffield's schooling was one of reasonable satisfaction as to 'numbers, discipline and attainments' but that 'there ought to be three times the number in attendance' in the public elementary schools. He focused on the Church-aided schools and out of the 24 ecclesiastical parishes within the borough, 17 schools had a certificated head teacher in every department. In five districts, the schools were run by uncertificated teachers. These were Darnall, Crosspool, Fulwood, Dyers Hill and St Philip's. In the parishes of St James, St Simon's, Gilcar and Hollis Croft there was 'little of note'.

Seven schools were singled out for special praise: St Peter's (Parish Church Schools); Holy Trinity, Wicker; Pitsmoor; St Stephen's; St George's; St John's Boys; and the Blue Coat School. Out of the 44 schools inspected only six were designated infant schools taught by certificated mistresses. 6,320 children were presented for examination— 2,852 boys, 2,211 girls and 1,257 infants. This is 54 per cent of the whole, which compared unfavourably with 61 per cent in Doncaster and 70 per cent in Retford.

The gaps indicated in the Report were filled by new schools before 1871. The black spots highlighted the serious deficiencies in the voluntary system. One was at Dyer's Hill in the Park district, a warren of alleys, streets and courtyards. Out of a population of 8,000 only a hundred children gathered regularly in the dark, damp, inadequately furnished schoolrooms. The extensive parish of St Philip's with an estimated population of 18,000 was even more poorly served.

At the Walkley end of the parish was a small school, run by a certificated master with 88 youngsters in attendance, which was said to be in 'a fair state of discipline and elementary attainments'. Closer to the Parish Church in Hoyle Street was St Philip's National School in a totally neglected state. The boys' school had been discontinued, and the girls and infants were taught by two uncertificated sisters who conducted the school as a private adventure school. Watkins believed the mistress deserved more credit than blame. She paid seven shillings per week to the incumbent, bought all the books, slates and apparatus, paid for the fuel and light, her sister's services and the girl monitors when required. By the time the School Board surveyed the district in 1871 the population had risen to 23,425 and the deficiency of efficient school places was twice that of any other sector.[13]

The combined effects of the reports and disclosures generated a marked shift in public opinion towards a system of compulsory education 'for the sake of society'. Few now needed convincing of the necessity to educate the newly enfranchised workers in the wake of the second Reform Act. Moreover, enforced schooling was considered a far more effective means of preventing little children entering Sheffield's deadliest trades than the extension of Factory Acts.

Disenchanted with the political gadfly John Roebuck, one-time Professor of Radicalism and MP for Sheffield since 1849, political dissenters turned to a pioneer in industrial relations and an enthusiast for education, A.J. Mundella, the Nottingham manufacturer, as their Liberal candidate in the forthcoming election. He admired the Prussian education system and enlarged on the high standard of literacy enjoyed by his workforce in Saxony.

Armed with a wealth of statistics culled from HMIs Watkins and Fitch, Mundella was convinced that the only answer to the 50 per cent of children not attending school was a national system of compulsory education supervised locally.[14] His election was secured by a combination of employer and working-class interests, replacing Roebuck as the co-Liberal MP for Sheffield in November 1868. Six months later Alderman Saunders successfully moved a petition in the Town Council in favour of such a plan. The petition focused on the inability of the voluntary system to keep pace with the rapid expansion of the population and the recognition that the state must step in to enforce the education of the people. The motion was carried unanimously—an event that five years earlier would have appeared inconceivable.[15]

The campaign for a free, compulsory education system and the setting-up of local boards was orchestrated locally by the formation of a branch of the National Education League. At a branch meeting in January 1870 the two rival newspaper editors, the Liberal Robert Leader and the Conservative W.C. Leng, united in calling for urgent government action.[16] Mundella supported much of the League's programme but was wary of the secularist position and parted company over free education because he could not accept the setting aside of the existing agencies. Churchmen, anxious to protect the voluntary school interests, affiliated with the National Education Union. They recognized the right of the state to say 'erect or we shall do it ourselves' but they were opposed to any attempt to exclude religion, to throw the whole cost onto the rates, or to destroy the present system.[17]

Nationwide pressure inevitably led to the drafting of an Education Bill. Mundella dismissed fears that the government were displacing parental rights to educate their children and stressed the Bill would rightly enforce the parent's natural responsibility 'not merely for the sake of the child but for the sake of society'.[18] The proposals to supplement the voluntary system by filling the gaps were generally welcomed but the League was disappointed by the repudiation of free schools, and the permissive nature of the compulsory clauses relating to the creation of school boards was attacked by Leader and Mundella. The question as to who should nominate the *ad hoc* bodies was eventually resolved by adopting the American solution of election by ratepayers.

Acrimonious debates on the religious character of the proposed 'supplemental' schools were forestalled by a resolution of Protestant clergy who agreed that religious instruction should be solely biblical, given by the regular class teacher, and all creeds and formularies should be excluded.[19] The Roman Catholics defended the present system and paid little heed to the ongoing discussions. Gladstone's reluctant acceptance of the Cowper–Temple conscience clause pleased most shades of political opinion and the removal of existing denominational schools from school board control enabled them to survive side by side in a 'dual system'.

Leader summed up the feeling admirably when he wrote:

> No measure was possible that would entirely satisfy either of the parties into which educationists are divided. In the need for compromise we went into the question so bent upon having an Education Bill that we were prepared to make any compromise essential to its success.[20]

The 'dual system' effectively denied the voluntary schools the benefit of rate support until 1902 and the unequal struggle was a persistent source of conflict. Free schooling was confined to the very poor until 1891 and the introduction of compulsory education was determined by the elected representatives of the school board. Nevertheless, a watershed had been reached. The state had finally accepted the responsibility for educating the nation's children. In the town of Sheffield there was no shortage of those prepared to meet the demands of what was arguably the most vital reform of the century, but beyond the fringe the response was distinctly variable. What is certain is that no measure more affected the lives of working people nor delivered a more effective response to the challenge of democracy.

Notes

1. *SI* (28 October 1837); R.S. Bayley, *A Lecture on National Education* (1837), LP 42, SCL.

2. *Sheffield Mercury* (21 October 1837).

3. *SI* (18 November 1837).

4. *SI* (4 March 1843).

5. *Sheffield Mercury* (3 April 1847); *Sheffield Iris* (1 April 1847); *SI* (13 March 1847).

6. *SI* (3 April 1847); *Sheffield Mercury* (3 April 1847). See also D.K. Jones, Isaac Ironside, 'Democracy and the Education of the Poor', *THAS,* 11 (1981), pp. 28-37.

7. *SI* (13 June 1857; 4 July 1857).

8. *SI* (2 January 1858).

9. *SI* (31 March 1862).

10. *SI* (23 January 1862).

11. CCE (1867), *HMI Watkins' Report*, pp. 279-80.

12. *SI* (27 January 1866; 7 February 1866; 24 April 1869).

13. J.H. Bingham, *The Period of the Sheffield School Board 1870–1903* (1949), Appendix IV.

14. *SI* (22 September 1868).

15. *Sheffield Times* (13 March 1869); *SI* (10 March 1869).

16. *SI* (18 January 1870).

17. *SI* (18 December 1869).

18. *SI* (18 January 1870).

19. *SI* (26 April 1870; 25 May 1870).

20. *SI* (25 July 1870).

Chapter 5

Teachers, Schools and Classes 1839–1870

I do not think it generally practicable or desirable for poor boys to be kept at school beyond 13 years of age and poor girls beyond 14. Boys might be required to attend school 5 days a week because there is no demand for their services at home. Girls might be required to attend 4 or 3$^1/_2$ days a week. There is a demand for girls at home to nurse the baby and mind the younger children while mother washes, irons and cleans the house.

Evidence of Revd Samuel Earnshaw to Newcastle Commission (1859)

School Expansion

Once parliament empowered the state to subsidize the voluntary schools, pressures built up for a supervisory body to control expenditure and distribute the grants which were conditional upon inspection. With the creation of the Committee of the Privy Council in 1839, Her Majesty's Inspectors were recruited to monitor and appraise the growth of the rapidly expanding school system. One feature of their work was to gather reliable information as to the quantity and quality of schooling and from their reports we glean some measure of their condition.

The implied criticism of the 'national education' lobby, the possibility of enhanced government funding and the profusion of educational statistics prompted the Church in Sheffield to extend its influence. The inadequacy of the Church school provision was outlined at a public meeting in Carver Street School in 1839 when the evangelical Thomas Sutton, Vicar of Sheffield, moved a resolution stressing the obligation of the Church 'to improve the education which is afforded for children of the poorest classes'.[1] He advocated periodical inspection of all the schools associated with the Church and the need to seek out and train young people to teach in them.

The provisions of the Peel Act of 1843 for 'The Spiritual Care of the Populous Parishes' facilitated the division of the sprawling parish into ecclesiastical districts. Evangelical clergy were appointed who considered parish schools a priority of mission and many of them doubled as worship centres until the local church was built. Invariably, the great financial burden was met by congregational giving and private philanthropy supplemented by grants from the National Society, the Church Burgesses and the Exchequer. The scale of National School expansion can be gauged from the list in Table 5.1.

Table 5.1

National school expansion, 1840–61

Fulwood National	1840	Whitely Wood School	1840
Attercliffe (enlarged)	1841	Darnall National	1841
St Mary's Nat. (Hermitage St.)	1841	Crosspool National	1842
Dungworth	1842	Greenhill National School	1843
Stannington National School (extended)	1844	St Paul's National	1844
St Philip's National	1844	St George's National	1845
St John's, Park (remodelled)	1848	Clifford School	1850
Hillsborough National	1852	St Peter's (Parish Church)	1852
Holy Trinity, Wicker	1853	Neepsend National	1855
St Luke's Nat. (Dyers Hill)	1855	St Jude's Nat. Eldon St.	1855
St Andrew's Nat. Sharrow	1857	Shiregreen National (rebuilt)	1857
St Jude's National Moorfields	1860	Oughtibridge National	1860
St Stephen's National	1861		

The growth of this widespread network of schools generated several insurmountable problems in the short term. Nationally there was a dearth of qualified or competent teachers. Many candidates were either inept, provincial or culturally wanting. Unsuitable appointments, often out of charity, were very difficult to dislodge as in the case at Parson Cross where Dr Gatty opened the school to HMI inspection in 1845 in the pious hope that the master would improve. Adverse reports followed one after another yet it took 18 years before parental pressure eventually enforced his dismissal.

The lack of secular reading books was equally serious. Many schools were dependent on broadsheets and Testaments until the cheap Irish and National Society readers appeared. All other sets of readers were forbidden. Limited resources kept apparatus to a minimum and the absence of small-scale teaching areas handicapped the progress of

Figure 14. When St George's National School in Beet Street opened in 1845 it was described in the *London Evening News* as 'probably surpassing any other'.

effective teaching. Grant-aided schools were usually built for large assemblies that could double for religious purposes. Because large schoolrooms suited the monitorial style of instruction, ability groups were often separated only by curtains or a blackboard. Galleries were introduced for younger children in the 1840s and 1850s. Classrooms and partitions developed with the advent of the adult assistant in the school board era.

The success or failure of a school was determined more often than not on the supervision of the clergy, and their financial contribution was considerable. In 1847, HMI Watkins maintained that the clergy gave between one fifth and one sixth of their clerical income to the support of the schools.[2] Revd William Bruce—commended for his efforts at Wadsley by J.C. Symons in 1842—gathered together 450 children in his Sunday school and 220 for weekday schooling at his sole expense in the overcrowded urban parish of Holy Trinity, Wicker in 1846.

A succession of devoted clergy in the parish of St Mary's, Bramall Lane, enabled the dedicated teachers to promote fundamental curriculum development throughout the 1840s and 1850s. The school earned a high reputation from HMIs when one third of the 600 pupils took geography, grammar and history and the oldest boys were introduced to algebra, mechanics and the intricacies of the steam engine. Even the girls advanced to the rule of three in arithmetic 'and five beyond it'. Every morning the Vicar devised a short liturgical act of worship for the school.[3]

Whilst many of the Church schools were making good progress others were 'merely existing', as was the case at St Philip's. In 1853 HMI Moncrieffe reported:

> Nothing can exceed the disorder of this school except the igno-
> rance. Teaching is out of the question when the voice is drowned
> by noise. No subjects are now taught except reading, writing, arith-
> metic and religious knowledge. The writing alone approaches to
> being good; the arithmetic is tolerable. But the general impression
> is, especially after the religious examination, that with fewer subjects
> than formerly, those few are decidedly worse taught. But what can a
> master do alone with 170 boys.[4]

Fully comprehending the problems that beset both teachers and school managers in an age when schooling was voluntary is far from easy. The wild fluctuation of school admissions in the high density areas of Sheffield was highlighted by HMI Watkins in 1855.[5] Focusing on

St George's Boys School in that year, 369 children over the age of seven were admitted and 360 left. On admission 72 per cent had never been to infant school, 74 per cent could neither write their names or letters, and 70 per cent had done no arithmetic. The perpetual turnover of children characterizes the nature of working-class life when families were constantly searching for work, scouring the town for better or cheaper housing, or—equally germane—fleeing from vermin or the debt-collector.

It is not surprising, therefore, that when the Revd Samuel Earnshaw, Assistant Minister in Sheffield, gave evidence to the Newcastle Commission on popular education in 1859, he described education among the poor to be in a very unsatisfactory state for reasons he found 'insuperable'.[6] He claimed there was no shortage of elementary schools in the town and whilst some parents were opposed to the confinement of schooling there were others who could not afford it and set their children to work as soon as they had absorbed a little learning. Excluding the infant stage, he believed only one fifth ever reached a satisfactory standard having had five and a half years of instruction. He recognized the needs of trade and industry to test the capabilities of boys before setting them to apprenticeship and was prepared to let them go at 13. Because the attendance of girls was punctuated by domestic responsibilities he felt they could—and often did—stay longer at school. In common with many of his generation, he doubted whether compulsory education could ever be achieved.

School expansion was not confined to the Church of England. With the prospect of inspection in mind the Wesleyans resolved to create a more effective management structure by forming the Sheffield Wesleyan Methodist District School Society in December 1838.[7] By 1840 they had opened an infant school, 'mixed' schools at Red Hill, Brunswick and Park; Ebenezer Girls' and Boys' schools at Bridgehouses and Norfolk Street with a total of 1,100 children on roll. In general, Wesleyan schools were intended for 'the children of tradesmen, of farmers, and mechanics of the higher class, rather than for the sake of the children of the poor'.[8] Their local admission policy was clearly defined:

Res. II That the primary object to be sought in the establishment of such schools shall be the religious instruction of the children of Methodist parents; the offspring of persons regularly attending their places of worship or any other willing to entrust them to their care.

In order to combat the secularist arguments, the fear of popery and 'the licentious infidelity under the name of Socialism', the Methodists were anxious to preserve religious instruction. But they were prepared to integrate 'the several branches of secular knowledge' so that the children would be equipped for 'the several duties of life', their future well-being and advancement.

The large Red Hill Wesleyan day school followed a modified monitorial plan. When Symons visited the school in 1841 the only individual instruction was in handwriting. Geography and grammar were added to the three Rs for the more able. The lesson books were those published by the Irish National Schools and the Sunday School Union. British and Foreign cards supplemented the Bible and Testaments. Because of the continual turnover of children in the neighbourhood little more than the basics were attempted in the 1850s.

Brunswick Wesleyan, described by Symons as among the best in Sheffield, was not regularly inspected. The school was held in the basement of the chapel. Pupils were charged 2d for reading and 3d for the three Rs. The 'interrogative system' was used and each child was heard to read both individually and collectively. Morning school was devoted to the basic subjects but in the afternoon the Wesleyan Conference catechism was taught together with spelling, additional reading and the 'extra' subjects. McCulloch's *Reading Lessons*, and Chamber's *Natural Philosophy and Drawing* were the main textbooks. Symons declared that the children in Brunswick were more proficient and answered more intelligently than those in the majority of Sheffield schools.[9]

Park Wesleyan School developed a more varied curriculum to include geography, history, grammar, linear drawing, ornamental writing, mapping, mensuration, algebra and vocal music. In 1851 HMI Morrell reported: 'There are the elements of an excellent school here.'[10] Park was amongst the first of the Wesleyan schools locally to adopt the Glasgow Training System of David Stow. Stow developed his ideas from good infant practice where children learnt from doing. He laid great stress on oral class teaching with emphasis on questioning 'thus awakening thought, stimulating and directing enquiry and evolving the energies of intellect'. Gallery lessons were introduced early in the Wesleyan schools and pupil-teachers were able to give their daily class lessons more effectively. Morell's main criticism of the Wesleyan schools was that 'when half of the school was under the energetic control of the teacher the other half remained listless and unemployed...'.

The Roman Catholic schools improved immeasurably during the 1850s. When HMI Marshall first visited the schools in 1851 there was not one really efficient Catholic school in the town. Most of the teachers 'imported from Ireland' to contend with the victims of the Irish famine from 1846 to 1847 were trained in the Model School in Dublin. Marshall found them 'competent and valuable men yet generally unsuccessful in imparting a good method of reading'. As late as 1855 there were only 552 children present in all the inspected schools; but one of them had become 'a model for the others'.[11] No comment was made on the task of disciplining the impoverished Irish children who were virtually beyond control. In the words of Father Burke: 'Their wild disregard for order or our authority almost disheartened me.'[12]

It was in 1855 that a party of eight Roman Catholic nuns arrived in Sheffield from Namur to teach all classes within the Catholic community. Their first task was to teach the high-spirited girls in the Surrey Street and St Vincent's schools, opened in 1853. Within twelve months the average attendance had doubled to over a thousand. In the opinion of HMI Marshall, many of these Sisters of Notre Dame were 'unsurpassed' as elementary teachers. It is clear that the Catholic Church was able to build on their success and gradually overtook the Wesleyan provision. With the support of the Duke of Norfolk they set about building another school at Sheaf Gardens for girls and infants which opened in 1858. St William's in Lee Croft opened shortly afterwards.

Secular instruction was given but the emphasis was essentially on that 'which moulds the heart in the precepts of the Gospel'. The habit of learning columns of words by heart was abandoned and writing from dictation was employed for teaching spelling. Gallery teaching was not introduced into St Marie's Surrey Street schools where nine very long desks accommodated up to 14 pupils on each form. The rest of the children were divided into four semicircles so that planned reading could take place using the readers of the Irish Commissioners.

Dissenting congregations were loath to provide day schools. The Baptist congregation at Town Head Street did open an infant school in 1836 but it appears to have been short-lived. Not until 1860 did the Congregationalists resolve to erect the Wicker Congregational Church and School in Gower Street. Heavily influenced by Edward Baines and the Voluntaryist lobby they opposed all state interference and spurned government funding until Baines had a change of heart in the wake of the second Reform Act. The Gower Street complex, built to accommodate 400 pupils, had a 60 ft long school room with additional classrooms. When the school opened in January 1861 Baines had reached the conclusion that education should no longer be a charity.[13] The spirit of independence should be infused and parents were expected to make sacrifices for their children. He charged the school managers not to keep the school fees low 'but boldly charge a good price and be resolved to give for it the money's worth in good education'.

Parents were asked to purchase essential books—by instalments if necessary—in order that the managers could introduce homework as a spur to greater achievement. By 1867 the Congregationalists admitted that the voluntary system was overstretched and accepted state assistance. Once the Board schools were established they approved the non-denominational nature of religious instruction and offered their school to the Board in 1882. Zion Congregational School in Attercliffe had an even shorter life. Opened in 1860 it received only minimal state subsidy and closed in 1874 when Newhall Board School opened.

Curricular Innovations

In his evidence to the Newcastle Commission, Samuel Earnshaw outlined his views on the elementary curriculum.[14] By the age of 13 he believed all children should be able to read, write and compose easily. Boys should be familiar with the ordinary rules of arithmetic up to the rule of three and practice. For girls he would substitute mental arithmetic so that they could cope with shopping. He also stressed the importance of needlework and the ability to make do and mend. Underpinning all the basic instruction was an understanding of the Gospels, the catechism and scriptural history. He considered music and drawing undesirable elements, but singing he did allow; plus a little geography sufficient 'to give a general notion of the distribution of land and water but nothing more'. These were minimum requirements that most of his contemporaries would have endorsed.

Vocal music was an area of the curriculum that was not constricted by the Revised Code. In 1859 Revd John Curwen, the creator of tonic sol-fa notation, was invited to Sheffield by the Sunday School Union. Hullah's adaptation of Wilhelm's singing manual gave way to the new movement and by 1862 the singing of tonic sol-fa was being taught in Wadsley, Pitsmoor and the infant schools of St Mary's and St George's. The following year the master of St John's Park 'commenced a singing class for the recreation of the first class boys and girls as a reward and encouragement'. The school already had a drum and fife band which entertained at local concerts. Crookes School extended their singing repertoire to four-part rounds. The clergy of all denominations were enthusiastic about the teaching of tonic sol-fa to stimulate choir practices and Sunday school anniversaries. The widespread enthusiasm for this form of music training contributed in no small measure to the eminence of Sheffield's choral traditions over the next fifty years.

Drawing was a lucrative grant-earning subject and skilled artisans welcomed its inclusion in the curriculum but Earnshaw dismissed it. 'Drawing is a useless accomplishment to a boy whose hand will soon have become horny and stiff when he has left school and to a girl who will have to make nails.' Nevertheless, pupil-teachers were encouraged to compete for prizes from the Department of Science and Art throughout the 1850s. When the School of Art in Arundel Street was opened in 1857 all the voluntary and private schools were informed that competent teachers were available at a low rate and in some cases gratuitously. Table 5.2 shows which schools entered pupils for the drawing examinations held at the School of Art in 1859.[15]

Table 5.2

School of Art examination candidates, 1859

Central National School	74	Trinity School, Wicker	26
Heeley National School	24	Lancasterian School	21
St Mary's National School	44	Ragged School	15
Free Writing School	12	Parish Church Nat. School	43
Sheffield Grammar School	9	Neepsend National School	34
Brunswick Wesleyan School	55	St Luke's Dyers Hill	21

Of the 378 pupils examined, 42 gained prizes.

Despite a marked improvement on 1858, HMIs were disappointed with the take-up in Sheffield: 'Where knowledge of drawing is more likely to be useful (than in any other town) there is at the same time no place in which pupil teachers and school children seem to have taken so little advantage of the School of Art planted in it', an institution described by the Inspector General of the Department of Science and Art as standing 'at the head of all the schools in the country'.[16]

By 1867 the Committee of Council recognized the severe limitations the Revised Code placed on curricular development and introduced grants in one or two 'specific' subjects such as grammar, geography or history on condition that a three-year course was offered to Standards 4, 5 and 6. Grammar and the outlines of geography proved the most popular. Elements of English history were confined to dates, chronology and deeds of heroism.

Evidence of the occasional chemistry lesson emerged in 1868. At a meeting of Sheffield schoolmasters organised by the Yorkshire Board of Education, certificated teachers were encouraged to qualify themselves as evening-class instructors in science subjects. Another outcome of the meeting was the formation of a centrally organized chemistry class for the more advanced pupils in the voluntary schools. Chapters of Macadam's *Chemistry of Common Things* were read and illustrated.[17] Science teaching developed more widely under the aegis of the School Board when they eventually promoted an experimental approach.

Religious instruction, at the heart of the curriculum for centuries in the voluntary schools, experienced the squeeze of a non-grant-earning subject after 1862 until it became liable to separate clerical inspections in the 1870s. For many years the Bible was the sole reading and spelling source, particularly in the under-resourced schools. Enlightened clergy like Thomas Ryder of Ecclesfield, preaching to parish schoolmasters in 1839, exhorted them to stimulate their pupils' attention, exercise their understanding and constantly question them as to the meaning of the Scriptures, otherwise the time was wasted.[18]

Unfortunately such advice went unheeded. Chunks of Scripture continued to be taught and the catechism was drilled thoroughly but the application of the Gospels to everyday life was rarely attempted. However, HMI Watkins did comment in 1859 that the candidates for confirmation were much better prepared than formerly.

In 1868, Charles Trigg, master of Parson Cross School, outlined his syllabus of religious knowledge.

> 1st Book of Samuel.
> Life of Christ especially principal miracles.
> Read Gospel of Matthew.
> Catechism: 1st class—whole of it.
>   2nd class—to the end of the desire.
>   3rd class—to the end of the commandments.

Appointed in 1864, Trigg set parts of the catechism as homework. The school was set amidst fervent Methodist communities at Birley Carr, Wadsley Bridge and Southey who were opposed to their children learning Anglican formularies. Pragmatically, the Vicar of Ecclesfield, Dr Gatty, recommended that it 'not be pressed too perseveringly'.

Hostility in the Sheffield townships was less marked because there was a greater choice of Nonconformist and private schooling.

The value of sport and organized games, central to the ethos and education in the greater public schools, was hardly recognized in the elementary sector. Recreation and playtime had crept on to the timetable, however, and where schools had no playground, play space was sought. In 1852 St Mary's Girls' playground was depicted as small but fair for a large town. St Paul's playground was defined as 'tolerable' but St Philip's, classed as 'fair', was utilized by neighbours to dry their clothes. The play space at St George's was sited under the boys' schoolroom, whereas the recreation area for the Boys' Charity School was constructed on the top floor of the school and only partially covered. The boys appropriated the adjacent church yard for their games.

In the 1860s St John's Park installed a swing in the playground and those boys who were present at 8.15 a.m. and practised copy-book writing until 9 a.m. were rewarded by being allowed to swing for a quarter of an hour. The master discovered extra play to be conducive to greater effort in school. In icy weather he found 'a merry slide' equally effective. Periodically the boys were taken to Norfolk Park for a game of cricket. Triangular cricket matches were held at the other side of town by St Stephen's, St George's and Crookes Endowed Schools. The Lancasterian school organized visits to Ecclesall Bowling Green after school hours. Apart from the marching drill practised by the infants there is little evidence of gymnastics or physical education.

The phenomena that created the most excitement and broadened the horizons of generations of children was the arrival of the railways in the 1840s. The era of school outings and educational visits dawned when the first mass expeditions set out to explore the neighbouring countryside and venues further afield. Annual excursions to Wharncliffe, Wortley and Worksop, Lincoln, Hull and York were arranged in association with local Sunday schools.

In August 1844 the Established Church chartered a monster excursion to York. Eighty-four carriages pulled by three locomotives were required to carry 2,252 scholars and 468 teachers and friends on the four-hour journey. Greeted by brass bands and handbell ringers the party split into two groups for lunch before touring the Minster, the Museum, Clifford's Tower and the Castle. Returning to the station at 6.30 p.m. the train was delayed and did not arrive back in Sheffield until after midnight, 'the journey having occupied a considerable longer time than was anticipated'. Undeterred, the Wesleyans made the same journey a week later with an even longer train. The 3,800 scholars and teachers needed 140 carriages. After trudging round the city walls and exhausted by sightseeing they descended on the station and consumed 1,000 lbs of bread and a dozen bushels of apples brought by the teachers. Transport to and from home to the station was provided by an assortment of gigs, spring carts and wagons.[19]

Despite the increasing number of children at school no more infant schools were built during this period. Infant departments and all-age girls' schools admitted babies from the age of two upwards where they huddled together in a corner until a babies' class could be formed. Little ones were rarely excluded because their admission permitted older children to attend who would otherwise have been at home child-minding. HMI Watkins disliked the mixing of young infants with older children, claiming that they could only be described as 'a burden to themselves, a hindrance to their school fellows, a torment and a puzzle to the teachers'.[20] Yet the practice persisted well into the School Board era.

On reception in the infant schools, the youngest were drafted into the alphabet class. They were then divided into anything between 12 and 15 monitorial divisions for reading, writing and ball-frame arithmetic led by 'unpaid little monitors'. The practice was modified when pupil teachers were employed but in many schools they continued to be gathered in parallel drafts of perhaps six or seven of each sex. Handwriting on slates consisted of adding pot-hooks to straight lines and then making words by a succession of curves and short lines. A large proportion of infants were able to read an easy narrative and write before they left the department. In February 1869 the oldest infants in Crookes Endowed School were set the following pieces of dictation.

> It will soon be time to go home.
> No more birds are to be heard singing in the bushes.

The exemption of infants from examination after 1862 led to many more older children being 'kept back' in infant departments. Neepsend National School overstepped all reasonable grounds in September 1869.

> My Lords observe there are a large number of scholars above 7 years of age in the infant school and that there are even some above 11 years of age...The methods of instruction of infants and older children are essentially different and cannot be advantageously carried on in the same department.

The development of good infant practice was negligible during this period. Through lack of training and the absence of any real concept of infant education teachers resorted to firm discipline, formal instruction and rote learning. Pressures on the schools to prepare the youngsters for the elementary school precluded Owenite notions of play from taking root. Periods of outside recreation alternating with intellectual instruction, 'the mark of the truly progressive infant school' according to Wilderspin, were adapted in St Mary's Infant School. The playground was fitted with rotary swinging ropes secured to a frame and a carriage ran on a circular railway to exercise the children. Generally such ideas were largely ignored in an age when juvenile employment beckoned them from the age of seven upwards. When teachers trained by the Home and Colonial Infant School Society percolated into the schools the collective lessons in the infant tiered galleries became more common. But so did simultaneous answering and the chanting of didactic verses in a high pitched singsong voice—the bane of the inspector's life.

Much emphasis was laid on moral training. Cleanliness, tidiness and good personal habits were instilled. Where the schools were inspected the infants were found to be 'neat, clean and healthy in appearance'. Punctuality proved much more difficult to inculcate. At St Mary's in the 1840s prayers were delayed until 9.30 a.m. when the majority had arrived. In 1869 many of the infants at St Paul's in Cambridge Street did not arrive until 10 a.m. so the teachers decided to commence school at 10 a.m. in December 'because mornings have been so dark they cannot get to school sooner'.

Young children's ailments and contagious diseases always created havoc with attendance figures. Measles and whooping cough were common but serious outbreaks of scarlet fever and typhus were devastating. In 1848 above one third (nearly 50) of St Philip's infants died from scarlet fever. In Attercliffe the following year HMI Watkins reported 'many deaths of late'. Five died out at Parson Cross in 1865. Lack of efficient heating apparatus and non-existent ventilation in noxious overcrowded rooms full of unwashed little bodies militated against a healthy existence.

Teachers
'Sound religious principles, a practical piety and sincere attachment to the Established Church' and preferably a married couple without children was the job description for the teachers at Darnall National

School in 1841. The ability to read a chapter of the Bible, and to be sober and of good character were often the only requirements before 1846. Consequently, the calibre of teachers in the first half of the nineteenth century was extremely variable. The versatility of the country schoolmaster is epitomized by Richard Furness of Dore on the outskirts of Sheffield.

> I Richard Furness, Schoolmaster, Dore,
> Keep parish books and pay the poor.
> Draw plans for buildings and indite
> Letters for those who cannot write.
> Make wills and recommend a proctor,
> Cure wounds, let blood with any doctor;
> Draw teeth, sing psalms, the hautboy play:
> At chapel on each holy day.
> Paint signboards, cart names, at command,
> Survey and plot estates of land;
> Collect at Easter, one in ten,
> And on Sunday say—Amen!

'A man of very considerable capacity' observed HMI Revd John Allen in 1841, but a disaster in the schoolroom.[21]

> The stage of neglect into which the school had suffered to fall under his hands almost exceeds belief. The children are dirty, many of them sit without any means of employing their time and no check is offered to their fighting and squabbling between themselves. Of the 43 children present on the day of my visit, no one could read a verse of the Gospels correctly, the spelling of all except two was disgraceful. Eleven were learning writing and only five arithmetic but in each case with indifferent success. The master said that he did not consider it to be part of his duty to question the children as to the meaning of what they read, nor to give them any religious instruction whatever, and the result is, that it is almost impossible to extract any sort of answer from them; their ignorance of the simplest elements of religious truth is most lamentable.

The endowed schoolmasters at Lound, Ecclesfield, Shiregreen, High Green and Parson Cross were equally ineffective. Joseph Bowler at Ecclesfield Feoffees School (1816–41) was almost insane. The infant school was kept by an illiterate old woman who signed with a cross when she was paid. Lound School was in ruins and the few scholars there were taught by a cripple—physically incapable of teaching more.

Figure 15. Dore School was built by public subscription in 1821.

Thomas Finch at Shiregreen was well into his seventies and spent most of his time making aeolian harps and teaching a handful of children. High Green School was so cold and damp it was useful only for storing faggots. The dame was assisted by a disabled old woman reputed to possess 'supernatural' information on the whereabouts of 'missing bodies, stolen goods and stray pigs'. About ten infants huddled round the dame's fire. 'Talk of education was a mockery in such a place.'[22] At Parson Cross, George Hawksworth, a one-armed file cutter who had lost his other arm in a brawl and had been placed there out of charity, 'had no notion of education, is violent and ignorant. The children learn nothing likely to be useful in their after life or make them better. The children and the place are both dirty. The school is a disgrace to the trustees.'[23]

This deplorable state of poor quality teaching was not representative of all country schools, however. Charles James Fox, who succeeded his father as master of Norton Free School and died in office in 1864, was so admired by Sir Francis Chantrey—an old boy of the school—that he bequeathed to him a handsome annuity. The Children's Employment Commissioner, J.C. Symons, commended the master at Gleadless Church School and pointed to the excellent teaching in the Endowed School at Handsworth where pupils stayed at least six years. The ten-year-olds he examined were able 'to read well, had a fair substantial knowledge of the scripture facts, and could explain the cardinal doctrines of the Church. Their spelling was fair and in both writing and arithmetic they were proficient.' It is clear, however, that the school attracted the wealthier classes because the fees were high—reading was 4 shillings per quarter, 7 shillings for additional writing and 9 shillings for geography and grammar. These were fees that deterred many of the villagers 'who were almost exclusively of the poorer classes'.[24]

Amongst the most noteworthy of teachers in the town centre was Charles Collier, who was master of Carver Street National School until he was appointed second master at Sheffield Grammar School in 1845, and elected Principal of Winchester Diocesan Training College in 1859. A contemporary at the Lancasterian School was Mr Elmsley who was elected first secretary of the Voluntary Teachers' Association for Yorkshire and Lancashire in 1854. When Mr Haughton was appointed to the Parish Church School in 1858 he was described as 'the efficient master of the Manor Boys' School, York', accounted one of the best in the country. His successor was John Paton who delivered an 'excellent' paper at the Social Science Congress in 1865. He was succeeded by

Mr Sutton who lectured in general science and physical geography at the Church Educational Institute. Similarly, Newlove Sanderson, master of St George's National School (1854–98), the first Sheffield schoolmaster to receive a first-class certificate and the Queen's Prize for Mathematics, lectured in the Institute for twenty years. B.D. Davis, master of the Wesleyan Red Hill School, became the first Superintendent of the Sheffield School Board (1872–85).

Opening up the voluntary schools to inspection led to a general undertaking to improve the quality of teacher training nationwide. The Minutes of 1846 inaugurated the pupil-teacher system which replaced child monitors by apprenticing promising pupils for five years from the ages of 13 to 18. In their final year, pupils could opt for competitive examination and admission to a training college. The opportunity to lift themselves into the working-class aristocracy and reach for a professional career appealed to many girls. Recruiting male pupil-teachers when the advantages were so long deferred was much harder.

At the heart of the matter were the paltry pay scales offered to pupil-teachers compared with the inducements of commerce and industry for the more intelligent youngsters. A pupil-teacher started at £10 per year (3s 10d per week) and eventually reached £20 per year at 18. The Sheffield Trades paid between 8 and 10 shillings per week from 13 upwards, whereas the railways, the most formidable competitors, offered up to 15 shillings weekly. Good conduct, the ability to write and spell well, plus a working background of geography were the major requirements. Telegraph offices held out between 10 and 11 shillings, with the prospect of gradual increases. An assured income was also secure in merchants', lawyers', and canal offices without any of the uncertainties created by annual examinations and the conditional rewards of teaching.

As teaching became recognized as a profession there was a gradual improvement in the quality of candidates and their pay. Even so, Yorkshire teachers' pay lagged behind that of much of the country. In 1853, the average annual salary was £66 compared with £132 in Middlesex and London, £88 in the North-West and £77 in Derby and the Midlands. Four years later, Watkins reported that the £90 received by many teachers in Sheffield 'was far less than the 14s. per day won by the brawny arm and hard hand of many a day labourer in the iron works'. He reckoned that clerks of various kinds received much higher remuneration than teachers who were both undervalued and underpaid.[25]

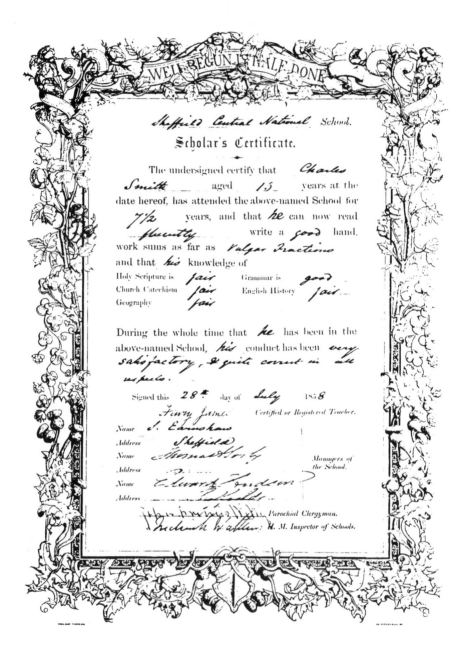

Figure 16. This record of achievement certified by HMI Watkins in 1858 enabled Charles Smith to begin a five-year apprenticeship as a pupil teacher.

Further support for the teachers came from the local clergy. Addressing the fifth annual conference of the Association of Church Schoolmasters meeting in Sheffield in 1858, Revd James Moorhouse contrasted the current schoolmasters with those of former years when 'any poor dilapidated creature' could be made a teacher. In his opinion, the higher schoolmasters were in the social scale the better it would be for the nation.[26] Four years later, Revd James Wilkinson affirmed 'the present system had raised up a body of masters whose equal no other kingdom could produce'.[27]

The teachers were not without their critics, however. Writing in the *Sheffield Independent*, Robert Leader reminded them that they had been raised to their present position by the expenditure of public money. The capital employed in teaching them their profession was not their own, yet they retained a monopoly of public instruction for no school could receive government aid without a certificated teacher. On their efficiency the income of the school from government depended.[28]

Private Schools
Because private schools produced little documentary evidence of their own, they have tended to be ignored or derided by educational historians who have accepted the blanket condemnation of nineteenth-century educationalists with a vested interest in their demise. Some did allow that wealthier artisans may have patronized them but not on any significant scale. Private schools for the working classes have been dismissed as totally irrelevant.

The absence of formal discipline, regularity and order, where children could come and go as they pleased, offended the sensibilities of middle-class observers. Moreover, religious and moral training was judged to be the foundation of real education. Schools devoid of that bedrock were not deemed schools at all, merely places of learning. Consequently, the notion has been nourished that official documents and statements hold the key to formal educational developments— alternative forms were either worthless or insignificant.

In his evidence to the Newcastle Commission, Earnshaw was particularly disparaging about their efficiency—writing being their only redeeming feature—and appealed for their inspection.

> The lower class of private schools are the weak point of popular education doing little more than waste the time of life allotted for the education of poor children.[29]

Gerald Fitzmaurice, 'Inspector of Returns', and HMI Watkins were of the same mind in 1871 when they condemned 59 out of 84 such schools in the Borough where fees did not exceed 9d per week. Significantly, more schools were denounced for defective premises; that is, poor ventilation, lack of decent sanitation, overcrowding, etc., than for incompetence or ineffective instruction. Of the 20 validated schools, admission limits were drastically reduced because the inspectors considered more than 35 children to one competent teacher unsatisfactory—a standard rarely achieved in the voluntary schools. Dame schools were decimated except for children under the age of five. In the initial trawl of dame and common day schools only 17 out of the first 50 were found worthy of recommendation. Specific schools rejected by the official investigators were reported by J.F. Moss, the clerk to the Sheffield School Board:

No. 1   School kept by a widow 72 years of age living in a back court. Says she gives instruction in reading, writing and grammar. Has a few simple books in good condition. They appear suitable. Says she never liked arithmetic herself and prefers not to teach it. Has children 11 or 12 years of age but finds difficulty in getting school fees especially if there are any extra for books etc.

No. 12   Teacher says she only teaches reading and spelling. There is a rude form and a couple of old grindstones for seats. Has only 12 scholars and wishes the school board would send her more.

No. 14   Return states, that there are 95 scholars. About 80 in attendance on day of visit. According to standard adopted in these calculations, rooms will accommodate 27. Teacher however appears far more intelligent than most of the others visited and school books etc. are more plentiful and in good condition.[30]

Nevertheless, the sustained popularity of the working-class private schools throughout the nineteenth century—labelled adventure schools in the 1850s—prompts us to re-examine the working-class response to the alternatives of publicly provided schools. Until recently, the contribution of the working classes to the 'growth of education' has been considered non-existent; they were apathetic or indifferent 'recipients of education ladled out to them by benevolent middle class agencies'.[31]

Schooling for most working-class parents was solely a means for their children to learn to read, write, and account; and for girls, the ability to sew. In general they were opposed to the inculcation of obedience and submission and, for many, moralizing and religious instruction was no more than an unwarranted distraction and superfluous. As we noted in Chapter 4, in the 1830s and 1840s there were overwhelming votes in favour of secular education and opposition to the influence of the Church. And on the eve of the 1870 Act, the Town Council stressed that religious instruction in any 'public' school should be non-sectarian in character and 'liberty given to parents to absent their children from school during the time of religious education'.[32]

Nowhere is the spurning of 'public' schools more apparent than in the popular rejection of infant schools. Between 1833 and 1872 babies' and infant classes were formed in the voluntary schools but there was no concerted demand for publicly provided infant education until the Board School era. Contaminated by the dislike of monitorial schools, parents rejected the practice of infant monitors, the regimentation of little ones, oversized classes and the excessive use of drills. Working-class parents much preferred the cosy maternal influence of the dame's hearth to the draughty, joyless schoolroom with its male obsession for neatness and order 'where they learnt nowt'. HMI Watkins admitted that 'many children who go to public schools go to dame schools first especially when there are no infant schools nearby'.

Although there was a steady expansion of the public sector between 1838 and 1851, the proportion of children attending the private schools was remarkably constant. In his commentary on the Educational Census of 1851, Horace Mann found that the private sector comprised one third of the total and acknowledged that that was 'unquestionably an understatement'. In the enumeration of schools and scholars in the Sheffield and Ecclesall Unions, 6,588 pupils were recorded in the private schools and 10,040 in the public day schools—39.6 per cent in the private sector compared with the 40 per cent in Sutton's earlier enquiry.

Table 5.3

Sheffield educational census, 1851[33]

No. of schools		No. of scholars on roll		
Public day schools		Both sexes	Male	Female
Sheffield Union	34	7,951	4,204	3,747
Ecclesall Union	17	2,089	1,221	868
	51	10,040	5,425	4,615

Private schools

Sheffield Union	130	4,534	2,246	2,228
Ecclesall Union	64	2,054	876	1,178
	194	6,588	3,122	3,466

In his report to the Newcastle Commissions, Assistant Commissioner Patric Cumin commented:

> It seems a remarkable fact that [between 1851–1859] the proportion of children who attend public schools as compared with those who attend private schools instead of increasing has actually diminished amongst the mass of the people. I found no great readiness to abandon the private for the public school.[34]

By 1871 the proportion of pupils in the private schools within the borough had declined marginally to 37.5 per cent, but the actual number in attendance had risen to over 10,000.

It is important to remember that private schools catered for all social classes. Working-class private schools defy accurate classification because they never fitted into the neat categories professionals sought to impose on them. Their significance rested more with the people who used them than the premises themselves. When probing working-class culture in Sheffield, Caroline Reid made a distinction between the 'rough' and the 'respectable'. Similar labels could be applied to the working-class private schools. The offspring of the more respectable miners—often Dissenters—more affluent railway workers and those in skilled manual trades sat alongside the children of clerks, shopkeepers, craftsmen and tradesmen in working-class private schools akin to lower middle-class establishments, depending on their location. Factors like squalor, overcrowding, poor ventilation and inadequate facilities hardly fit respectability.

Woefully inadequate as many private adventure schools were, they offered 'the kind of education many of the working class wanted rather than the education the middle class thought they should have'. Traditionally a part of everyday life, they were the product of a distinctive culture anchored in the community to which the children belonged; a place where parents could 'drop in' as opposed to the public sector controlled by clergy and regulated by government inspectors. In every sense the working-class private schools 'were ours, not theirs'. In 1867 Joshua Fitch, HMI confirmed that 'a considerable portion of the children usually found in the National Schools in

Sheffield are taught in private adventure schools of which there is a large number of a humble kind'.[35]

Ever critical of these schools, Earnshaw was convinced that 'the children of the poor are here better educated, at least they have a better education offered to them in schools under inspection than is to be had in the common private schools to which the middle class are sent'. Moreover, he alluded to middle-class parents who had asked for classes to be formed in the National Schools so that 'they may have the same advantages as the poor to education'. He did not go so far as to advocate inspection for the superior and middle schools but he inspired their revitalization by urging the adoption of the Cambridge 'Local' Examinations. 'These examinations will supply a deficiency and do much more to give them sound education than anything hitherto devised.' Welcomed by the *Sheffield Independent*, they were seen as 'a measure calculated to preserve to these classes the intellectual rank corresponding to their social position'.[36]

A spirited defence of the private sector came from Thomas Chambers, Liberal MP for Marylebone, in his opening address to the Social Science Congress in Sheffield in 1865:

> We have reason to be thankful for those who came forward to supply that demand for education for which there existed no adequate public provision...Indiscriminate censure of those establishments would be as unjust as indiscriminate eulogy would be absurd.[37]

In common with his contemporaries he devoted his criticism to the lack of any effective means of assessing the performance of these schools.

Arguably the most influential private school was the Collegiate School with its department of practical science (1843). Many of Sheffield's distinguished sons were educated there, including Archdeacon Favell, Surgeons W.F. and Richard Favell, the scientist Henry Clifton Sorby and the industrialists Sir Robert Hadfield and Thomas Vickers. The steel giants Mark Firth and Samuel Osborne attended John Eadon's academy at Red Hill. At this time the Grammar School was organized as a high-class commercial school and the classical element was almost absent according to Joshua Fitch in 1868.

Samuel Eadon, John's brother, was the most innovative. He experimented with a child-centered approach based on the work of Pestalozzi and De Fellenberg. In the 1850s he went on to develop hydropathy

Figure 17. The Collegiate School built in 1835 was extended and converted to the City of Sheffield Training College for Teachers in 1905.

exercises with 'Spartan perseverance' so that youths 'at the close of their scholastic career will enjoy blooming health and feel better fitted to encounter the battle of life. They will be organically stronger, intellectually mightier and more impressionable for all that is great and lofty in the advancing movements of society'. It took another fifty years before elementary schools accepted that physical health was 'the basis on which mental education must be founded'. Middle-class schooling was untouched by the 1870 Education Act and one seventh of the child population was deducted from the required 'public' school accommodation. The demise of the working-class private school, however, was clearly approaching.

Two privately run industrial schools which must not be confused with reformatory style institutions were the Girls' Industrial School established by Revd W. Wilkinson in South Street in 1859 and Elizabeth Harrison's Industrial School for the Blind in West Street set up about the same time. The aim of the Girls' Industrial School was not 'to reclaim the vicious but qualify virtuous well conducted girls for respectable situations'. Admitted at the age of 13, the girls were prepared for domestic service by improving the three Rs, developing their understanding of home economics and given practical experience of taking in washing and 'getting up' linen. Their fees ranged from 2s 6d to 3s 6d per week to cover board and lodging. Basket and mat making was the focus of the blind training. Their products were marketed by the Blind Institute. The school and workshops were later integrated into the North of England Manufactory of the Blind in 1869.

Sunday Schools

Throughout these mid-Victorian years, Sunday Schools were considered as complementary to the day schools in reinforcing religious instruction. Popery, secularism and apathy were the besetting sins of their generation and the huge capital investment by the Nonconformists induced R.S. Bayley to remark that Sunday schools were 'as common as sunbeams'. In 1843 G.C. Holland portrayed them as instruments of great good but altogether inadequate for the times. The knowledge imparted was exceedingly superficial, but what could be expected from the few hours under instruction? The following year HMI Watkins confirmed the utility of the schools 'as the only means of religious instruction for thousands of young people'.[38]

The popularity of Sunday schools can be gathered from the recruitment statistics published over the period. Almost 13,000 scholars were recorded in 1840. The Education Census of the Sheffield and Ecclesall Unions recorded 15,753 pupils on the registers of 78 schools. Robert Leader reflected on the 24,000 children on the roll of Protestant Sunday schools and the 35,000 copies of the Whitsun Anniversary Services ordered in 1862, compared with the 12,000 copies printed in the 1820s.[39]

Table 5.4

Protestant Sunday Schools in Sheffield 1862

Sunday Schools		Teachers	Children
Church of England	21	485	5,500
Wesleyan	34	1,096	5,694
Sunday School Union	41	1,708	12,776
(Affiliated Dissenting Bodies)			
	96	3,289	23,970

In 1863, the Sheffield Festival Committee distributed buns and medals to more than 17,000 Sunday school children and 3,500 teachers on the marriage of the Prince of Wales.

However carefully we treat these figures—and children being children were attracted to more than one school—the social impact of the movement was considerable. The Whitsun anniversaries were so popular that by 1851 a wide variety of venues were needed. Norfolk Park provided the focus of the Whit walk and sing for the Sunday School Union and the Roman Catholic processions later in the day. When the Brightside contingents found Norfolk Park too far they resorted to the gardens at Osgathorpe. The grounds of the Collegiate School and Wesley College afforded open space for the Church and Wesleyan gatherings where football, cricket and general sporting activities were enjoyed. Even the occasional 'romp' in the Botanical Gardens was permitted at Whitsuntide.

Penny readings, choral concerts, soirées, Band of Hope meetings, sick and friendly societies all helped to foster family interest, mutual improvement and attachment. This happened in spite of the repressive discipline where silence was golden and the fear of hell-fire was reinforced by the oft-repeated verse,

> There is a dreadful hell, and everlasting pains,
> Where sinners must with devils dwell in darkness fire and chains.

Sunday schools were still regarded with much affection by the working classes. The imposition of the necklace *I must not talk to boys* rarely prevented the sexes from clandestine meetings or finding future marriage partners. In 1868 the *Sheffield Independent* printed the Bishop of Oxford's advice to church trustees: 'Banish the chance of a little innocent courting after school and you will banish many teachers from Sunday school work.'

Secular instruction was abandoned in Church Sunday schools once the National Schools were established but Nonconformists were divided on its effectiveness. There was no opposition to teaching children to read and understand the Scriptures but teaching writing on Sundays was condemned as sinful by the Wesleyan circuit ministers and contrary to the expressed opinion of Conference. The Wesleyan flagship Sunday school at Red Hill reached a crisis over the matter in 1855. Discipline was being eroded because some boys were defying their teachers and pleasing themselves as to whether they did any writing or not. The teachers favoured retaining writing in conformity with the design of the school's founders, and carried the vote so that writing continued to be taught.[40] Independents, New Connexion and Primitive Methodists persevered with writing until the advent of compulsory schooling when they accepted there was no longer any justification for their involvement on Sundays. By this time it was generally agreed that Sunday schools were nurseries of the church, to promote conversion and provide leaders for the church and pastors for the pulpit.

As the century progressed, voluntary teachers proved more difficult to recruit. Schools became more reliant on younger candidates and there was a growing recognition that the social mix was being fragmented by the migration of the more affluent to the new suburban housing developments. Social control became increasingly difficult as the schools evolved as indigenous working-class institutions. John Askham confirmed this in 1866 when he appealed for a better class of children who could set a good example 'to the lower portion of the working classes' generally to be found in the schools.[41] Nevertheless, the movement enabled many to climb the first steps of the educational ladder. Sir John Brown, the industrial baron, learnt his ABC in Sunday school and acknowledged his debt, not only by teaching Sunday school evening classes but also by creating the Atlas Works Sunday School which even eclipsed the large Wesleyan Red Hill Sunday School in the 1860s. With Evangelism as their underlying function, Sunday schools were at the hub of their communities, offering a social, educational, religious and cultural focus.

Evening Classes and Adult Schools

Elementary education in the nineteenth century was perceived as education for the 'labouring poor' and as such it could be offered to young adults. Adult education warrants an in-depth study of its own and here I can only sketch a brief outline of its development. The concept of self-improvement nurtured by the Sunday schools attracted adults from the beginning and was taken up by all denominations and a few enlightened employers. In 1812, Roscoe Place Sunday School, established for the apprentices of brass founders Shaw, Jobson and Company, expanded to admit not only workers' children but adults who needed instruction. Revd Mark Docker called for an adult literacy campaign in 1814 and the Allen Street New Connexion Methodists opened their adult school a year later. Differences of opinion led the Wesleyans to open evening classes to supplement their Sunday school instruction but the sexes were carefully segregated.

Between 1819 and 1821 three schools for young men aged 16 to 21 were opened. In their *Address to Uninstructed Youth* the promoters outlined why 'those of riper years never sought the advantage of useful learning'. Amongst the reasons given were 'indifference, poverty and never having felt the want'. Intent on rescuing the young from depravity they recounted how, within the space of an hour after dark, they had seen 'upwards of one hundred and ninety abandoned females walking through High Street and Fargate, many of whom did not exceed the age of sixteen. These are seeking whom they may devour and young men frequently become their prey, and to gratify their corrupt propensities are led from one act of depradation to another.'

The provision of libraries in the large monitorial schools and the major Sunday schools led to the foundation of a Mechanics' Library in 1824. Unfortunately, it failed to attract the labouring and artisan class of readers for whom it was intended, largely because novels, plays and works subversive to the Christian religion were prohibited. A more serious attempt to improve the education of artisans materialized with the opening of the Mechanics' Institute in 1832. The aspirations of the working classes were rapidly extinguished, however, once the deficiencies of their education were exposed. The Institute attracted the labour aristocracy and a prestigious structure was erected in 1847 and 1848 but it failed to capture the interest of the masses.

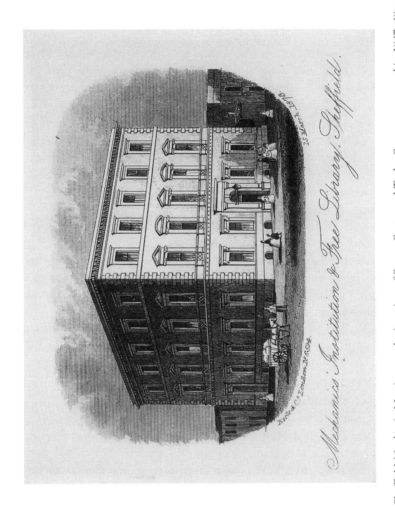

Figure 18. The Sheffield Mechanics' Institute at the junction of Surrey Street and Tudor Street was erected in 1847–48 at a cost of about £7000. From 1856 the Free Library occupied the ground floor. The site is now occupied by the Sheffield City Library which opened in 1934.

In the 1830s Owenism adopted the Methodist 'class meeting' activity and a Hall of Science was organized in 1839 where Owenites and Chartists could meet. In addition to giving basic and scientific instruction, it tended to address political issues and provide a haven for secularist theory.[42] The dissemination of Owenite philosophy spurred renewed denominational activity and Vicar Sutton promoted the Church of England Instruction Society in 1840. Classes were arranged, not only in the basic subjects but also in drawing, geography, scriptural history plus specialist lectures in natural history, natural philosophy and theological topics. A library and museum were also created. The early productive years in competition with the Mechanics' Institute were followed by a gradual decline until revitalized in 1855 by James Moorhouse who remoulded the Society on the lines of the People's College. The Society was then renamed the Church of England Educational Institute and new premises were sought.

Encouraged by his father-in-law, the Revd Canon Sale, Moorhouse laid the foundation of an extremely successful Institute of Further Education. With the exception of modern languages—French and German—all the classes were taught voluntarily and ranged from the classical languages, Euclid and mathematics, English and Bible-related subjects to shorthand, drawing and singing. The basic three Rs were provided until the demand diminished with the introduction of compulsory schooling. Canon Sale took a reading class regularly for over twenty years.

Revd James Moorhouse, son of a Master Cutler, curate of the Parish Church and later Bishop of Manchester, believed his real education began in the evening classes where he sat alongside working men in the Sheffield People's College. This institution for the people stemmed from dissatisfaction with the Mechanics' Institute by one of its lecturers, the Independent Minister of Howard Street Chapel, Revd R.S. Bayley. He considered a higher range of really useful studies should be available for young working-class people, and started classes in 1842. So as not to interfere with employment, evening classes were supplemented by classes arranged before breakfast at six thirty in the morning. Bayley had no intention of segregating the sexes—a practice emulated in the Church Institute. The effect was 'an increased degree of decorum and self respect exhibited by both sexes'.

In contrast to the Mechanics' Institute, Bayley stressed the impor-tance of the humanities for personal development—literature and composition, logic, history and languages. On his departure in 1848 the ethos changed and the students called for a distinctly vocational bias. They argued that 'a College for the People must include in its curriculum classes that would have a direct bearing on the industrial pursuits that distinguish the town'. Eventually the college was absorbed into the 'growing body of Technical education'.[43] This experiment in working-class education not only stimulated the longer-lived Church Institute, the Attercliffe Literary and Scientific Institute, and the Surrey Street Christian and Educational Institute but also the more notable Christian Socialist London Working Men's College in 1854. Clearly, all these adult initiatives had the objective of extending the period of working-class education but it was obvious to many that few 'youths were disposed to spend evenings learning after a day in the close poisoned atmosphere of a workshop'.

Literacy

With the widespread expansion of elementary education in mid-Victorian Sheffield, public schooling became more accessible to the working classes. Educational standards rose with the introduction of certificated teachers and pupil-teacher assistants, and fees tended to be lower than in the private sector. Yet school enrolment increased but slowly. By 1851 it was estimated that only 60 per cent of the school-age population of Sheffield were actually on roll and 40 per cent of them were in private schools. Twenty years later the total school enrolment had reached 69 per cent.

Although Victorian observers were convinced that most children did attend school at some point in their lives and in 1861 the Newcastle Commission believed few were totally unschooled, many children failed to retain the little they learnt, having attended spasmodically, and continued to leave school as early as ten. Relatively few children rose above Standard 3 whereby they could demonstrate the ability to read a short passage from a school reading book, write a sentence having heard it read once and then dictated in single words, and do a sum in any rule as far as short division. Having left school, the vast majority of youngsters enjoyed a couple of 'fallow' years before life's work began.

As the heavy steel industry progressively transformed the face of Sheffield, the standard of living improved, public attitudes towards child labour stiffened and the demand for it declined. Restrictive legislation assisted the process but the opportunities for casual work remained. There is evidence, however, that male literacy was significantly influenced by occupational demands and this is reflected in the rise of literacy during this period. The acceleration of female literacy was perhaps more closely linked to environmental factors and the chances offered by migration, especially in the more rural parts of the region and across county boundaries.[44]

The economic benefits of acquiring literacy were most visible in the growth of job opportunities for literate youngsters. The railways and road haulage expanded; the Royal Mail extended its operations; manufacturers augmented their clerical and warehouse staff; the middle classes sought more cultivated domestics, cooks and housekeepers; and shopkeepers demanded literate assistants able 'to keep the books'.

The concerted drive for mass literacy by Church and State, allied to the significant proportion of children drawn to the private sector, delivered a clearly visible upward trend in the percentage of literate brides and grooms after a long period of stagnation. By extracting details from the Registrar General's Annual Reports we can compare the local scene with national estimates. Such a rise reflects a growing demand for popular literacy by the working classes themselves and has led some historians—notably E.G. West and Phil Gardner—to question the wide-scale intervention by the state since 1870.[45] The growth in literacy, however, tends to conceal the poverty of overall educational standards reached by the poorer segments of the population.

Table 5.5

Literacy by registration districts, 1849–73
(Percentage of brides and grooms signing their names at marriage)

Registration district	1849		1856		1866		1873	
	M	F	M	F	M	F	M	F
Wortley (including Ecclesfield)	64	56	75	58	79	74	80	73
Ecclesall Bierlow	71	61	81	69	79	70	80	68
Sheffield	69	49	70	53	73	60	78	63
England and Wales	69	50	71	60	78	70	81	75

Whilst literacy may have been a precondition for employment in many commonplace occupations, for those who toiled in foundry, forge and furnace skill, proficiency and physical performance were much more eagerly sought. The vernacular response most commonly heard from Sheffield workmen when asked about education was 'I'm no scholer. I ger on reight enough—tha mun do tsame'. Yet the grinders rejected any insinuation that they were ignorant.[46] At a general meeting of the Grinders' Sick Society in 1852 it was claimed that out of 80 men and boys employed at the wheel only two could not read and four were unable to write. Of the several hundred operatives employed in the prestigious works of Joseph Rodgers 'there are not more than ten who cannot read and write'. The grinders in John Walters' Globe Works could not match the same level of literacy but 176 (65 per cent) of the 269 workers could both read and write, 223 (82.8 per cent) could read, and only 46 (17 per cent) of the semi-skilled workers—mainly table blade forgers and hafters—were totally illiterate.

The publication of criminal statistics between 1845 and 1862 provides a clear insight into the literacy levels of the submerged working classes—less than one per cent received a 'superior' education. The data also serve to illustrate the impossible task of the voluntary 'public' sector and the painfully slow progress made in raising overall educational standards in a period of continuous population growth when schooling was voluntary. In the thirty years between 1841 and 1871 the population of the town more than doubled, expanding from 110,891 to 239,946.

Table 5.6

Declining percentages of illiteracy of prison inmates in Sheffield, 1845–62[47]

				Neither Read nor Write				Able to Read			
Year	Total	Male	Female	Male	%	Female	%	Male	%	Female	%
1845	2,556	2,221	335	932	42	203	60.5	1,289	58	132	39
1850	3,187	2,803	384	1,180	42	210	55	1,623	58	174	45
1855	3,377	2,791	586	1,341	48	344	59	1,450	52	242	41
1860	2,787	2,199	588	855	39	306	52	1,334	60.5	282	48
1862	2,784	2,204	580	860	39	291	50	1,334	61	289	50

What emerges clearly is that parental attitudes towards education, personal wealth, social status and occupation impinged upon the levels of literacy in every community and neighbourhood, effecting wide variations between the urban and more rural parts of the region. The literacy of prison inmates reflects the poorest segments of the town and highlight enormous fluctuations to be found within areas of high population density—a fact concealed when examining marriage signature marks alone.

Increasingly, literacy was seen to be a product of schooling though it is difficult to ascertain the scale of those who acquired it in adolescence and adulthood. What is certain is that the production of cheap reading matter such as pamphlets, periodicals and novelettes; the publication of affordable newspapers; the launching of railway bookstalls; and the opening of the free municipal library combined to foster the development of lasting reading habits.

Newspaper circulation in Sheffield was reactivated in 1855 when the *Sheffield Daily Telegraph* appeared—the first local penny daily to be issued in the wake of the abolition of newspaper stamp duty. Capitalizing on the insatiable interest in the progress of the Crimean War, circulation over the first year exceeded one million copies (3,200 per day)—small by today's standards but a considerable achievement for a provincial paper. The long-established *Sheffield Independent* followed suit in 1861 with the publication of the *Daily Independent* and the short-lived *Daily News* surfaced at one halfpenny. With the advent of daily newspapers, sales increased to an estimated 3 per cent of the adult population, but that was meagre compared with the more popular Sunday papers at 12 per cent and the magazine-buying public of almost 20 per cent.[48]

Circulating libraries were commonplace in Sunday schools. Reading rooms were accessible to the working classes whilst the Town Subscription Library and the Literary and Philosophical Society catered for the élite. Agitation for the creation of rate-supported libraries culminated in the adoption of the Public Library Act of 1850 which entitled boroughs to use the product of a halfpenny rate to provide staff and buildings. Ensuing discussions in the Town Council enabled Sheffield to become the first town in Yorkshire 'to embark on public library provision'.

The Public Free Library opened in 1856 when the Town Council rented space on the ground floor of the Mechanics' Institute. 19,000 books, magazines and newspapers were freely available in the 1860s and between 1861 and 1865, 126,380 books were issued from the lending library and 11,760 from the reference section. Over the first few years an average of 2,400 new borrowers joined annually of which one third were in the age range 14 to 20. 'The greater number were drawn from the poorer classes' reported Mary Walton, and among them 'were a surprising number of servant girls'.[49]

As cheaper editions became available, new titles steadily increased. Amongst the most popular were two American novels, *Uncle Tom's Cabin* and *The Lamplighter*, Charlotte Yonge's *The Heir of Redclyffe* and

The Daisy Chain, Charles Kingsley's *The Heroes* and Thomas Hughes' *Tom Brown's Schooldays*, all recently published. Of a slightly older vintage were Frederick Marryat's seafaring tales, Thomas Mayne Reid's 'new world' adventures and the historical romances of Alexander Dumas. Children under 14 were not admitted to the public library but this mid-Victorian era witnessed a flowering of children's literature.

The overall improvement in basic literacy on the eve of the 1870 Education Act persistently disguised the chronic failure of the voluntary system to meet the needs of the whole population, especially those in socially deprived areas. Nevertheless, the popular demand that subscribed to the success of the *Sheffield Daily Telegraph* in June 1855 and the creation of a public library service eight months later serve as a bench mark in the growth of a reading public. Even without the support of compulsory schooling there is sufficient evidence to indicate a grass-root recognition of the benefits of popular literacy.

Notes

1. *Sheffield Mercury* (4 June 1839); *Sheffield Iris* (4 June 1839).
2. CCE (1847–48), *HMI Watkins' Report*, 1, p. 191.
3. CCE (1844), *HMI Moseley's Report*, 2, p. 516.
4. CCE (1853), *HMI Moncrieffe's Report*, p. 236.
5. CCE (1855), *HMI Watkins' Report*, 1, p. 260.
6. *Report of the Royal Commission on the State of Popular Education in England (Newcastle Report)*, 1861, 5, pp. 184-85.
7. Sheffield Wesleyan Methodist District School Society Minute Book (1835–45), SCA.
8. Quoted in J. Lawson and H. Silver, *A Social History of Education in England* (1973), p. 270.
9. CEC *Second Report*, Trades and Manufactures, Appendix, E25.
10. CCE (1850–51), *HMI Morrell's Report*, p. 636.
11. CCE (1856–57), *HMI Marshall's Report*, p. 582.
12. C. Hadfield, *A History of St. Marie's Mission and Church* (1889), p. 117. I am indebted also to D.M. Marsden for her unpublished manuscript history of St Vincent's Schools.
13. *SI* (19 January 1861).
14. *Newcastle Report*, 1861, 5, p. 184.
15. *SI* (10 December 1859).
16. CCE (1856–57), *HMI Watkins' Report*, p. 306.
17. *Sheffield Daily Telegraph* (11 October 1868); St Stephen's National School Log Book (22 October 1869).
18. Miscellaneous Papers, Ecclesfield Parish Church.

19. *SI* (30 August 1844); *Sheffield Mercury* (7 September 1844).

20. CCE (1850–51), *HMI Watkins' Report*, pp. 123f.

21. CCE (1841–42), *HMI Allen's Report*, p. 160; J. Dunsmore, *I Richard Furness* (1991).

22. CEC *First Report*, Mines, 1842, p. 199; A. Gatty, *A Life at One Living* (1884), pp. 55-56.

23. CCE (1845), *HMI Watkins' Report*, 2, pp. 78f.; 1 (1847–48), p. 373.

24. CEC *First Report*, Mines, 1842, p. 198.

25. CCE (1852–53), *HMI Watkins' Report*, pp. 123f.; (1857), pp. 290f.

26. *SI* (2 January 1858).

27. *SI* (23 January 1862).

28. *SI* (31 March 1862).

29. *Newcastle Report*, 1861, 5, p. 185.

30. *Report Presented by the Clerk of the School Board to the Statistical Enquiry Committee* LP 5 (1871), SCL. More schools are described in Bingham, *Sheffield School Board*, pp. 7-8.

31. P. Gardner, *The Lost Elementary Schools of Victorian England* (1984), p. 1.

32. *SI* (14 July 1870).

33. *Census of Great Britain 1851*, 1852–1853, vol. XC, p. 266.

34. Gardner, *Lost Elementary Schools*, p. 183.

35. C. Reid, 'The Pursuit of Respectability', in Pollard and Holmes (eds.), *Economic and Social History*, p. 278: *PP* 1868, *Schools Inquiry Commission (Taunton Commission)*, 2, p. 335; Gardner, *Lost Elementary Schools*, p. 83.

36. *SI* (10 September 1859).

37. *Transactions of the National Association for the Promotion of Social Science* (1865), p. 32.

38. Holland, *Vital Statistics*, p. 221; CCE (1844), *HMI Watkins' Report*, 2, p. 252.

39. Pawson and Brailsford, *Illustrated Guide to Sheffield* (1862), p. 86.

40. *SI* (24 November 1855).

41. *SI* (24 October 1866).

42. J. Salt, 'The Sheffield Hall of Science', *The Vocational Aspects of Secondary and Further Education* (1972), 25, pp. 133-38. See also H. Silver, *The Concept of Popular Education* (1965), pp. 229-31.

43   G.C. Moore Smith, *The Story of the People's College, Sheffield 1842–78* (1912).

44. See Mitch, *The Rise of Popular Literacy*, pp. 57f.

45. E.G. West, *Education and the State* (1970), pp. xvii-liii; Gardner, *Lost Elementary Schools*, chs. 6 and 7.

46. *SI* (31 January 1852).

47. Criminal Statistical Records for Sheffield 1845–62, SCL.

48.   R. Williams, *The Long Revolution* (1965), p. 188. See also *The Sheffield Daily Telegraph 1855–1925* (1925).

49.   M. Walton, *Sheffield: Its Story and Achievements* (1952), p. 223; M. Walton, *A History of the Parish of Sharrow* (1968), p. 38n.; *The City Libraries of Sheffield 1856–1956* (1956).

Chapter 6

Children Apart 1839–1870

> I deplore, therefore, year after year, the continued evil of the present system of pauperising the children of paupers. Consigning them to that caste—encircling them with its concomitants—inuring them to dependence and domiciling them in workhouses. I shall hail the day as one of the greatest achievements in social progress which shall witness the entire severance from workhouses.
>
> Jelinger Symons, HMI Parochial Union Schools (1854)

Attempts to educate the most deprived and disadvantaged children in the middle years of the nineteenth century generated three distinct institutions: workhouse schools, ragged schools, and industrial and reformatory schools. Prior to the Poor Law Amendment Act of 1834, the parish was responsible for all poor relief and youngsters born and bred in the workhouse were farmed out as pauper apprentices on reaching the age of seven. Sympathetic efforts at the end of the eighteenth century to improve the system and provide vocational training until old enough for manufacturing apprenticeship failed, though it was widely recognized that many boys ran away to enlist as soldiers or became vagabonds and thieves. Pauper girls were enmeshed in a vicious circle; at risk from child abuse, they later turned to prostitution, returning to the workhouse as adults 'the victims of disease and profligacy'.

With the passage of the 1834 Acts, the parish of Sheffield was divided into two unions. The Sheffield Union comprised the townships of Sheffield, Brightside, Attercliffe and the parish of Handsworth; whilst the Ecclesall Union embraced Ecclesall Bierlow, Upper and Nether Hallam, the Chapelries of Dore and Totley, and the parish of Norton with Beauchief. The object of the Act was to concentrate all poor relief within the workhouse, ensuring that it was only a marginal improvement on starvation. The education of pauper children, however, became mandatory. Boards of Guardians were elected by the ratepayers and the Unions were set up in 1837.

Workhouse Schools

The Sheffield Union inherited the remodelled silk mill at Kelham Island, purchased in 1829 as a workhouse. The Guardians decided to convert the Brightside workhouse in Rock Street, Pitsmoor, for the benefit of the children in 1843. The tendency to provide outdoor relief for the able-bodied—housing only the helpless, aged and incapable—led to inordinate expenditure on poor relief which was severely criticized by ratepayers and the Poor Law Commissioners. The decision to separate children from their parents was an extension of that policy in a bid to stave off the stigma of pauperization and improve their prospects of employment.

In 1843, 12,000 people were reported to be wholly dependent on parochial relief, demanding assistance as a right and not a charity. Of the 300 dependent children who had to be fed, clothed and educated, they were said to be 'living in every room from bottom to top without order or regularity'.[1]

In a more extensive report on the Rock Street premises in 1844, 112 boys, 70 girls and 19 adults were housed in accommodation calculated to cater for 110.[2] The severe overcrowding caused the children to sleep three to a bed, in beds so close together one could hardly walk between one bed and another. Ventilation of the dormitories was non-existent, aggravated by the extremely low ceilings. The children washed and dressed unsupervised. The beds were made directly they had risen and consequently never aired. The schoolmaster was described as a feeble old pauper aged seventy-eight with no previous experience as a teacher. He was assisted by another pauper with three children in the house. The boys were tolerably proficient in writing, read very indifferently and had reached the rule of three in arithmetic. The Bible was their only class book. No industrial occupations or activities were performed except that the older boys were expected to assist in the wash-house. This practice was condemned by the inspectors because it encouraged their association with the women and older girls thus producing 'a tainted atmosphere, the direct tendency of which is to vitiate and corrupt the feelings and habits of both sexes'.

The outcome of Commissioner Tufnell's visit was the immediate replacement of the geriatric schoolmaster by the more proficient Thomas Wolstenholm who held a Class 3 certificate of competence. By 1848 there was clearly a marked improvement. The writing was reported to be good and the arithmetic very fair. Industrial training had been introduced. Ten boys were given instruction in shoemaking and eight in tailoring. Elements of geography and grammar were taught but 'the mode of questioning was not searching'. The girls were taught to read and instructed in sewing and knitting but were said to be in a very low state and indisciplined. The mistress, on a salary of £15 per year, superintended the repair of clothing. Although 152 boys and 114 girls were registered the average daily attendance was 89 boys and 77 girls.[3] As trade improved in the 1850s children were withdrawn at the earliest possible moment. Consequently there were fewer to be examined and those who remained made little progress.

The harsh existence of the workhouse child was obviously tempered by the humanity of the schoolmaster. Consumer experiences are meagre but the years from 1845–55 were years of relative compassion. In 1854 T.B. Browne HMI asserted that the boys' school was one of the best in the kingdom. Twenty years later, one old boy who had prospered looked back in gratitude.

> The Union was my cradle, nursery and school. I had not the tender solicitude of a fond mother yet retrospect of those early days is not sad but joyous. We were comfortably housed, warmly clothed and well fed. The scene in Oliver Twist is an overdrawn one...
>
> Every morning and evening all who can join together in praise and prayer and we always learned to prepare for the Sabbath! How glad we were to have cocoa (an agreeable change having boiled milk on weekdays). Dinner was more enjoyable and a blessing was cheerfully sung before and afterwards which is usual at every meal. On Sunday afternoons and evenings in the dining hall earnest and warm hearted local preachers unfolded to us the simple gospel and urged upon us the necessity of complying with its conditions.
>
> Our education is equally associated with pleasant recollections. Mr T. Wolstenholm, than whom no person was better fitted for a schoolmaster, was untiring in his zeal to fit us for the duties of life; he was a musician, artist, botanist and horticulturalist. A true lover of nature, he would in the early Spring and Summer take us to the woods and awake admiration in our breasts...When walking out the bystanders expressions were oftner complimentary than otherwise. 'See thee there's t'workhouse childer! They dont look as if they were clam'd! Noa they dont t'schoolmasters a rare en! Thats im' pointing to a middle aged but kindly looking person busily engaged in conversation with some of the boys which was always his custom when we were out for a walk. At home he would beguile the evenings with his violin, learning us to sing some new piece or sketch some scene we had visited.[4]

Compared with the Sheffield Workhouse, the Ecclesall Institution was palatial, but the treatment of its indigent children was grimmer. In 1839 the Ecclesall Guardians accepted that neither Sharrow Moor House, built around 1793, nor the poorhouse at Crookes could be converted into an efficient Union workhouse. A site at Nether Edge was purchased, and handsome premises built of freestone in an elegant Elizabethan style were erected 'in the country'—the nucleus of the present Nether Edge Hospital. Portrayed by Samuel Roberts in 1841 as that 'Horrible God-defying PLACE of TORMENT!'[5] it was built to house 500 inmates and their offspring. But no attempt was made to segregate the youngsters from the geriatric, the lunatic, the sick or any other condition of indigent pauper.

In 1847 there were 58 boys and 52 girls under instruction. The schoolmaster was entered as a 'lazy' old pauper and the boys failed abysmally in the examination. The girls did much better. Eleven were being taught geography, six grammar and seven were making good progress in dictation. The girls were allowed to mix quite freely with the adult women.[6]

Six years later, only 29 boys and 18 girls of school age were in the institution. Samuel Ellis, a certificated master, had been appointed. The apparatus, consisting of blackboards, maps and Irish reading books, were reported to be in good shape and there was an obvious improvement in the boys' ability. Lest the education should improve beyond what was consistent for pauper children, H.B. Farnell, District Poor Law Commissioner, offered the following fatuous advice to the Guardians: 'Too much mental education induced pride and idleness among pauper children. Three hours a day is quite sufficient to be in school. The remainder of the time should be occupied on the land even if they dig trenches in the ground and refill them for want of more profitable employment.'[7]

To the north of Sheffield, Parochial Union Schools were established in Ecclesfield and Bradfield but there was rarely more than a handful of children in either school Nothing more than the three Rs was ever attempted and like the Sheffield schools in the 1850s they were taught by paupers.

In 1855 both Sheffield and Ecclesall Unions required new teachers. The advertisement for the Sheffield vacancy read:

> Schoolmaster wanted. Single man or widower fully competent to perform the duties of the office prescribed by the General Consolidated Order of the Poor Law Commissioners. A person

possessing certificate of qualification from Committee of Council on Education preferred. Salary £45 per annum with board, washing and apartments to replace Mr. Thomas Wolstenholm resigned.[8]

The vacancy to replace Samuel Ellis at Ecclesall offered £30 per annum.

Teachers in Parochial Union schools could qualify under the Poor Law Commissioners' Certificate. Consequently the Guardians were not obliged to employ religious men and women. In 1859 lady visitors to the Union schools expressed concern about the lack of religious education and indirectly about the quality of teaching and the general welfare of the children. The following year a charge of severe corporal punishment was levelled at the Sheffield schoolmaster. In his defence, Mr Turner asserted that all children were clean, regularly washed and had plenty of pocket handkerchiefs. The rooms were warmed by two fires lit before the children came down in the morning. He admitted striking the boy Storey two or three times. When the boy tried to defend himself by raising his arm the blows intended for his shoulder hit his head. He stopped punishing when he saw the blood and sent the boy to have his head washed. The lad then resumed his place and carried on with his work.[9]

Two months later, Joseph Rowntree, the Quaker educationalist and social investigator, visited the Union workhouses and severely criticized the Pitsmoor School.[10] He described how the master divided the 40 boys into two groups and listened to the 12 older boys reading a chapter very laboriously and incorrectly. When Rowntree questioned some of the boys who had been in the school four years on their pence tables they were unable to calculate the following:

> How much was 99 pence?
>
> If 2s 6d was taken to the grocer for 1 lb of sugar at $7^1/_2$d and 1 lb of soap at $4^1/_2$d how much change would there be?

In Rowntree's opinion the master 'did not evince an aptitude for imparting the needful instruction'. He had dropped all vestige of industrial training—'even the more common oakum teasing for mat making'. The corporal punishment he inflicted failed to develop the mental faculties of such poor boys. Two strong canes were laid on the table: one was 'shivered up' and a new one laid ready for use. When shown the punishment book he was astonished to discover ten entries made during the first two months of the year—one of which caused a boy's head to bleed. In his view, the reasons for punishment were trivial: such things as inattention, dirty habits, etc. by which was meant the childish problem of bedwetting. In justification, the master claimed the medical officer's support but Rowntree was not impressed considering that 'too many boys had swollen glands and symptoms of tuberculosis'.

Rowntree found the condition of the girls to be much better. Thirty-five girls were taught by a competent mistress who helped them to understand what they were reading. Several of them read quite well and answered his questions on the multiplication tables—though clearly many were retarded. He also praised their knitting and sewing. He did question her use of the cane, however, because corporal punishment of girls was contrary to the standing orders of the Poor Law Board. She argued that she was entitled to use her own judgment irrespective of the views of ratepayers and Guardians because she had a good certificate.

The Guardians defended the staff and criticized his mode of inspection. The chairman reckoned the children were frightened of Rowntree's method of questioning because when he asked similar questions they answered correctly on their slates. As for reading, Rowntree set the second chapter of Ephesians which the children could not understand whereas when he gave them the twenty-first chapter of St Luke they read very well.

The Poor Law Commissioners did all in their power to get the Sheffield Guardians to replace their school premises in the 1860s because they were constantly overcrowded. By the standards of the day there was accommodation for 78 yet they housed 172. When the Guardians suggested the play room should be used the Commissioner stated that 'it was so low, damp and unhealthy and not fit for the reception of human beings'. Visitors could 'barely breathe in such an atmosphere for ten minutes'. Even the workhouse governor said his stable was a superior room. Many teachers refused to take up vacancies; claiming the school was gloomy, unhealthy and more often than not filled with smoke.

The Guardians came up with all manner of excuses but they were not prepared to increase taxation. The whole question of poor relief was aggravated in the lean years because nearly all the destitute of the borough were to be found in the Sheffield township, including the entire Irish population who regularly looked to the Union for subsistence. The chairman pointed to the improvement in health in

1863 when he reported that with over 200 children in care, months passed without a single child in hospital. Moreover 'children were never allowed to remain for any length of time. They were removed and put to work at the local trades which did not allow them to receive a good education...77 out of the 108 boys in school ranging from 5 to 15 had been in school for less than a year so it couldn't be expected they had learnt very much'.[11]

Pressure by the Inspectorate eventually paid dividends. By 1865 there is evidence of an overall improvement in school attainments and the children were found to be 'remarkably clean, well dressed in suitable clothing and looking very well'. Occasional treats were arranged. Trips to Miss Harrison's grounds at Weston and Wombwell's Menagerie were regularly organized. Some children were permitted a holiday once per month until the Guardians discovered they had been roaming round the town unsupervised. A few had been enticed into public houses on Furnace Hill where they were dressed up to dance and sing to amuse the customers.[12] Alternative arrangements were made in 1867 when a three-week holiday was organized on the Hollow Meadow Farm.

The Ecclesall Guardians experienced different problems. Because the institution was unable to cope with all the various classes of vagrants and paupers they had to extend their wards. This necessitated building a new school on Cherry Tree Hill Road parallel to the workhouse to accommodate 176 children. When the Commissioners tried to coerce the Guardians to double their planned admission they refused.[13] 'They had the Hallamshire audacity to suppose they knew their own affairs best.'

A gallery was erected above the dining room to facilitate worship for the pupils and staff. The long narrow schoolroom was divided; half for the boys and the other half for the girls with a rear projection for the infants. A large attic formed a 'magnificent' play room in bad weather and swings and rantipoles were erected in the school yard. Although a high proportion of the children were orphans or deserted, the compulsory separation from their parents was almost as rigid as in the detached provision created in Sheffield.

An inquest in 1869 sheds light on the callous nature of care behind the workhouse door.[14] A little girl of ten had been admitted with her mother three months earlier, but mother was only allowed to see her daughter once per fortnight. The schoolmistress informed the mother that her daughter was ill but she was not allowed to visit until the child was transferred to hospital on the day she died. When the house surgeon first saw her the little girl was suffering from an inflammatory fever, sore throat, bronchial pains and severe pains in the head. He did not regard the symptoms as serious and prescribed mustard poultices, medicines and removal to the sick ward. The child was poulticed every twelve hours but the surgeon neglected to see her again before she died. Standards of welfare and schooling in the Parochial Union Schools generally improved over the next few years but an enlightened attitude towards the care of these sorry children had to wait until the end of the century.

Ragged Schools

Concern for the condition of destitute children in the 'Hungry 40s', roaming round the streets, ill-fed, ill-clad, begging, pilfering and illiterate led to the foundation of Ragged Schools. It was clear to many observers there was a stratum of society—unable to benefit from the existing voluntary schools yet not employed—just running wild. The notion of Ragged Schools stemmed from the action of a disabled Portsmouth cobbler, John Pounds, who set out to rescue as many of the poorest and degraded children he could in his spare time. The plan was taken up by Sunday school teachers in the London City Mission who invited Ashley Cooper, later seventh Earl of Shaftesbury, to become president of the Ragged School Union in 1844.

Out walking with a party of friends in the summer of 1848, the Revd John Manners, Principal of Sheffield's Wesley College, was accosted by a gang of street children and resolved to set up such a school. Premises in Barley Fields were opened and twenty little urchins crowded through the door at six in the morning. No child was admitted into school whose parents were able to pay the merest school fee. By February 1849 75 children were in fairly regular attendance. School opened for morning and afternoon sessions every day of the week, including Sundays, and on three evenings a week. The greater part of the children were barefooted, bareheaded, ragged and invariably hungry. Some brought what they called a dinner—a crust of bread— which was all they had to eat from morning to night. The promoters soon realized that a meal of sorts must be provided. Youngsters were regularly to be found scavenging in the markets. The sweepings were heaped in one corner and allowed to rot—'upon which, children not pigs are grovelling whilst one infant sits playing with offal and gnawing a decayed leek'.[15]

Meetings were held, lectures given, subscriptions raised and in September 1849 the Ragged School opened in new premises in Baker's Yard, Peacroft, originally Allen Street Sunday School. Of the 280 children on roll in October 1849, 80 boys (50 per cent) and 95 girls (93 per cent) were unable to read a letter when they started. 40 boys (15 per cent) had never been to school before, 30 had since found a job and nine were reported to be begging. The aim of the trustees was to ensure that the children were ones other schools would refuse to admit or that their parents were unable to afford one penny per week. The catchment area was the Water Lane, Castle Green district where 'as many as fifteen lived in one house and as destitute of all sense of right and wrong as could well be conceived'.[16]

The first priority was to impose discipline and tailor the instruction to their level of understanding. The non-denominational school opened with prayers, a general confession and a few collects which the children repeated. Biblical instruction emphasizing the Ten Commandments and the moral code plus the three Rs was the basic curriculum. Girls were taught knitting and sewing, and industrial training was introduced to the older lads which allowed them to earn between 1s 6d and 2 shillings per week. Commenting on the movement generally in 1852, Thomas Mann wrote, 'The primary object of the Ragged Schools is to convert incipient criminals to Christianity'.[17]

In 1854 the Town Council warmly endorsed the work of the school and claimed that shopkeepers could now leave goods at their shop doors without fear of them being stolen. Many of the children who once depended on plundering and thieving for their daily bread were no longer feared. Something of an exaggeration, perhaps, but the Police Superintendent was convinced the lessons taught in the school were far more effective than the discipline of prison.[18]

Regular attendance was largely secured by the provision of bread from a special fund set up by the trustees. In the first six years of the school's existence, 761 destitute children were admitted; 54 were orphans, 236 fatherless, 83 motherless and a large proportion were either deserted, or stranded by parents who were in prison or had been transported. Upwards of five hundred obtained work on leaving or were promised a job. Most of the youngsters were so grateful for the shelter and provisions that they proved biddable, and corporal punishment was rare.

A survey of the nearby Hollis Croft neighbourhood revealed that out of a population of 7,000 not more than 20 families attended any form of public worship, whilst in the same district there were 85 public houses and beer shops. In three streets and adjoining courts, out of the 311 children, 93 received no instruction 'except that gathered in the streets and vicious houses. The swarming courts as full of life as sewers are of rats and quite as foul.' Juvenile delinquency was increasing and young people generally between the ages of seven and twenty were guilty of 25 per cent of the crime.

Periodically the schools annual report would contain touching anecdotes revealing abject poverty and misery. One little boy of six had been earning a living for two or three years by singing in public houses, tumbling, standing on his head and clowning. His friend had been sold for 1s 6d to accompany a blind beggar. School visitors would also describe the housing conditions. One house, small and damp in a dirty backyard, was almost destitute of furniture. A sleeping room contained a quantity of straw and one quilt for the entire household of widowed mother, two sons and a daughter. In another family, the father had been unemployed for 20 weeks. Three of his children attended the school and often subsisted for the whole day on the piece of bread given to them by the teacher. When the school was invited into the Botanical Gardens for a treat, some were unable to go because they were so wretchedly clad. The lucky ones begged for spare buns so that they could take them for their brothers and sisters.

By 1855 it was clear that larger premises were needed. Many of the 380 children just had to sit on the floor. There was no provision for infants, and the promoters were anxious to provide a night refuge. The committee were stung into action by the example of the Roman Catholics who had opened St Vincent's School in the adjoining yard. Their Sunday instruction was attended by hundreds whereas the Ragged School only attracted about one hundred. The affluent and philanthropic were canvassed—not only for funds but also for promise of employment to those leaving school. The Town Council, previously loath to get involved in education, did eventually agree to support the school financially by 26 votes to 6.

The new school, designed to accommodate 200 boys on the ground floor and 200 girls on the floor above, had separate entrances, class-rooms and lavatories. Ministers of every Protestant denomination supported the venture. Invited to the official opening in May 1856, the Earl of Shaftesbury congratulated the Committee and considered the children were stronger and healthier than the mudlarks who crawled in the ooze and the low alluvial slime of Lambeth and Westminster.[19]

Nevertheless, he was convinced of the need of schools 'for the wandering Arabs and Bedouins of society. Without such schools I do not believe the Government could have kept the country in order and subordination in 1848'.

A penny bank was started and a clothing fund set up enabling children to purchase clothing at half price. A Shoe Black Brigade was also tried but failed due to lack of supervision and want of leadership. Four shillings' worth of bread (16 lbs) was distributed daily and the landlord of the King's Head provided 300 pints of soup each week. Without such provision many would have been compelled to beg as formerly. On Sunday evenings, the majority of youngsters attended evening service at West Bar conducted by the Vicar, Dr Sale. It was a service intended 'for those classes who excused themselves from not going to Church on the grounds that they had not clothes fit to mix with those who attended'.

Four salaried teachers were employed in 1859. When the trustees advertised for a schoolmistress they offered up to £25 per annum 'for one who has some experience in teaching and a good voice to lead the singing'. The pupils were examined regularly in reading, writing and mental arithmetic, the Bible, geography and history. Dr Sale examined scripture, the school secretary, Mr Ford, examined the three Rs and Mr Atkin, the master (previously master of Greenhill National School), assessed the history, geography and singing.

Home visiting was introduced in order to satisfy the committee on the condition of parents and guardians. 'Children who were not fit objects of charity were not admitted.' The Vicar made it abundantly clear that he was only prepared to support the school so long as they excluded all children whose parents could afford the fees normally charged in the voluntary schools. He argued that the admission of such children would have a pernicious effect upon the habits of the poor and the Guardians provided for the education of outdoor pauper children from the rates (Denison's Act 1855).

The evening classes had a much more disorderly beginning. One visitor enlarged on the mayhem when a newly appointed teacher's attention was diverted. There were 146 older boys supervised by one teacher and the ensuing commotion 'beggared all description!'– whistling, shouting, singing, laughing, followed by horseplay. A sparring match got out of hand and one boy was thumped in the eye. When the teacher tried to restore order someone turned off the gaslight and the lads outside the room held the door to prevent others going out. On another occasion, the secretary discovered about 20 boys venturing to whitewash the teacher who 'submitted to the indignity from a desire to gain the goodwill of the boys by kindness'. The outcome was an appeal for voluntary assistance. Boys from 9 to 15 were admitted into night school. Most of them were illiterate and one fourteen-year-old had been in prison eight times.[20]

For a time a policeman patrolled the evening sessions but gradually the tone improved. By 1857 the behaviour was reported to be under control and the anxiety to learn said to be admirable. Some boys arranged to start work earlier in the day so that they could attend at night. The emphasis was on religious instruction and the three Rs. Towards the end of the decade pupils were regularly entered for the School of Art examinations. In the 1860s the average attendance rose from 76 to around 130 scholars between the ages of ten and 18, most of whom were working. A tailoring class was started in 1862. They were taught how to mend their clothes by 'a tailor whose heart was in his work and who also planted Christian instruction in their minds'.

Girls' attendance in night school was more spasmodic than the boys' because the Sheffield Trades demanded they work later in the evenings. Although 167 girls were on roll in 1851 the average attendance was only 42. The majority were under 14 but 43 were aged between 14 and 20. As most of them had never attended day school, reading instruction had to begin with the alphabet. A mothers' sewing meeting of about 30 was given instruction in sewing and reading. It combined with a girls' class to make and distribute the half price clothing: 2s 6d a suit of clothes, 4d for a shirt, 1 shilling for a girl's frock. In 1861 they completed 378 garments including 42 boys' shirts, 43 suits, 5 coats and 7 vests.[21]

Sunday school attendance fluctuated wildly. Between 150 and 300 attended, taught largely by voluntary teachers. Whereas children were admitted in the day school up to the age of ten, they remained in the Sunday school till about 13 or 14. 'Then they come to a period', commented Dr Sale, 'when they have no master to control them and they think themselves their own master which is one reason why they don't enter church or chapel.' For that reason he believed the evening school to be the most important part of the institution.

Midway through the 1860s, extensive improvements were put in hand.[22] The Crofts on the far side of Tenter Street was regarded as extremely suitable as 'it resembled the Irish quarter of Liverpool'. Irish immigrants had settled almost exclusively in the district and the dirt and squalor were fearful. Large families were herded into squalid rooms. Ragged, dirty and unkempt children in all stages of development swarmed the footpaths. In the view of the Ragged School promoters it was cheaper to snatch the young urchins from the street, educate and train them to be useful artisans than erect costly gaols for their reception or fit out commodious transports for their conveyance to the Bermudas or Australia.

The altruistic aim was a comprehensive welfare and educational complex. Included in the scheme were improved infant school provision, a night refuge for the destitute, an orphanage and an industrial school. Several recessed berths were set into the walls for the toddlers. A gallery was erected and forms fitted with arm rests and securing bars for the two-year-olds. The upper rooms were equipped for tailoring, shoemaking (including clogging and repairs) and paint making. A large all-purpose play room for use in wet weather and an open playground was added.

The night refuge had twenty sleeping berths alongside the matron's quarters. The orphanage could house up to twelve in dormitories. The kitchen and refectory, washing rooms, bathrooms and separate lavatories were located in the basement though raised well above ground level. Mary Carpenter, defender of neglected children, speaking in Sheffield later in the year confirmed that the aim of the institution was 'to civilise as well as educate'.[23]

The whole new complex was due almost entirely to the exertions and leadership of Alderman Henry Elliot Hoole, the stove grate manufacturer of Green Lane Works and, more importantly, his wife. Mrs Hoole coordinated the collection of subscriptions and organized a bazaar which raised over £1,000. Amongst the company of noble helpers were Lady Halifax, Countess Fitzwilliam, Lady Wharncliffe, the Mayoress, Miss Lacock and the Misses Vickers. Appeals were made for cast-off shoes and clogs. The children were supplied with home knitted stockings, chemises, linsey petticoats and calico shirts. Sir John Brown and others opened their grounds for occasional treats and buses and drays were offered freely by the Sheffield Carriage Company and Tennants the Brewers. These schools captured the hearts and minds of all sections of the community.

The school was officially opened by Lord Wharncliffe and his brother the Hon. Stuart Wortley, attended by the band of the 83rd Regiment and the girls' choir. In his opening address, Stuart Wortley affirmed the charity was educating the lowest ranks of society—every child rescued from a career of crime and pauperism was withdrawn from being a charge on the poor rate. Boys were put in a position to earn their own living and become producers of what constituted the country's wealth instead of being absorbers of it. He contended it was useless to teach reading and writing and give a basic education unless accompanied by religious education, although he stressed there was no denominational teaching given. Only knowledge of Almighty God was taught, other questions were left to parents. Lord Wharncliffe reminded those present that a very valuable adjunct to the schooling was that they were taught 'habits of discipline and obedience to their superiors as well as habits of honesty and truthfulness'.

The standard of schooling improved immeasurably in the more spacious accommodation. HMIs reported that the new infant school had made an excellent start, the children were happy and orderly and a fair number would have passed the examination if they had been presented. Although both reading and writing were well taught, staffing ratios required improvement to raise the overall level of attainment reached in the best infant schools.

In March 1869, the Earl of Shaftesbury revisited the school after 13 years. He admired the work of reclamation and praised the devotion of the committee. 'Here is activity while others sleep. The grand principle of the ragged school system is that it takes children in rags and turns them out washed. It takes them in ignorant and turns them out taught. It takes them in heathens and turns them out Christians.' When applauding the singing, he told the children how the people of Sheffield were recognized throughout England and even throughout the world for their musical talents. From all his experience he knew nothing more humanizing than to teach children to sing hymns and pleasant cheerful songs.[24]

At that time (1869) the school was progressing excellently with 946 children on roll; 650 attending day school, 140 night school and 156 in the Sunday school. Sixteen mothers regularly attended the sewing class. Sir John Brown recounted that out of the 11,600 children admitted to the Ragged School in the past 14 years, scarcely a child had been sent to prison or set before the magistrates—many proving themselves good workers and excellent members of society.[25]

Two months later the school was reduced to ashes, totally destroyed by fire and uninsured. Mrs Hoole lost no time in gathering working men together to discuss rebuilding. Workers and political parties met in schoolrooms throughout the town to arrange fund-raising events.

Subscriptions and donations flooded in from companies, societies, sewing classes, individuals and scholars. On his return from America in January 1871, Mundella donated the fees from his lecture tour on the American system of education.

The erection of the new school facing Pea Croft began in 1871 at a cost of £4,500, £3,000 of which was already raised. When the deeds were examined, however, it was discovered that Unitarians and Roman Catholics were precluded from supporting the institution and any alteration would involve the committee in hefty legal fees. Not until 1873 was the school fully operational again and a quarter of the children were prepared for their first HMI examination.

As the school was overcrowded and oversubscribed, supporters lobbied for additional accommodation. Some argued for comparable schools in other parts of the town, believing the new School Board had little sympathy for this underclass and preferred to take them before the magistrate if they did not attend. The Mayor, Alderman J. Fairburn, added fuel to the argument when he said that he could not see his way clear to bring the ragged children amongst the orderly clean children whom they expected in the Board Schools.[26] Other patrons became reluctant to continue their financial support when they detected that some parents could afford normal school fees and were taking advantage of the subsidized schooling of one penny a week and the daily issue of bread and soup. In 1875, 20 cases were investigated. One parent was found to be earning £5 per week whilst others varied from 22 to 50 shillings per week.[27] Further enquiries revealed that 266 parents were skilled artisans. This abuse of the school led to its discontinuation as a charity and in 1876 the School Board resolved to purchase the property and rename it the Crofts Board School. Surveys undertaken by the Board disclosed only 80 to 100 children in the town under 14 years of age really necessitous and entitled to have their school fees remitted.[28]

For over 25 years the Ragged School had impressed a wide spectrum of public opinion. In addition to the Earl of Shaftesbury and Lord Wharncliffe, the school attracted such notable figures as Lord John Russell and Lord Brougham to chair the annual meetings. The blend of Christian mission and social welfare rescued hundreds of neglected and half-starved little bodies from 'Beggary, Filth and Crime'. The social influence of education on child care since 1870 has been impressive but the example set by the Ragged School was unique and its achievements should not be discounted.

Industrial and Reformatory Schools

Contemporary with the creation of the Ragged School was a movement towards the opening of an industrial school for the offspring of
parents on outdoor relief. In 1851 the Town Council claimed that the
Union School was full, that 1,120 pauper children in the township
were running wild and parents on relief receiving between 1 shilling
and 2s 6d a week could ill afford school fees. The motion was defeated
by councillors who argued that the introduction of industrial schools
would bring them into conflict with artisans, whilst others suggested
that it could encourage some folk to become paupers in order to get
free education.[29] When the Poor Law Board proposed the conversion
of Hollow Meadows Farm to an industrial school, the Guardians
dismissed the idea as impractical because 'there was such a demand for
boys in the different branches of the Sheffield trades and for girls as
domestic servants'.[30]

Once the Guardians were empowered by Denison's Act of 1855 to
pay school fees for those in receipt of outdoor relief, enquiries were
made as to which schools would accept them and on what terms. Some
were directed to the Ragged School but St John's, Park, St George's,
and the Lancasterian School proved the most popular. By 1859, only
240 out of 1,081 young paupers with parents on outdoor relief were
neither at school nor at work.

Educational solutions, however, failed to stem the rising tide of
juvenile delinquency. Many neglected children found themselves at
odds with the law for the most trivial offences. Petty larceny predominated, but stealing turnips, begging, and sleeping rough were equally
punishable misdemeanours. Some lads were so hooked on 'low
theatres' where lurid dramas such as *Jack Shepherd, Highwayman and
Thief* were performed, they pilfered to indulge their addiction.
Criminal statistics reveal that during the twelve years 1845–56, over
2,000 children under 16 were taken into custody—roughly 5 per cent
of the criminal intake: 101 boys and 18 girls were under 10 years old,
1,754 boys and 164 girls were aged between 10 and 15. Statistics for
1871 show little change.[31]

Most of them were whipped or birched and discharged. Three girls
of 15 were transported for seven years. Imprisonment varied from one
month to two years. Not until 1858 is there evidence of a child being
sent to a reformatory as an alternative penal institution. Reformatories,
an innovation of 1854, were 'designed to assist young offenders below
the age of sixteen by removing them from the scene of criminal life

before they could become fully hardened'.[32] Nonetheless, youngsters had to spend a fortnight in gaol before being sent to a reformatory where sentences could vary from two to five years.

In 1861, the Roman Catholics opened St Joseph's Reformatory at Howard Hill, Walkley, for girls in their northern dioceses. Run by the Sisters of St Vincent de Paul, they gave instruction in elementary education and the Catholic religion. Their purpose was to reclaim girls from delinquency by a rigorous training in domestic service. Prizes were awarded not only for good conduct and proficiency in the three Rs but also for cooking, baking, washing and ironing.

Ten years later a Catholic orphanage and industrial centre was set up at Kirkedge on a bleak, elevated moorland above Worral. It was planned to provide for 300 boys and girls but was later classified as an industrial school for girls. A new wing was added in 1885 to accommodate a chapel, dormitory, lavatories and infirmary but, owing to the insoluble problem of securing an adequate water supply, the girls were transferred to St Joseph's Home in Walkley (1887). Catholic boys convicted of criminal offences were sent to industrial schools at Shibden near Halifax or St Joseph's, Manchester.

Constructive models of penal reform which prompted the creation of reformatories led also to the passing of the Industrial Schools Act of 1866. A significant outcome locally was the decision of county and borough magistrates to commit juvenile delinquents to industrial schools, normally the Humber training ship *Southampton*. Established for 'the reception and training of boys who through poverty, parental neglect or being orphans are left desolate, and homeless and in danger of contamination from association with vice and crime', the industrial schools were completely isolated from the influence of family and friends. Instruction was given in tailoring, net making, the three Rs and a general training in seamanship. Alderman Webster took a personal interest in the welfare of the boys and persuaded the School Board of the institution's worth. 'These boys are our own children... some of our workmen, of our fellow townsmen. They are not strangers—they are our own, only moved to a place of safe keeping and rational education. They are the victims, not of their own faults but of the recklessness or misfortune of their parents and the unsatisfactory conditions of modern civilisation.'

Some boys thrived on the experience and sought a future in fishing and in shipping. Others, not so enamoured, returned home as soon as possible. On taking office Sheffield School Board undertook the responsibility for the supervision and maintenance of all young offenders and disclosed that currently 38 Sheffield boys were aboard the training ship. When the Truant School at Hollow Meadows was opened, those children who might previously have been charged and perceived only to be lacking discipline were tackled there. Intractable cases demanding stiffer penalties were committed to industrial schools in York, Leeds, and Cockermouth in Cumberland.[33]

Charity Schools

The distinctive uniforms of the charity school children set them apart from all their contemporaries. Rooted in the eighteenth-century concept of patronage and subservience, the Boys' Charity School trustees selected the orphans and jealously safeguarded the school's authority. By 1845 the school had increased its intake to 100 scholars who were divided into five classes under one master. Not until certificated teachers were employed in the 1860s did the school merit praise. The monitorial system was phased out and former pupil-teacher assistants were appointed. A common curriculum was pursued as in other public elementary schools and no industrial or vocational instruction was given except for the regular kitchen duties. With the exception of the six Hanbey boys who were dressed akin to Christ's Hospital scholars, the rest wore the old-fashioned garb of blue cloth coat buttoning up in front with cutaway tails behind, yellow braid and brass buttons, green corduroy trousers, white bands and blue muffin caps.

Clues as to the welfare of the lads is scarce but in 1875 evidence of their Spartan existence emerged. Rations were meagre. The boys complained of being half-starved, the bread was hard and the milk was watered down. Breakfast consisted of a pint of milk and an 8 oz. chunk of bread. Meat was allowed four times per week which the trustees thought ample. Sweet puddings and treacle on Thursdays—'most nutritious diet'—and 20 oz. of bread daily, never more than three or four days old, was thought sufficient. Cold-water washing and bathing in the outside troughs was customary. The boys were only allowed to leave the premises to visit relatives or friends on Saturday afternoons. Nevertheless, affection for the school by many who succeeded in the world of work contributed to the formation of an Old Boys' Association.[34]

The Girls' Charity School unashamedly trained girls for domestic service. In contrast to the boys' school, the girls' school was not open to inspection though neither institution received parliamentary grants.

Figure 19. The staff and pupils of the Boys' Charity School c. 1900. With the exception of the five 'Hanbey' boys wearing the garb of Christ's Hospital boys, the charity scholars are dressed in their uniform of blue cloth coats, green corduroy trousers, white bands and blue muffin caps.

By the time the girls left school at the age of 15 many had reached the fifth standard of the Government code—a standard achieved by few in the public schools before the 1880s. Plans to move the school to Mount Pleasant, Highfields were delayed until 1873. Shortly afterwards, a reporter described how the girls, trim and neat as Quakers, were probed in mental arithmetic before being led through gymnastic exercises that brought a bloom to their cheeks which 'augurs well for the vigorous use of the broom and scrubbing brush in after years'.[35]

Notes

1.   *SI* (20 May 1843).
2.   *SI* (20 July 1844).
3.   *HMI Browne's Report*, CCE Parochial Unions 1847–50, pp. 199f.
4.   *SI* (16 December 1854; 27 January 1876).
5.   J. Flett, *The Story of the Workhouse and the Hospital at Nether Edge* (1985), p. 8.
6.   *HMI Browne's Reports*, CCE Parochial Unions 1847–50, pp. 199f, 1852–57, pp. 259f.
7.   *SI* (21 February 1852).
8.   *SI* (10 January 1855).
9.   *SI* (3 March 1860).
10. *SI* (10 March 1860).
11. *Sheffield Times* (5 May 1860); *SI* (19 January 1861; 23 March 1861; 24 July 1862; 30 April 1864).
12. *SI* (29 April 1865; 19 May 1865).
13. *SI* (5 May 1866).
14. *Sheffield Times* (1 May 1869).
15. Quoted from *The Builder*, *SI* (7 October 1861).
16. *SI* (27 October 1849); *Sheffield Times* (24 February 1849).
17. *Census of Great Britain 1851*, 1852–1853, *Mann's Report*, p. 77.
18. *SI* (13 May 1854).
19. *SI* (3 May 1856). See *SI* (13 February 1872) for the sanitary state of the Crofts.
20. *SI* (3 January 1857).
21. *SI* (17 November 1861).
22. *SI* (7 September 1865).
23. *Transactions of the National Association for the Promotion of Social Science* (1865), pp. 321f.
24. *SI* (4 March 1869).
25. *SI* (20 May 1871).
26. *SI* (23 May 1873).

27. *SI* (16 April 1875). See also Bingham, *Sheffield School Board*, pp. 65f.

28. *SI* (18 April 1876).

29. *SI* (15 March 1851).

30. *SI* (19 August 1854).

31. Criminal Statistical Records for Sheffield 1845–56, SCL; *SI* (27 October 1871).

32. P. Horn, *The Victorian Country Child* (1985), p. 189.

33. *SI* (15 December 1870; 3 February 1871); Bingham, *Sheffield School Board*, p. 199.

34. *SI* (22 February 1875; 25 February 1875; 27 February 1875).

35. *SI* (23 February 1875).

Chapter 7

Children Working 1839-1870

Children go to school earlier so that they might work earlier.
Revd Frederick Watkins HMI (1859)

There was nothing new about children working. Setting the child to
work was the custom of centuries. For the mass of children, school was
merely a place to go until old enough to start work. What was revealed
by the Children's Employment Commission of 1842 was the sheer
physical grind and exploitation of countless children, sufficient to
disturb the nineteenth-century conscience. The Commission, the
outcome of tenacious lobbying of Lord Melbourne's government by
Lord Ashley, the Earl of Shaftesbury's heir, was asked to enquire
into the conditions of life and labour of children in the northern
manufacturing towns.

In the Sheffield region, children of seven and eight were employed
in the mines and younger children could be found assisting adult relatives at the grinding wheel and forge. With the onset of steam power
there was a steady migration of rural cutlers into the town centre.
Household chores for boys diminished in the warren of back-to-back
houses erected around Shalesmoor and Park Hill, whilst the chances to
acquire a little skill as outworkers in the converted workshops and lean-
to sheds escalated. For girls 'born to work' the demand for help around
the house did not slacken. Consequently, very few daughters were
wage-earning before the age of twelve.

As the population increased, so did the necessity for poorer children
to supplement the family income. With industrial expansion the
demand intensified for semi- and unskilled workers. Formal apprenticeship declined and more opportunities opened up for children to acquire
wage-earning significance and a measure of independence. Jelinger
Symons, the Children's Employment Commissioner, focused on the
youngsters 'exposed to the corrupting association of older youths and

men while at work'. Drinking habits began early and the upswing of
sexual promiscuity led Symons to reflect on the melancholy amount of
immorality among the young, 'working more closely together than
those employed in cotton, woollen and flax factories'.[1] Many were
totally independent of parental control, 'entirely their own masters as to
habits, hours, education and religious instruction before they are fourteen years of age'. Canon Sale referred to the problem of 'infant independence' time and time again.

The opening of the Sheffield Canal basin in 1819 and the arrival of
the railways in 1838 accelerated the development of the South
Yorkshire coalfield. Collieries to the east of Sheffield—Soap House,
Tinsley Park, Handsworth, Intake and Deep Pits—furnished evidence
of the youngest boys employed as trappers, confined to infernal dark-
ness for hours on end. Others 'harnessed like dogs' to the corves (coal
trucks) would drag them on all fours through underground tunnels.
Girls too, often naked to the waist and dressed like boys in trousers,
performed the similar tasks of trapping, hurrying, tipping and filling the
coal trucks as they trundled backwards and forwards in the mines.

The 'cry of the children' was real, and evidence of the soul-
destroying drudgery captured the imagination of many writers.[2] Yet
local coal owners were reluctant to admit that children entered their
mines before the age of nine. Most of the children interviewed were
aged between 9 and 13. The colliery owner of Intake, William
Newbould, who endowed ten school places for girls at Gleadless,
asserted that being in the pits kept the children out of mischief.
Hannah Richardson of Intake told the Commission, 'It would hurt us
if childer were prevented from working till 11 or 12 because we've jobs
enow to live as it is'. Trapping could bring in 6d per day. Those over 11
could earn up to five shillings per week.

Although Yorkshire emerged as one of the largest coalfields in the
country, Sheffield was not primarily a coalmining town and the
number of children employed was limited. In the course of his
inquiries, Symons could only discover 1,028 children in 80 of
Yorkshire's principal collieries and most of them were over ten years
old.[3] The overall picture nationwide respecting the employment of girls
and women in the mines was sufficient to ensure restrictive legislation
but ten-year-old lads could still be employed. Not until 1862 was the
minimum age raised to twelve for boys.

Factory legislation and reform provided a degree of protection for
the mass of children harnessed to power-drive machines in the textile

mills of Lancashire, the West Riding and the Midlands, but was totally irrelevant to the Sheffield Trades. Investigations into the cutlery industry revealed traditional practices that were difficult to eradicate. Parents and relatives were accustomed to taking their lads with them to the anvil, bench and wheel. The opportunity to run errands, to try their hand at hammering, filing and boring or generally hanging about the place was irresistible and the assortment of hearths and small-scale workshops in the secluded courts and alleys hindered effective inquiry.

The common age for starting work was 9-plus but some children as young as six were discovered wiping knives and putting scissors together. One example cited by Commissioner White in 1865 was of a six-year-old grinding on a dry stone and glazing by his father's side at the Globe Wheel. One woman who was 'set on' in the cutlery trade at the age of six and had to be lifted on to the stool to reach her work because she was not big enough to climb up herself, 'put her own lass now dead on at three weeks turned six'.[4]

In workshops almost devoid of ventilation, children would inhale flying steel or sandstone dust as they crouched behind the wheel. Grinding the blanks of rough-hewn forks constituted the greatest health hazard. In his treatise on the Sheffield grinders' disease Dr J.C. Hall declared 'that to send a boy of 8 or 10 years of age to work polishing forks in the grinding hull is an act of refined cruelty'. Fork grinding was the most pernicious of occupations but the term 'grinding' comprised a wide range of processes related to knives, forks, razors, edge tools and files. Ebenezer Elliott affirmed that grinders had a law that 'no grinder under 28 years of age shall take an apprentice, and as the life of a grinder is about 30 years he must have no assistance or set his uneducated child at the age of ten or twelve to work so deadly that under good government none but criminals would be allowed to labour at it'.[5]

File cutting was both dangerous and unhealthy and a 14-hour day for ten-year-old youngsters was quite normal. As files varied both in shape and size, younger children could be given lighter tasks using lightweight hammers to chisel the toughened steel. Some girls proved quicker and achieved greater dexterity than boys and often worked at home. George Hawksworth, master of Parson Cross School, a file cutter by trade, was alleged to spend more time teaching pupils how to cut files than the three Rs. Bending over the vice or 'stiddy' badly affected the physique of young file cutters. This 'stunted race of men' gave rise to the comments of George Orwell a century later: 'In

Sheffield you have the feeling of walking among a population of troglodytes'.[6]

Children were also drawn to the varied processes of silver plate and Brittania Metal manufacture. Buffing and burnishing were exceedingly dirty operations undertaken by women and girls. Boys more often than not were engaged in 'raising' or 'chasing' which entailed hammering the plate or creating a raised pattern on the surface of the metal. Occasionally they ladled molten metal into moulds.

Compared with the Victorian country child or children employed in the textile mills, children in the Sheffield trades were well paid. Youngsters leaving school at the age of 9-plus could earn between three and five shillings per week. Some boys leaving Pitsmoor School could earn up to eight shillings per week. The ironworks paid between 9d and 1s 4d per day whilst colliery lads could earn between 7s 6d and 9s 6d for a five-day week. In collating the pay scales for children in the various trades, HMI Watkins argued that it was futile to consider compulsory education 'in the manufacturing and mining districts when child labour is much used and highly remunerated'.[7]

Because children were rarely employed by the manufacturers but by journeymen and relatives it is extremely difficult to unearth the true extent of child labour. When Symons arrived in the town in 1840 he endorsed the opinion of the *Sheffield Independent*. 'It is true that we have not in the trades of Sheffield any considerable number of tender age. There are however some.'[8] In 1842 Symons calculated that 754 children (652 boys and 102 girls) under thirteen were employed in the Sheffield Trades which was roughly 4.1 per cent of the school-age population.

In contrast to the 'dark satanic mills', where thousands of children were pressed into remorseless physical toil, industrial Sheffield harboured no great concentration of child workers. Not until the heavy steel industry developed in the late 1850s were large-scale foundries and workshops established. The 'little mesters' forge and smithy remained the typical place of work where children could do odd jobs or amuse themselves with no compelling reason to attend school.

Inevitably, some youngsters found employment outside the major industries. Shopkeepers, tradesmen, merchants and the people in professions were continually on the look-out for someone to run errands, shop lads and messenger boys. Hawking attracted the street children prepared to sell anything from firewood and clothes pegs to matches and trinkets. Climbing boys in Sheffield were never numerous but little boys between the ages of five and ten were apprenticed by master chimney-sweeps until the practice was finally abolished in 1875. Their champion, Samuel Roberts, campaigned vigorously on their behalf from 1807 onwards and organized an annual dinner for them. In 1824, 24 boys attended. Forty years later 22 boys accepted invitations.

The range of casual jobs outlined by Revd James Blackburn, curate of Attercliffe, clearly illustrates the vital necessity of earning compared with learning for families living in poverty in the 'hungry forties'.

> Some children are employed in the coke yards picking out the white shale etc. Little boys of six or seven blow the bellows for the spade and shovel makers. Six or eight boys of eight or nine strike for the chain makers—each man has a boy as a striker. Boys under thirteen are employed to take milk on donkeys to Sheffield.

> Horse lads begin at ten. Girls under thirteen are commonly employed to drive coal carts drawn by donkeys and ponies. Girls very young go from hence to Sheffield to work in hair seating manufactories. Girls work in the potteries and brickyards. Girls not so young go into various manufactories in Sheffield, hardware, Brittania Metal, silver plating, buttons etc. These are all sad and demoralizing schools. Girls of five years old and upwards are employed by mothers to nurse, or let out to nurse; by which they are deprived of education.[9]

When the steel age arrived in the 1860s after a long gestation period, mergers, amalgamations and expansion created the industrial empires of John Brown, Charles Cammell, Mark Firth, Thomas Jessop, Edward Vickers and many others. The Atlas Works, Cyclops Steel, Brightside and River Don Works all emerged as huge magnets for skilled artisans and a host of unskilled labourers. As trade boomed, wages rose and job opportunities for boys offered more scope for evading school and the workhouse. Yet Commissioner White resisted all temptation to estimate the number of boys employed in the iron and steel industry in 1865.

> Taking the manufactures of the district generally the proportion of children to adults employed in them is small. It is in few that they are employed where ever light work and in some cases work that is not light, can be found for them.[10]

The lighter work included the treading of clay as part of the process of making lids for the steel melting pots. The most dangerous jobs were in the rolling mills where lads were exposed to terrific scorching. The 'most objectionable' was the work of cellar boys who operated in pitch-black cellars beneath the steel smelting furnaces.[11] White described how one ten-year-old in Saville Street Works would stand a few feet in front of the furnace and 'hold up' the door as the fiery metal was drawn out and others were showered by flakes of blistering steel from the shingler's hammer.

The wearing of crinolines became exceptionally fashionable midway through the nineteenth century and initially Sheffield produced all the crinoline steel that was used. Whilst the women and girls covered the wire with cotton, boys would tent the reels on which the steel wire was wound, fire up (stoke) the furnaces and scour the wire. Night shifts were common and manufacturers were severely criticized for their lack of supervision of the lads 'who were drawn into old women's houses' so overcrowded no one could stir. Many lads were scarred for life, not only by their experiences but also by the scorching wire that could spit and snap.[12]

Manufacturing confectionery was a cleaner and healthier occupation and attracted tidy children who made up half of George Basset's work force of 150. Boys assisted the adults in the preparation of spice, the production of acid drops and transporting pastilles and candied peel and other ingredients to the warehouses where the women and girls worked. Factory hours and regulations did apply.[13]

Girls working in the hair-seat and curled-hair workshops were not so well served and little protection from sweated labour was attainable before 1867. Sitting and bending for twelve hours per day as the shuttle wove in and out of the fabric was exhausting for twelve-year-old 'servers'. Mattress and upholstery manufacture expanded with the demand for contemporary furnishing at a time 'when a cloth sofa and matching chairs was considered indispensible to the respectable working class home'.[14]

The plight of girls plunged into domestic service—estimated to be 71 per cent of all girls under 20—received no attention whatsoever. Ignored by Royal Commissions and Trades Unions alike, hundreds of girls were pressed into service to satisfy the inexhaustible demand from Sheffield's expanding suburbia. 'To keep one skivvy in the kitchen as surely announced middle class membership as the possession of a cottage piano indicated the respectability of a working man.'[15] Just as the discipline of the workhouse made pauper boys into very obedient sweeps, so pauper girls made very good servants.

Stung by national press criticism in the wake of the Employment

Commission's report in 1865, Sheffield Town Council undertook its own investigations into the extent of child labour in the borough. 2,000 of the leading manufacturers were circulated and 1,986 responded. From these enquiries it is evident that 1,606 manufacturers employed no child whatsoever under twelve. Of the remainder, just over a thousand were employed: 856 boys and 186 girls—3 per cent of the school-age population. The Association of Organised Trades considered the reports 'fair and correct'.[16]

The majority of employers was now prepared to dispense with the labour of young children altogether and 'thoughtful members of the working classes accepted that to a certain age they should be at school'. Opinion diverged, however, on the question of further restrictive legislation. There was wide agreement that it could only depress poorer parents and, considering that only a small proportion of school-age children would be affected, the Town Council felt justified in petitioning the Queen, 'Praying that Sheffield may not be placed under the extension of the Factory Acts'.

In the event, the Factory Acts were redefined. Together with the Workshop Regulation Act of 1867, safety measures were introduced, night working under the age of eleven was prohibited, and the number of school-age children permitted to work was again curtailed. Nevertheless, infringements and loopholes led to the patchy observance of the legislation. In February 1870, 19 cases of children under 13 employed in Bull Week—the week before Christmas—were brought before the courts. One boy was discovered polishing the wheel between 2 a.m. and 5 a.m. His father was prosecuted. Some boys were not actually working but were found on premises where men were at work. More prosecutions were brought against electroplate manufacturers in May. Seven girls were found burnishing and polishing at five minutes to nine at night. The excuse given touched on the time the jobs arrived and the fact that the girls had little to do in the morning.[17]

The evidence of working-class children leaving school early is overwhelming. In 1859 Watkins inferred that children went to school earlier so that they might work earlier and Earnshaw confirmed that only one fifth stayed on to 12 or 13. The benefits of possible earnings clearly outweighed the cost benefits of education for the majority of the population.

Increasing prosperity in the fifties and sixties imperceptibly changed parental attitudes towards children working and the introduction of heavy industry, new technology and restrictive child labour regulations markedly affected the use of children in the workplace. Official investigations in the 1860s failed to discover any extensive involvement of young children in trade or industry which prompted Robert Leader to comment in 1869:

> We have emptied the manufactories but we have not filled the schools. The employers, rather than submit to the restrictions imposed upon them, endeavoured to dispense with the labour of the children who are thus thrown out of employment and into the streets.[18]

With the decline in job opportunities, parents continued to secure the maximum schooling they could afford and withdrew their children before the age of eleven. In 1871, 29,000 children were on school registers but only 25 per cent were over the age of ten.[19] Neither at work nor at school, many were allowed to drift aimlessly, some no doubt searching for casual jobs until permanent work could be found. As in earlier times, there was a tendency to mix work experience with school and a little healthy amusement until compulsory schooling became a reality.

The downturn in job prospects for boys and girls is borne out by two recent surveys of industrial villages within the borough.[20] Census evidence for Grimesthorpe in Brightside Bierlow identifies a concentration on fork and shear manufacture. Darnall evolved as a steel and mining community. Analysis of the returns uncovers those 'at work' in each age group and reveals that the number of children employed under the age of ten is negligible. Nationwide, 2 per cent of boys and 1.5 per cent of girls were classified as 'occupied' in 1851. This proportion had dropped to 1 per cent by 1871.[21] In Grimesthorpe a nine-year-old boy was fork dressing in 1851 and in 1861 a seven-year-old was shear grinding. In Darnall one nine-year-old cutlery worker was recorded in 1841, an eight-year-old coke burner was working with his father in 1851 and a nine-year-old servant girl, possibly an orphan, was listed in the schoolmaster's household in 1871.

In the ten to fourteen age-range a significant proportion of boys were working, higher than the national average. Even so, whilst the majority of boys was employed by the age of twelve in the 1850s and 1860s, by 1871 only 20 per cent of twelve-year-olds were at work. The common age for starting full-time employment had risen to 13. On the other hand, girls under the age of 14 divided most of their time between home and school and very few were sent out to work. These statistics may not generalize to the whole region but they indicate the extent of child labour in the expanding urban environment.

Table 7.1

Children at work (aged 10 to 14) in Grimesthorpe and Darnall, 1841–81

		Child population		no. employed		percentage	
		Boys	Girls	Boys	Girls	Boys	Girls
1841	Grimesthorpe	86	77	9	2	10.5	2.6
	Darnall	77	78	13	1	16.9	1.3
1851	Grimesthorpe	41	44	16	–	39.0	–
	Darnall	76	53	35	5	46.0	9.4
1861	Grimesthorpe	49	46	28	10	57.0	21.7
	Darnall	79	73	39	6	49.4	8.2
1871	Grimesthorpe	173	136	47	11	27.0	8.0
	Darnall	122	108	36	10	29.0	9.3
1881	Darnall	243	253	53	27	22.0	10.7

Sheffield boys bear a marked similarity to those in the West Riding as a whole, which had the greatest proportion of boys officially at work in the country, namely 51.6 per cent in 1851.[22] The participation of girls is closer to the national average of 20 per cent. Clearly the impact of child labour on educational standards was enormous. Depressed even further by erratic school attendance before the age of nine and the early withdrawal of children, the retention of a 'little learning' became that much harder.

Compulsory education laws contributed to the increase in school enrolments and extended the age-span of schooling but had limited success in improving school attendance. How far child labour was the root cause of this post-1871 is difficult to ascertain. Child employment under the age of ten was not finally eliminated until Mundella's Education Act of 1880. Half-time working was not widely used in Sheffield and rarely rose above 300 in any one year though it survived until 1918.[23] Delays in raising the school-leaving age allowed many to leave school at the age of twelve until the first World War. The abundance of spare-time jobs did not diminish, however. Mounting concern towards the end of the century led to a City Council response to a government initiative in 1901.

A very large proportion…of boys were engaged in barber's shops or as newsboys or errand boys for small shopkeepers. A much smaller number of girls were reported as engaged in domestic work and both the hours and the renumeration varied, some of the children working for between 30 and 40 hours a week, while others were reported as engaged for three or five hours a week.[24]

Educational legislation effectively checked the practice of setting the child to work but there were many children still anxious to find employment for themselves.

Notes

1. CEC *Second Report*, Trades and Manufactures, 1843, Appendix, E13, e1, p. 178.

2. J. Tann, *Children at Work* (1981); Horn, *Victorian Country Child*, and *The Victorian and Edwardian School Child* (1989); T.J. Caulton (ed.), *Children of the Industrial Revolution in Sheffield* (1985); A. Bennett, *A Working Life; Child Labour Through the Nineteenth Century* (1991).

3. CEC *First Report*, Mines, 1842, *Symons' Report*, pp. 210-211.

4. CEC *Fourth Report*, Trades and Manufactures, 1865, pp. 3-5.

5. CEC *Second Report*, Trades and Manufactures, 1843, *Symons' Report*, Appendix, e13.

6. G. Orwell, *Road to Wigan Pier* (1962 reprint), p. 86.

7. CCE (1857), *HMI Watkins' Report*, pp. 295-96.

8. *SI* (28 November 1840). This point is emphasized in Stephens, *Education, Literacy and Society*, pp. 22-23; and Mitch, *Rise of Popular Literacy*, pp. 158-59.

9. CEC *First Report*, Mines, 1842, p. 269.

10. CEC *Fourth Report*, Trades and Manufactures, 1865, pp. 2-3.

11. CEC *Fourth Report*, Trades and Manufactures, 1865, p. 5.

12. CEC *Fourth Report*, Trades and Manufactures, 1865, pp. 144-45.

13. Pawson and Brailsford, *Illustrated Guide* (1862), p. 183; Caulton (ed.), *Children of the Industrial Revolution*, p. 24.

14. *SI* (19 October 1866).

15. J. Burnett, *Useful Toil: Autobiographies of Working People from the 1820s to the 1920s* (1984), p. 136.

16. *SI* (31 October 1865; 10 December 1865; 27 January 1866).

17. *SI* (5 February 1870; 11 May 1870).

18. *SI* (16 March 1869).

19. *SI* (2 August 1873); SSB *Statistical Survey* (November 1871), SCA.

20. Earl Marshall Local History Group, Sheffield, 'From Farm and Fork to Foundry' (1991); S.E. Turton, MA Dissertation on the Darnall Area of Sheffield, Sheffield University (1992).

21. Mitch, *Rise of Popular Literacy*, p. 168.

22. Stephens, *Education, Literacy and Society*, Appendix B.

23. Bingham, *Sheffield School Board*, p. 87.

24. Bingham, *Sheffield School Board*, p. 86.

Part III

Innovation and Inequalities 1870–1902

Chapter 8

Implementing the 1870 Education Act 1870–1902

Our object is to complete the present voluntary system, to fill up gaps, sparing the public money where it can be done without, procuring as much as we can the assistance of the parents, and welcoming as much as we rightly can the co-operation and aid of those benevolent men who desire to assist their neighbours.

W.E. Forster introducing the Elementary Education Bill (17 February 1870)

The 1870 Education Act enabled school boards to be set up where there was a deficiency of school places and gaps to be filled. Within a month of being approached by the Education Department, Sheffield Town Council approved the measure unanimously and promptly set the wheels in motion to form a school board. It was hoped that a contest could be averted but the election was vested in the ratepayers and a ballot was inevitable. Candidates were canvassed in the wards and vestry halls, churches and Sunday schools; manifestoes were published and hoardings were plastered but the election passed quietly—no treats, no refreshments, no frantic demand for cabs to ferry reluctant voters. On 28 November the full complement of fifteen members was elected to serve on the Sheffield School Board.

For what was arguably the most democratically elected body in local government, each voter was allowed as many votes as there were places on the Board. The opportunity to plump for one candidate by using the cumulative vote safeguarded minority interests and the sole Roman Catholic candidate topped the poll. The secret ballot was not available until after 1872 and consequently every voting paper had to be signed by the elector. Unlike what happened in the City of London, a good proportion of female ratepayers exercised their rights.

Because it was elected entirely on denominational grounds, any fears that the Board would be monopolized by the Anglican Church were swiftly dispelled. On the proposition of Dr Sale and the full agreement of all the clergy and Nonconformist ministers, no clerical nominations were submitted until the Anglican clergy reversed their decision in 1876. On the first Board only four of the elected members represented the Established Church whereas ten members represented the various branches of Nonconformity. Women were eligible to stand for nomination but when one was nominated in 1879 the editor of the *Sheffield Independent* regarded it as a practical joke. However, Mrs Sarah Ruth Wilson was elected in 1882.[1] Two more women, Mrs Mary Ripper and the indefatigable Maud Maxfield were elected in the second half of the Board's existence. Working-class representation was limited. John Wilson, a grinder of Andover Street, served for twelve years and W.H. Smith, a file hardener, filled a vacancy for twelve months in 1885. Charles Hobson represented Labour from 1894 to 1901 as did Robert Holmshaw in the final two years. Elections in the latter years were fought on a sectarian versus non-sectarian platform and candidates rarely used party political labels. The business and professional classes predominated. Serving voluntarily, they fulfilled their duties conscientiously and fitted them into very busy work schedules.

The first twelve years were dominated by the steel giants, Sir John Brown, Mark Firth, Charles Doncaster, and the enterprising draper, Skelton Cole. Of the 47 schools built or transferred to the Board between 1871 and 1902, 12 were in process of being built by 1873, 16 were in use by 1878 and by 1882 the Central School and the Administrative Offices in Leopold Street were opened.

In the beginning, the School Board concentrated on building the schools rather than the quality of education, ensuring that school accommodation was provided 'for all the children resident in such district for whose elementary education efficient and suitable provision is not otherwise made'. Initial surveys estimated there was provision for almost 31,000 children. Using the yardstick of one sixth of the population, currently 39,978, there was a net deficiency of 9,276 places. A house-to-house census by the police revealed a significant number of children attending private adventure schools and estimates had to be adjusted upwards to a more realistic deficiency of 12,000 places. When calculating the shortfall, due allowance of one seventh of the child population was made for middle-class parents prepared to pay in excess of 9p per week for private education, plus a further fifth for absences, which included physically and mentally handicapped children who were considered ineducable.

Before the onset of compulsory education, school attendance was

SHEFFIELD
SCHOOL BOARD ELECTION

WHY VOTE FOR THE
CHURCH & EDUCATION ACT CANDIDATES?

1.—Because they wish to supplement, where necessary, and not to close existing efficient Voluntary Schools.

2.—Because the Church of England has endeavoured to provide a School for every Parish in the Kingdom.

3.—Because, previous to the passing of the Act of 1870, the Church of England had already spent over £28,000,000, by Voluntary effort, in EDUCATING SIX OUT OF EVERY SEVEN of the Children receiving Education.

4.—Because, since 1870, the Church of England has contributed upwards of £13,000,000 in Education, without any addition to the rates.

5.—Because, if the Voluntary Schools were closed, it would COST THE TOWN ANOTHER LUMP SUM OF £360,000, FOR BUILDINGS ALONE, and another £30,000 A YEAR FOR MAINTENANCE, which means that the present School Board Rate would at once be doubled.

6.—Because the Education advocated by them is thorough, training the whole man intellectually, morally, and spiritually.

7.—Because such Education instructs children in their duty to their parents, their country, and their God.

This is why you are recommended to **VOTE FOR** the following Candidates :—

REV. J. GILMORE,   MR. A. 8. WINNILL,

MR. B. FLETCHER,   REV. J. DARBYSHIRE,

MR. S. H. WARD,   MR. W. PARKIN,

MR. J. D. FAWCETT,   MR. W. COLVER,

BECAUSE

1st.—They will carry out, loyally, the Education Act of 1870.

2nd.—Maintain Bible Teaching in the Schools.

3rd.—Give an Efficient Education, without throwing unnecessary burdens on the Ratepayers.

4th.—While in office, they have kept all their promises, increasing the efficiency of the Schools, and Reducing the School Board Rate Twenty-five per Cent., or Twopence in the Pound.

You have only 15 Votes. Divide them as equally as possible amongst the above Eight Candidates.

Printed and Published by Sir W. C. Leng & Co., High Street, Sheffield.

Figure 20. Two School Board Election Manifestoes 1888. In 1888, twenty candidates stood for the fifteen seats. **A**. The Conservative and Church Eight.

SCHOOL BOARD ELECTION.

WHY the Ratepayers should Vote for the Liberal and Unsectarian Eight:—

BECAUSE they have been selected by the Liberal Hundred, assisted by Representatives from the Labour Association, and the Federated Clubs.

BECAUSE that choice has been ratified by the Liberal Council for the whole Borough.

BECAUSE they are the friends of the Board School system, and not its opponents.

BECAUSE they will maintain the present system of Unsectarian Biblical Instruction in the Schools.

BECAUSE they are in favour of Free Schools.

BECAUSE they would not throw any extra burden on the rates.

BECAUSE they are prepared to build additional Board Schools, so that all parents who desire it may find places for their children.

BECAUSE they desire to offer to your children the best education they will accept.

BECAUSE they are opposed to the further endowment of Ecclesiastical organisations with public money.

BECAUSE they believe that Public Education should be managed by the People for the People.

BECAUSE they desire to see the people of England intelligent, prosperous, and free.

Printed and Published by Leader and Sons, Bank street, Sheffield.

TO THE RATEPAYERS OF SHEFFIELD.

LADIES AND GENTLEMEN,

We have been selected by a representative committee as Candidates for seats on the next School Board, advocating Liberal and Unsectarian principles. Three of us are able to point to past services on the Board, and the remaining five have been actively engaged and interested during many years in the work of Education, both Secular and Religious. We base our claim to your suffrages on the fact that we are advocates of Education in the interests of the children and of the nation, not in that of any sect or section of the people. We desire to see placed within the reach of the people an education as wide and as liberal as they are willing to accept—a National Educational System managed by the people for the people—and not manipulated or controlled by Ecclesiastical organizations for their own ends.

We shall loyally maintain the system of Unsectarian Biblical Instruction hitherto in force in the Schools of the Board.

We are all agreed in regarding Free Schools as the inevitable and desirable outcome of a National System of Education, and we believe they can be secured without increasing the local rates.

We seek to throw no impediments in the way of any so-called Voluntary Schools, properly constructed, equipped and maintained, but we object to sacrifice the interests of the children for the convenience of any School Managers; and we hold that parents should be able, if they desire it, to find places for their children in Board Schools.

Our constant aim will be to cultivate economy by the wise expenditure of money. We shall endeavour to educate, not to cram, the children; to treat them as intelligent beings, not as little grant-earning machines.

The completion of the labours of the Royal Commission on Elementary Education, and the issue of its final report, renders the present time a crisis of immense importance. Should the recommendations embodied in the report of the majority be made the basis for legislation, a serious and most damaging retrograde step will be taken, and it will be our earnest endeavour to prevent so grave a mischief.

Experience has shown that the best educational results are secured in Schools under the management of Elected Boards; and it is of the highest importance to the future of the Country that her sons and daughters should be as well equipped for the battle of life as the children of our trade competitors in Germany, Switzerland, or the United States. We appeal, confidentially, to the Ratepayers to be true to themselves and to their own Schools, and not to place these priceless institutions in the hands of avowed enemies or lukewarm friends.

On these grounds we confidently appeal for your VOTES on SATURDAY, the 17th November.

HENRY ADAMS.	CHARLES PEACH.
THOMAS WILLIAM HOLMES.	EDWIN RICHMOND.
GEORGE HENRY HOVEY.	MARY ANN PALMER RIPPER.
JOHN DANIEL LEADER.	SARAH RUTH WILSON

Printed and Published by Leader & Sons, Bank Street, Sheffield.

B. The Liberal and Unsectarian Eight.

Figure 21. Architectural detail of the Sheffield School Board Offices.

both 'irregular and unpunctual'. The second statistical review undertaken by the School Board in the autumn of 1871 revealed 29,000 on school registers—69 per cent of school-age children in the borough attending some form of school—plus 4,500 (36 per cent) children of nursery age. In 1872 HMI Watkins recorded that 94 per cent of children between the ages of 4 and 14 were on school rolls in his South Yorkshire area compared with the national average of 92.13 per cent. Yet only 25 per cent were over the age of ten.

Table 8.1

Children at school in Sheffield between the ages of 3 and 13, 1871[2]

Aged 3 to 5

In public elementary schools	2,648	21%
In private adventure schools	1,867	15%
	4,515	
Children not attending school	8,308	64%

Aged 5 to 13

In public elementary schools	18,178	43%
In private adventure schools	10,915	26%
	29,093	
Children not attending school	12,762	31%

Clearly, more children were going to school than is commonly supposed but a truncated school life, intermittent attendance and the questionable quality of instruction combined to yield 'below standard' attainments. When HMI Watkins reviewed the years 1871–72 fewer than 46 per cent were examined compared with 59 per cent in 1870–71. He observed that 'the children in my district neither come to school so young nor stay so long at it as in other parts of the country'. Consequently they could not be expected to profit from it to any great extent.

Anticipation of the Education Act and the ensuing six months of grace provoked a flurry of voluntary sector activity. Even so, school accommodation in many districts was so inadequate that temporary premises were eagerly sought. Methodist school rooms at Newhall, Weston Street, Allen Street and Manor were among the first to be leased. Searching out land in appropriate situations before 'modern schools' could be built was time-consuming but essential. When Henry Wilson, an Anglican representative on the Board, offered a plot of land near to his works in Sanderson Street, the offer was instantly accepted and work on the country's first new Board School building commenced. Unfortunately, industrial disputes delayed the opening until 27 January 1873. Two months later Broomhill School opened.

Forster's declared aim in 1870 to cover the country with good schools was interpreted literally in Sheffield. School buildings were far less sophisticated than now but structurally more sound and architecturally they enriched their neighbourhood. The jewel in the crown of the School Board's properties was Springfield, opened in 1875 and still standing proud today.

> Springfield schools are without exception the most handsome block of buildings the board have erected...Capital view especially coming up Thomas Street. High turret in foreground rising well towards the sky and a remarkably pleasant and well defined line—early geometrical Gothic. Various roofs and gables are full of character—here surmounted by a carved finial, there by a sculptural bird and again by bright red terminals. Built of Grenoside stone and roofed with blue Welsh slate.[3]

When the Board purchased the site in 1873, 'not in a choice situation near the centre of the town but in those quiet and recently opened up retreats that lie between Broomspring Lane and Convent Walk', the charge of recklessness was levelled at the Board. £3,851 was paid for 2,251 square yards—over £1 14s per square yard—more than twice the cost of any previous site. Built to accommodate 830 children, it cost over £8,000 which was the average outlay in the 1870s. It was all beyond the comprehension of the Liberal MP, David Chadwick, invited to the opening of Park Board School the same year. He was staggered at the Board's audacity in persuading the ratepayers 'to tolerate their extravagance in spending £100,000 in the building of 14 or 15 schools as substantial as so many castles'.[4]

Sir John Brown dismissed all charges of extravagance when he stated that the Board's duty was to provide the best accommodation it possibly could under the powers given to it by the Act. Confirmation of the Board's cost-effective approach can be gathered from the parliamentary returns issued in March 1879. In Sheffield the cost of elementary education per scholar was £1 19s 6¹/₄d compared with £1 19s 10³/₄d in Birmingham, in Manchester £2 2s 0³/₄d, Bradford £2 2s 1¹/₂d, Liverpool £2 7s 4¹/₂d, and £2 13s 5d per head in London. This conclusion was endorsed a year later by the radical politician George Dixon of Birmingham, chairman of the National Education League, when he affirmed that 'the great merit of the work of the Sheffield Board [was] that it cost less than that probably of any other school board in the country'.[5]

The Architect praised the designs of Innocent and Brown who were the Board's first architects because they had not repeated themselves over the first six years. Their designs were 'cheerful and attractive in appearance and not likely to have the repelling effect on pupils that board schools elsewhere undoubtedly had'. *Building News* considered there was 'a twinge of quaintness' in the Gothic style adopted. Generally, no one was in any doubt that the schools were 'improving and elevating the public taste'.[6] This view was shared by Sheffield MP John Roebuck who declared that it could no longer be said that Sheffield had no public buildings of which it could be proud. 'We have schools to show that surpass those of any other town in England.'[7] Today they are considered 'one of the most architecturally interesting set of Board Schools in the country'.

When Mark Firth proposed the creation of a university college in 1876 he approached the architect T.J. Flockton. Anxious to locate the Central School and Offices in close proximity, the Board appointed E.R. Robson, architect of the London School Board, to work in conjunction with Flockton on the Smith Street project, later renamed Leopold Street. Robson was offered the opportunity to design Heeley Bank and Brightside Schools also and henceforward acted as consultant. After 1881 school building was opened to competition but ornamental features were phased out as more emphasis was placed on interior layout and design—central halls, separate classrooms and specialist areas.

To counter suspicions that the School Board would build where it suited itself and ignore existing voluntary schools, it was repeatedly stressed that its purpose was 'to supplement and not supplant'. James Crossland, a Church representative, was concerned about proposals for new schools in the Park district and asked that a return be provided of the children admitted into the temporary Board School in Cricket Road which opened in September 1874. The return shed light on the wealth of public and private schools in the vicinity and revealed that a few children were drawn from the local church schools and others in the town centre over half a mile away. There were others, however, prepared to travel from Ellesmere Road, a mile and a quarter across the Don valley, and some transferred from the Attercliffe and Carbrook

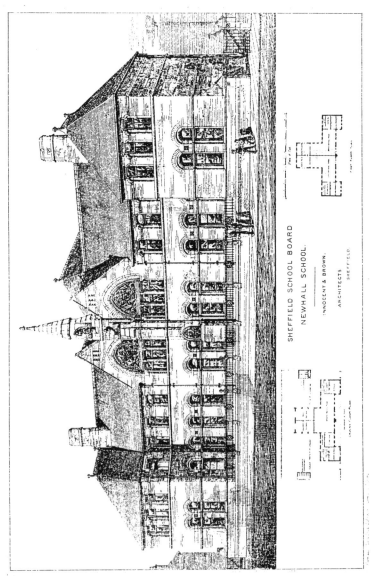

Figure 22. Architecture of the Sheffield School Board. *Illustrations of Public Elementary Schools*, Innocent & Brown, Sheffield 1874.
A. Newhall School, Sanderson Street, opened in January 1873.

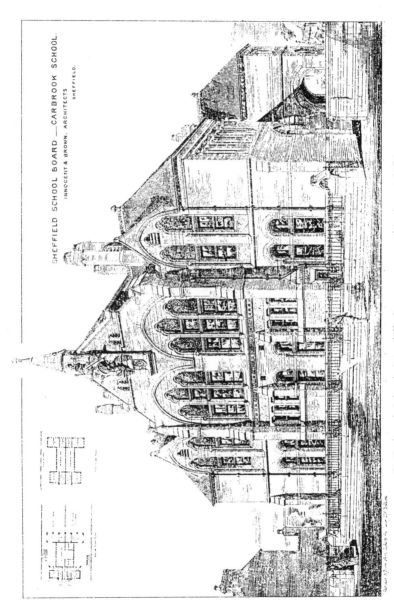

SHEFFIELD SCHOOL BOARD — CARBROOK SCHOOL.

INNOCENT & BROWN, ARCHITECTS

SHEFFIELD.

B. Carbrook School, Attercliffe Common, opened in August 1874.

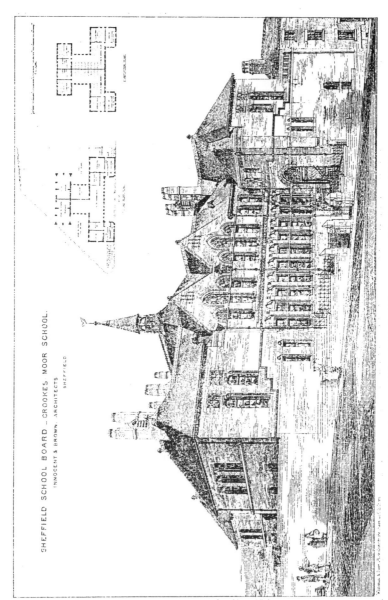

SHEFFIELD SCHOOL BOARD — CROOKES MOOR SCHOOL.

INNOCENT & BROWN ARCHITECTS

SHEFFIELD

C. Crookesmoor School, Oxford Street, opened in August 1874.

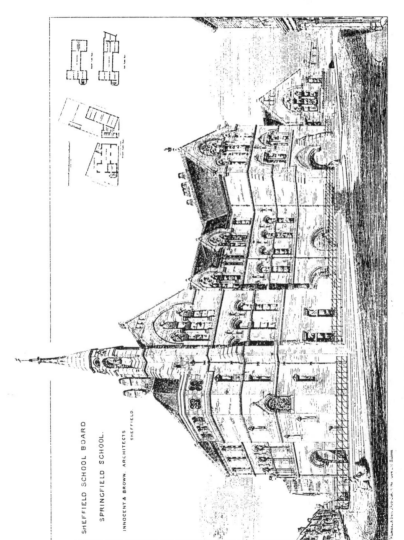

SHEFFIELD SCHOOL BOARD

SPRINGFIELD SCHOOL.

INNOCENT & BROWN. ARCHITECTS
SHEFFIELD

D. Springfield School, Broomspring Lane, opened in December 1875.

Board and Voluntary schools over two and a half miles distant.

John F. Moss, the Board's Secretary, cited the Cricket Road school in a paper given to the Social Science Congress in 1874. When outlining the task facing the Board he described how thousands of children were being driven into school having received so little education. Out of the 310 first admitted, there were 185 (many over ten years of age) who did not know a letter of the alphabet. Only 30 were fit to be put in Standard 2 and three in Standard 3.[8]

The most contentious issue of the 1870 Act was the implementation of Clause 25. Parliament recognized the financial demands made on poorer families compelled to educate all their children. Parental choice of school was written into the Bill and the remission of fees was available for indigent parents unable to meet the cost of schooling. What disturbed the Nonconformist members of the National Education League was that Sheffield School Board was prepared to remit fees for children attending the voluntary schools. Totally opposed to public monies being set aside for denominational purposes they saw it as a reintroduction of the 'accursed church rate'. The League argued that the decision could only perpetuate sectarian conflict and infringe religious liberty.

Birmingham refused to remit fees for any child attending a denominational school. Leeds deferred the question. Manchester paid for 3,000 children attending voluntary schools compared with less than 300 in Sheffield. In the eyes of non-participants the difficulty was confined to a 'religious squabble'. The *Sheffield Independent* expressed gratitude that Sheffield was more serene than either Birmingham or Manchester. 'Not only do the wearers of the surplice and the gown take part in the affray but "fair ladies" stump the wards in the company of revered warriors.'[9]

Nonetheless, some Nonconformists were prepared to be penalized for non-payment of the education portion of the poor rate. Giles Hester, the Baptist minister, and George Sharman, the London Road grocer, were totally opposed to the School Board paying the denominations for children to be taught in their schools. Percy Rawson, of the Globe Works, claimed the system paid teachers to teach that 'he as a Protestant Dissenter was a heretic, schismatic and deserving of eternal damnation'. The stipendiary considered such objections 'wholly untenable' and required the Overseers 'to seize a portion of their goods'. Sacramental wine, furniture, a double-barrelled shotgun and 10 oz. of silver were among the variety of items appropriated by the bailiffs and sold at auction. Lettis Short, the Unitarian minister, deplored the action of giving rate aid to denominational schools but in his view the amount given was 'such a mere bagatelle as compared with the positive good they [the School Board] have accomplished that I feel constrained to condone it'.[10] That sentiment was reinforced when it was revealed that only £96 14s 11d was disbursed on fees for indigent children over a fifteen-month period. An Amending Bill in 1873 partially resolved the difficulty and in 1876 the clause was finally repealed and the Guardians were empowered to pay the fees for children whose parents could not afford them.

The 1870 Act was implemented by electing a school board in most urban boroughs and cities. Rural parishes and small towns were not so convinced of their necessity. In 1872 only 809 out of 13,844 parishes had elected a Board. Seven years later HMI Sandford commented that 'boards continue to be the exception rather than the rule', and only six rural parishes in his South Yorkshire district—Arksey, Askern, Barnburgh, Treeton, Epworth and Keadby—had a School Board.[11] At the end of the century, one third of the country avoided the 'imposition' of a School Board altogether. Sheffield's local scene admirably reflects the situation nationally.

In neighbouring Derbyshire there was a prompt response, and by 1872 an elected board was in office in Chesterfield, Dronfield, Unstone, Eckington and Norton. In contrast, the South Yorkshire neighbours were reluctant to create a Board. Many clergy resented any attempt to undermine their influence in education and opposed the formation of School Boards as unnecessary waste, time-consuming and expensive. Offers to raise funds and extend existing provision were readily accepted by ratepayers. Where voluntary schools could meet the needs of the neighbourhood the Education Department made no attempt to force the issue though public opinion could be tested in a public forum.

Norton School Board was delayed by a wrangle over the purchase of the Bocking Fields by the Cemetery Board having recently increased the parish rate. The issue was forced by the industrialist, Charles Cammell, who had established the infant school at the foot of Cobnar Road. In the spring of 1872 it was estimated that there were 465 children of school age in the parish and the Greenhill, Norton Endowed, and Woodseats infant schools could only cater for 350.[12] Led by Francis Bagshaw of Oaks Park, a vote in favour of a Board was passed by 43 to 20 and five members were elected without a poll. Profit from

Figure 23. Cammell's School, Cobnar Road, Woodseats, opened in 1865.

Figure 24. Norton School Board plaque marked the transfer of Greenhill
National School to Norton School Board in 1872.

the sale of the Bocking Fields was utilized to meet the initial cost of the
Derbyshire Lane School which opened in 1875. Woodseats and
Greenhill schools were leased to the board and Bradway School was
closed.[13] As the population of the parish expanded, Meersbrook Bank
School on Derbyshire Lane experienced gross overcrowding. In 1895,
Norton County School (Mundella) was opened and, together with

Meersbrook Bank, was transferred to Sheffield in 1901.

In the parish of Handsworth it was the colliery owners who effectively frustrated the movement towards a School Board by increasing the number of school places available. Thomas Dunn of Richmond Hill erected the school at Normanton Springs for the children of his colliery workers and the Sheffield Coal Company leased the Primitive Methodist Chapel at Intake for a school in 1874. The churchwardens organised a series of meetings but the only sector actively campaigning for a School Board was Woodhouse.[14] Sustained pressure did lead to Handsworth becoming a contributory district of Aston-cum-Aughton School Board which met in the Rotherham Colliery Offices at Woodhouse Mill, but apart from an improvement in school attendance little was achieved.

With the expansion of the colliery village of Intake, the Coal Company relinquished responsibility for the school in 1880. The Privy Council pointed to the deficiency of 263 school places and directed that a School Board be elected.[15] The seven-member Board immediately renegotiated the lease on the chapel until Intake Board School was erected in 1884.[16] Five years later Woodhouse County School was built to meet the growing needs of the village. Gleadless Church School was transferred to the Board in 1893 until Gleadless Board School was erected in 1898. Woodhouse West School opened in 1900. The following year the responsibilities of the Board were transferred to the West Riding Education Committee.

The sparsely inhabited chapelry of Bradfield avoided the election of a School Board altogether and the adoption of a board in Ecclesfield was effectually blocked for twelve years by the vicar, Dr Gatty, and the efforts of the voluntary societies. In November 1870 he informed the Earl of Wharncliffe that he would appeal to the Privy Council should any active ratepayer apply for a Board.[17] He argued that the voluntary system had served the parish well and with a few extensions to the efficient schools a Board was totally unnecessary. 'The expense of setting up a school board to say nothing of the *jaw* was economic irresponsibility.'

Table 8.2

Efficient schools in the parish of Ecclesfield, 1870[18]

	Accommodation
Ecclesfield Feoffees School	200
Rawson's Infant School	172
Parson Cross School	169
Shiregreen National School	101
Grenoside National School (to be built)	157
Lound National School (100 to be added)	208
Wadsley Church School	310
Hillsborough Church School (with additions)	176
Lower Wincobank (with additions)	270
School at Union Workhouse	100
Malin Bridge Day School	87
Wincobank School	199
High Green School (with additions)	355
Burn Cross School	133
Grenoside—requiring alterations	—
	2,637

Between 1870 and 1882, 400 additional places were provided but when the Education Department were informed that St Thomas's National School in Lower Wincobank was about to close the Wortley Guardians were instructed to hold an election and new schools were to be located in Hillsborough, Wincobank, Grenoside and Burncross. Many Hillsborough children sought admission to Sheffield's Langsett Road School which was permitted as an interim measure until Ecclesfield School Board was formed and new schools built.

The size of the parish determined that Ecclesfield was entitled to nine members and the poll in 1882 resolved that two Anglican clergymen, one gentleman, and six industrial manufacturers—including Thomas Chambers Newton of Newton Chambers and Company, Thorncliffe and George Dawson of Chapeltown—constituted the corporate body. Within the first three-year term the building programme was completed. Hillsborough and Wincobank Schools opened in 1884, Burncross and Grenoside opened the following year.

Concerned about the rising rate burden, 32 ratepayers petitioned the Board in 1885 to keep the expenditure down. The newly elected Board replied that 'they were in entire sympathy with its objects', confirming HMI Blakiston's opinion that the ratepayers of Ecclesfield, hostile to the imposition of a Board, 'elected men who were determined to do nothing'.[19] School fees were fixed slightly above the Sheffield scale, and slates and copybooks were charged extra. Because Ecclesfield School Board refused to admit children in their schools who did not bring their pence and the Guardians were niggardly in reimbursing the schools for those too poor to pay, the schools and the children were penalized until the abolition of school pence in 1891.

Lacking both vigour and zeal, Ecclesfield School Board provided little more than an adequate service. Unable to exact a rate precept in the same measure as urban boroughs they were always at a disadvantage and the Board was always conscious of the stronger voluntary sector. Owing to boundary changes, Hillsborough and Wincobank Schools were transferred to Sheffield in 1901. Burncross and Grenoside were absorbed into the West Riding structure until its demise in 1974.

Had it not been for the extensive voluntary school network established by 1871 Sheffield would have found it much more difficult to meet the challenge of the Education Acts as successfully as it did. Setting up School Boards in the rural communities would have proved even more formidable.[20] Yet for all their faults, by 1902 School Boards had fully justified their creation. The gaps were filled and publicly subsidized schooling was accessible to everyone.

Notes

1.   See Bingham, *Sheffield School Board* for a complete list of elected members. Appendix XII, pp. 310-18; *SI* (8 November 1879).
2.   SSB *Statistical Survey* (November 1871), SCA; *SI* (2 August 1873).
3.   *SI* (1 December 1875).
4.   *SI* (2 December 1875).
5.   *SI* (7 March 1879; 16 July 1880).
6.   *SI* (1 June 1875).
7.   *SI* (14 August 1874).
8.   *SI* (7 October 1874); Park Board School Log Book 1874–1903.
9.   *SI* (8 November 1873).
10. *SI* (27 February 1873; 16 May 1873; 28 June 1873; 3 May 1873).
11. *SI* (23 October 1879).
12. *SI* (18 March 1871; 16 April 1872).
13. *SI* (14 May 1872; 29 May 1872; 15 October 1873).
14. *SI* (2 February 1871).
15. *SI* (9 December 1880).

16. *SI* (13 December 1880).

17. *SI* (15 November 1870; 11 March 1871); Wharncliffe Muniments 418/xv/1, pp. 63-66, SCA.

18   Miscellaneous Papers, Ecclesfield Parish Church.

19. Ecclesfield School Board Minutes, CA 244, SCA. See also D. Postles, 'The First Years of the Ecclesfield School Board 1882–88', Essays in Local History, typescript SCL.

20. Compare Mitch, *Rise of Popular Literacy*, pp. 132-33.

Chapter 9

Compulsory Schooling 1870–1902

A great and ever present difficulty in the way of enforcing the compulsory clauses of the Acts is to be found in the existence of so large a number of waifs and strays of the streets. To compel the great majority of these children to attend school, unless they are provided with the necessary food and clothing, would be an act alike of cruelty and indecency. So long as they remain in the gutters, they have the chance of escaping starvation by the charity of the passing public, but compel them to attend school and this chance is lost to them…it is idle to hope that these gutter children can be driven into the ordinary school with advantage to the school or the children themselves.

Response of the Sheffield School Board to the Royal Commission on Elementary Education (March 1887)

By 1870 the arguments for compulsory education had been so well rehearsed in Sheffield that the School Board lost no time in framing bye-laws enforcing school attendance under the powers conferred by the Education Act.[1] All children between the ages of five and 13 were compelled to attend school unless they were prevented by sickness, lived beyond two miles from the nearest school, or were 'under efficient instruction in some other manner'. However, the impression that the 1870 Act made schooling compulsory nationwide is misleading. Where the setting up of School Boards was averted—as in Bradfield, Ecclesfield and Handsworth, no attempt could be made to enforce attendance until Lord Sandon's Education Act of 1876.

In Sheffield, the police distributed notices informing all parents and guardians of the legislation and the penalties for negligence. The first Superintendent, together with two attendance officers, was dispatched on house-to-house visitations to investigate the reasons for absence and explain to parents how to appeal for remission of fees in case of hardship. A compilation of their visits in September 1872 in the town centre parishes of Wicker, Neepsend, St Philip's, St James's, St Mary's, St Simon's, St Silas's and St Jude's, illustrates the size of the task. 7,800 families were visited; 5,964 school-age children were recorded but only 4,257 children (70 per cent) were on school registers. A similar trawl a month later produced a slightly better return of 73.5 per cent.

Evasive promises, excuses and indifference were rejected and the Board prepared to resort to the Courts. Locating elusive parents in order to spell out their duty proved much more difficult. The first summons was issued in August 1872 when Henry Richardson was charged with failing to send his son to school. The case was withdrawn on a promise that his son would attend St Paul's School—which he did, but not very regularly.

Twelve months later the School Board authorized the prosecution of all parents whose children were found on the streets during school hours. Fines ranged from one to five shillings for habitual offenders. Some parents were fined because their youngsters were beyond control. In a few cases the children, predominantly boys, were taken into custody by the police, charged with vagrancy and committed to industrial schools. Conflict between children and the law in the last quarter of the nineteenth century was aggravated substantially by the various Education Acts and bye-laws passed between 1870 and 1880. In fact some magistrates believed the School Board dealt too harshly with poorer parents and were reluctant to charge.

Discriminating between valid and fictitious excuses over the existence of contagious diseases was a perennial problem. Parents were cautioned against sending children to school when there was danger of causing an epidemic but evasion of the bye-laws was so rife that medical certificates were required. Occasionally, surgeons were accused and prosecuted for issuing 'doubtful' certificates. In October 1875, 156 summonses were issued against parents for neglecting their duty. The list included 111 skilled workmen, 26 labourers, a surgeon, a surgeon-dentist, seven charwomen or widows, four publicans and two hawkers. 125 were fined the maximum penalty. Those targeted were the 'idle' and 'dissolute' class who were earning high wages.

The success of this rigorous approach was summed up by J.F. Moss in his address to the Social Science Congress in October 1874.[2] 'Owing to the migratory character of the population of Liverpool the increase in attendance was reported to be a little over 24%. A similar situation in Manchester. In Birmingham the increase is 86%, Leeds 89%, in Bristol 32%, Newcastle 50%, Salford 45%, Hull 97%,

Nottingham 59%, Sheffield 100%.' Barrington Ward HMI confirmed that no board in England attended better to the enforcement of compulsory attendance than the Sheffield School Board, yet in 1875, Skelton Cole insisted that instead of the 40,000 children who should be at school there were 28,000 at the most. 'There were 12,000 to 13,000 children in the borough habitually absent.'[3]

One of the problems faced by the Board was the employment of children over the age of eight permitted by the extensions to the factory and workshop legislation. Children incapable of achieving Standard 1 could still begin working part-time in any process of manufacture subject to certain restrictions. This loophole enabled children to evade school by not working regularly. It contravened the Sheffield bye-laws which fixed Standard 4 as a minimum before half-time working was allowed. In the early years of compulsory schooling about 1,000 children were classified as half-timers which was minimal compared with Bradford's 10,000.[4]

Enforcing the attendance of street children was a much more intractable problem and persisted throughout the period. Many youngsters were found to be ill-clad, bare-footed, sadly neglected and 'pauperised by the militia'.[5] The refurbished Ragged School was overcrowded and many lived too far away to benefit. Other schools were reluctant to admit them. In one family visited there were nine children deserted by their father.[6] 'Some were running about at midday amid filth and dirt without a vestige of clothing whilst others wore the merest shreds', yet their mother refused to take her family into the workhouse. The Board's officers were expected to enforce their school attendance but the difficulty was finding a school willing to take them.

One avenue exploited by working-class parents to frustrate the 'School Board man' was the use of dame and private adventure schools. Although such schools were maligned by the authorities, parents still persisted in patronizing them; some to elude the strict routine of the public schools, others to avoid regular attendance, and some simply because they were convenient. In 1875, 230 notices were served on parents with children attending these schools. Between 1871 and 1877 the number of working-class private schools was whittled down. Fifty-six schools with 2,007 children on roll were closed.[7] In one school inspected in 1876, 49 children between the ages of eight and 14 were crowded into a room appropriate for 17 by government standards. An even smaller room was used mid-week when 65 were crammed inside. The quality of instruction was not denounced but the premises were 'so thoroughly unsuitable' that the Board was compelled to regard all children over six years old as not attending school within the framework of the regulations. Many proprietors did not keep registers; some issued false certificates, whilst others charged over 9d per week to circumvent inspection and then returned the excess fees to parents.

Inability to pay school fees was a recurring plea. Initially they ranged from 2d to 6d per week but the Education Department ruled them inadmissible as their payment penalized 'hard work and success'. The fees were then adjusted to 2d for infants and 4d for older children; but they were modified in 1881 for boys and girls in Standards 1 and 2 to 3d. The fee structure in the National and Wesleyan schools was generally 1d or $1^1/_2$d per week more. In October 1873, 447 fees were remitted. When the responsibility for educating outdoor pauper children devolved upon the Guardians in 1876, they decided to pay the fees direct to parents and expected the schools to collect them from the children. The voluntary schools experienced the greatest difficulty in recouping fees and the ensuing child absences reduced attendance percentages. In consequence, school capitation grants decreased, schools were starved of resources and the education of the poorest suffered. The School Board repeatedly asked the Guardians to pay the fees directly to the schools but co-operation was not forthcoming. The friction stemmed from earlier controversies over Clause 25 of the Act of 1870.

Attendance targets were frequently undermined by the staggered nature of school holidays and the condoned absence by parents during visits of Barnum and Bailey's circus and menagerie, Doncaster Race week, searching for water and fuel, picking blackberries, etc. In 1874 the Board approached the voluntary school managers with a view to fixing August as the holiday month although the maximum allowed in the summer was only two weeks. The following year headteachers petitioned for an extension to three weeks, as in London, and the Board agreed. A further approach was made to the voluntary schools to secure a uniform system of holidays—a fortnight at Christmas, Good Friday, Easter Monday, Whit week and three weeks in the summer—but the attempt was not wholly successful.

In 1876, Lord Sandon's Elementary Education Act enforced the creation of School Attendance Committees with the same compulsory powers as School Boards where no Board was established. Wortley Board of Guardians appointed their Relieving Officer for the whole Union which included Ecclesfield, Tankersley and Wortley. In

February 1878 he reported that 220 warnings had been served in Southey, Grenofirth and Ecclesfield. The effect of his visits had an immediate impact on the voluntary schools and the Sheffield schools on the boundary. Whereas Sheffield had increased its attendance officers to eight, the Wortley district employed but one part-time officer and evasions continued. One important aspect of the 1876 Act was to transfer the duty of ensuring the child was educated from the School Boards to the parents. The employment of children under ten was forbidden and those between 10 and 14 were obliged to attend half-time. Exemptions could be earned if the child had passed Standard 4 or had made more than 250 attendances for each of five years.

The 1876 Act also sanctioned industrial day schools for vagrant and delinquent children. Fining parents of persistent truants was proving ineffectual. On taking office the only option open to the Board was to send offenders to the Certified Industrial Schools set up after the Industrial Schools Act of 1866 and the Presentation of Crimes Act of 1871. Currently the Humber training ship *Southampton* (see page 160) held 40 Sheffield boys who had been committed for periods varying from 18 months to five years. Consultations with the Home Office led to the refurbishing of the branch workhouse at Hollow Meadows, six miles to the west of the town on a bleak Pennine moorland, as a detention centre for young truants between seven and thirteen for a three-month trial period.

The first batch of 'incorrigible truants' was admitted in June 1879. Longer sentences were permitted for more difficult youngsters not convicted of crime. Neglected children at risk from 'baneful home influences' were also admitted. Sunday suits and plain useful outdoor clothing for everyday were provided. A plain wholesome diet to keep them healthy and capable of outside employment was worked out.[8] Sunday breakfasts of coffee, bread and treacle were more appetizing than the milk-and-water gruel of weekdays. Hot meat, potatoes and bread were served for Sunday dinner, and tea, bread and butter at supper time. On weekdays it alternated between Irish stew and suet pudding with treacle, and gruel or cocoa with bread for supper.

Daily instruction began at seven o'clock in the morning and went on until 8.30 a.m. and in the evening from 5.00 p.m. until 6.30. The middle of the day was kept clear for work! The teachers concentrated on the basic subjects and religious instruction, beginning and ending each day with 'simple family worship'. Punishments ranged from the forfeiture of rewards and privileges, reduced mealtime portions, to solitary confinement and 'moderate personal correction'.

Before a child was sent to the Truant School, magistrates investigated the financial background of the parents in order to prescribe maintenance costs. Widows were charged a shilling per week but skilled artisans, such as joiners and masons, were charged between 3s 6d and 4 shillings per week. Recommended boys could return home provided they regularly attended an efficient elementary school. Licences were revoked if they failed to conform which meant a return to Hollow Meadows and a short period of solitary confinement.

Periodic escapes from the institution were attempted and, I suspect, not always reported. One lad made a run for it immediately after his Christmas dinner but he was caught within a mile of the school. A ten-year-old from Nottingham, having made one futile escape as far as Bell Hagg, made another attempt before school through a thick moorland fog. Although 'missed' within ten minutes, he vanished into the mist and drizzle—only to be picked up by Nottingham police two days later and promptly brought back. On his first absence he was caned six times. On this occasion he was given nine strokes followed by three days' solitary confinement. Because the school was not a reformatory, confinement in practice implied sessions of picking oakum and only being allowed to mix with the rest at mealtimes, schooltimes and prayers.

The school experimented with livestock farming on the adjacent Surrey Farm for six years but the project proved uneconomical and it reverted to market gardening. Root crops, mushroom beds, rhubarb and hurdle fencing proved the most rewarding. It continued as a truant school until 1926 when it was transferred to Sheffield Corporation for mentally handicapped children.

The compulsory attendance clauses were tightened considerably by Mundella's Education Act of 1880. The Education Department was empowered to enforce compulsion where School Boards and attendance committees were unable or unwilling to frame the necessary bye-laws. The employment of young children was prohibited without a certificate of education related to attendance and the number of half-timers in Sheffield was drastically reduced. In 1877 there were 329 and in 1902 it was 319 but in the intervening years it fluctuated wildly.[9] In general there were more boys than girls, but in 1902 there were 169 girls compared with 150 boys attending half-time. Compulsory full-time schooling became statutory for every child under ten. The minimum leaving age was not raised to eleven until 1893 and twelve in 1899. The system of half-time working was finally abolished in 1922

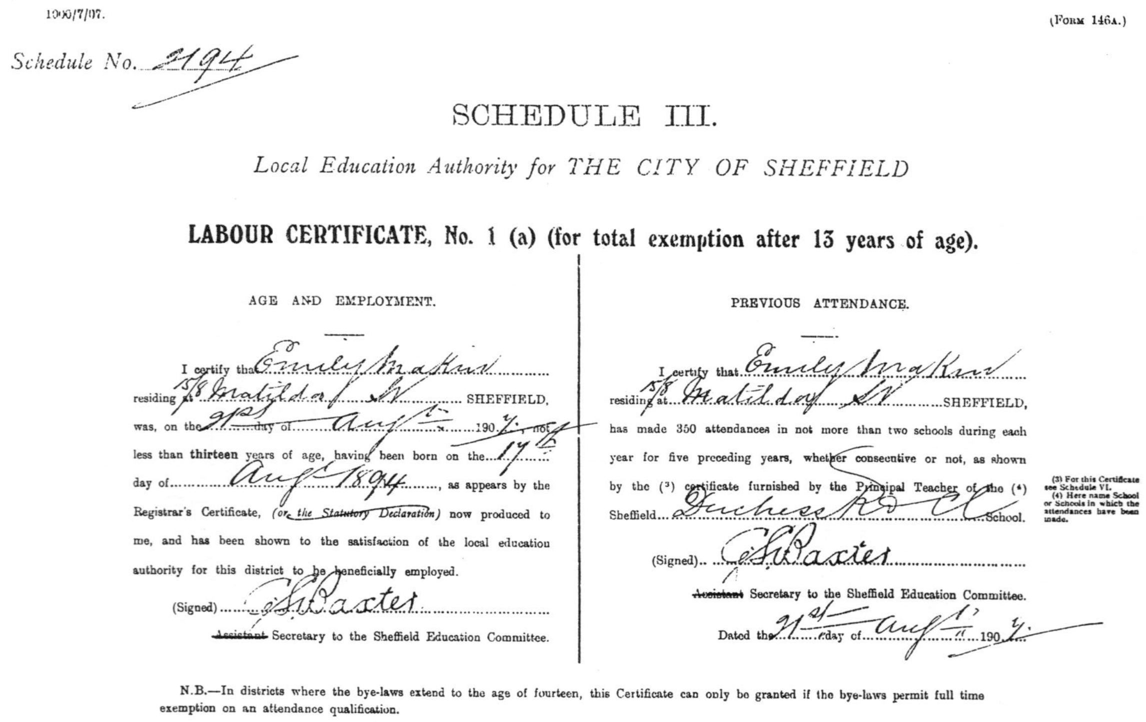

(Form 146A.)

1906/7/97.

Schedule No. 1944

SCHEDULE III.

Local Education Authority for THE CITY OF SHEFFIELD

LABOUR CERTIFICATE, No. 1 (a) (for total exemption after 13 years of age).

AGE AND EMPLOYMENT.

I certify that Emily Makin residing at Shottfield Rd, SHEFFIELD, was, on the ...day of.... Aug ...190 , as appears by the Registrar's Certificate, (*or the Statutory Declaration*) now produced to me, and has been shown to the satisfaction of the local education authority for this district to be beneficially employed.

(Signed) ....master

.... Secretary to the Sheffield Education Committee.

PREVIOUS ATTENDANCE.

I certify that Emily Makin residing at Shottfield Rd, SHEFFIELD, has made 350 attendances in not more than two schools during each year for five preceding years, whether consecutive or not, as shown by the (²) certificate furnished by the Principal Teacher of the (⁴) School.

Sheffield.........................

(Signed)...........master

.... Secretary to the Sheffield Education Committee.

Dated the ....rday of.......Aug....190 .

(³) For this Certificate see Schedule VI.
(⁴) Here name School or Schools in which the attendances have been made.

N.B.—In districts where the bye-laws extend to the age of fourteen, this Certificate can only be granted if the bye-laws permit full time exemption on an attendance qualification.

Figure 25a. This Labour Certificate (1907) permitted Emily Makin to take up employment at the age of 13 and offered her free tuition at any evening school in the city except the central school.

Printed for H.M. Stationery Office by Waterlow Bros. & Layton, Ltd., 24, Birchin Lane, E.C.

SCHEDULE VI.

Board of Education·
Form **144 (c)**.

Certificate of School Attendance for the purpose of employment under Section 5, Elementary Education Act, 1876, or for total or partial exemption under the Bye-Laws.

Gleadless Council   *School.

I hereby certify that the following particulars with respect to the Attendances made by the Child named below, at this School after attaining the age of 5 years, are correctly taken from the Registers of the School.

Name in full, and Residence of Child.	Number of Attendances made within the 12 months ending the 31st December	
Leonard Marples *Gleadless*	1899	425
	1900	398
	1901	410
	1902	425
	1903	423

Signed this ___2nd___ day of ___June___ 19 04

W. Roberts

Principal Teacher of the above-named School.

* Enter name in full, and state whether a Public Elementary, or Certified Efficient, School.

Figure 25b. Form 144(c) was issued to Leonard Marples in 1904. He was permitted to leave school under the age of 14 having made the requisite number of attendances.

and compulsory school attendance was effectively raised to 14.

Although school enrolments in the borough had risen to 55,651 in 1887 and climbed to 75,795 in 1902, school attendance required constant vigilance and provided ample scope for criticism. HMI Blakiston drew attention to the problem in Heeley. In 1884 he observed 'The street called Little London has a dense and growing population and their school attendance is highly unsatisfactory.' The following year he commented in the Heeley Bank school logbook: 'I have just walked through the slums of Heeley and I have seen hundreds of children at play who ought to have been at school.'[10] Both Norton and Sheffield School Boards were asked to investigate the problem. At the same time the schools in the Park had reached their admission limit and 'swarms of children of school age were playing about the courts, yards and streets'. Blakiston considered 'efforts should be made to get the children into school, fees or no fees, and not left to run wild'.

The vexed question of canal-boat children was also raised. Many of the parents were engaged in the local coal trade and families seldom remained in the wharf long before they were consigned to empty barges belonging to the same owner. Before there was any chance of prosecution the boats were off again to another colliery for a fresh load. Negotiations with Park Wesleyan School—the nearest to the canal wharf—for $1/2$d per day on account of poverty were agreed, but little benefit could be gained from occasional appearances. Officers were asked to monitor the situation but to little effect.

By 1887 the school attendance staff had expanded to one superintendent, two divisional officers and 18 officers renamed 'visitors'. Easily identified in their new uniforms of black facings and buttons and square felt hats, they descended on the markets and railway stations in specially prepared 'raids' and intensified the house-to-house visits. Competition was injected by offering an extra £1 for the highest proportional increase in school attendance. In spite of that, the School Board recognized that the teacher's influence could be the most persuasive method of raising school attendance and encouraged home visits by both teachers and pupil-teachers. The invasion of privacy whereby parents were interrogated in their own home introduced an entirely new aspect into English law but no real outcry surfaced.

The cumulative effect of the compulsory measures, the abolition of school fees for most children and the accessibility of public elementary schools raised the average attendance to 31,275 in 1877 (70 per cent), 44,500 in 1887 (80 per cent) and 65.699 (86.6 per cent) in 1902.[11] With 66,000 children attending school regularly and conforming to the discipline of the public schools the emerging city could breathe more easily. The changes effected by compulsory attendance were remarkable. 'Infant independence' described by Symons and Sale midway through the nineteenth century had vanished, child labour was thrust to the margins, and the conduct of children and young people was markedly improved. The average age-span of schooling was at least eight years by the end of the century and the quality of education (see Chapter 12) was enhanced year by year.

Sheffield School Board.

Report on School Attendance presented by Finance and General Purposes Committee, and adopted by Board, February 17, 1886.

The Staff to consist of one Superintendent, two Divisional Officers, and sixteen Visitors.

1.—The Town to be divided into two divisions, with an Officer in charge of each division.

2.—The Divisional Officer to be held responsible for the effective working of the division over which he is placed, and to give instructions to Visitors as to the working of the districts under his charge, excepting where special orders are given or issued by the Superintendent.

3.—The Divisional Officer to frequently take Visitors' ordinary duty in his own division, under the instructions of the Superintendent, where the work being done is not satisfactory, and report on his division daily to the Superintendent.

4.—One Visitor to be allotted to each of the sixteen districts into which the Town is now divided, each Visitor to report to the Divisional Officer any special cases needing immediate attention, otherwise the daily report to the Superintendent to be considered the Visitor's report for the day.

5.—Frequent surprise visits and searching house to house visits to be made by a sufficient and selected number of Visitors, in the various districts, under the immediate instructions of the Superintendent or a Divisional Officer.

   (*a*) It is believed that the irregular attendants in each and all the districts can be effectively looked up in three or four days in each week, leaving one or two days at liberty every week for house to house visitation by Visitors.

6.—The days on which Visitors are drawn from their own districts for special visitation and house to house visitation will be a convenient time for the Divisional Officer to take Visitors' duty.

   (*a*) Visitors to be drafted alternately.

   (*b*) The district to be specially visited, or in which house to house visitation is conducted, to be settled by the Superintendent ; more particularly on special occasions, such as festive periods, fair time, and the bathing season.

Figure 26. Sheffield School Board *School Attendance Report* 1886. In the instructions to school attendance visitors note especially the authorisation for house-to-house searches (5 and 6) and the bonus offered for the 'highest proportional increase in attendance' in each district (14).

7.—The Superintendent to have authority to temporarily remove any Visitor into any district he may think desirable, such removal to be reported to the next meeting of the Finance and General Purposes Committee.

8.—Printed slips to be provided for Visitors to place under the doors where parents are out, cautioning them against the irregular attendance of their children at School.

9.—Teachers in all Elementary Schools to be communicated with and earnestly invited to co-operate with the Officers and Visitors in the work of obtaining better attendance.

10.—The " slip registers " system to be adopted for all Schools in place of the present duplicate register.

11.—For the present, Visitors to continue wearing private clothing in lieu of uniform.

12.—No Officer or Visitor on any pretext whatever to undertake any other work or duty during the time he ought to be occupied with the work of the Board.

13.—The Evening Appeal Committees to remain as at present; but the Chairman of the Finance and General Purposes Committee to have power to arrange for a Special Committee at any Elementary School where the attendance is not satisfactory.

14.—Every six months a bonus of £1 to be given to that one Visitor in each division who, in his district, has obtained the highest proportional increase of attendance as compared with the percentage obtained in his district during the corresponding six months of the preceding year.

19ᵗʰ September 1887.

Recᵈ a copy of these regulations

Figure 26. Continued

Notes

1.   Bingham, *Sheffield School Board*, pp. 298-301.

2.   *SI* (7 October 1874).

3.   *SI* (2 December 1875). See Table 10.2.

4.   *SI* (14 July 1875); Bradford Corporation, *Education in Bradford since 1870* (1970), p. 11.

5.   *SI* (19 July 1873). Between March 1872 and July 1873, 109 wives and 320 children of militiamen became dependent on the Ecclesall Union.

6.   See Bingham, *Sheffield School Board*, pp. 63f.

7.   Bingham, *Sheffield School Board*, p. 69; *SI* (13 June 1877); see also pp. 294-297 below

8.   See Bingham, *Sheffield School Board*, ch. 9, and SSB Finance and General Purpose Comment Minutes 1879–1903, SCA, for more detailed reports and discussion.

9.   Bingham, *Sheffield School Board*, p. 87.

10.   SSB School Management Committee Minutes (1884), SCA; and logbooks of Heeley Bank Girls, Heeley Bank Infants and Park Boys Board Schools.

11.   Bingham, *Sheffield School Board*, p. 87.

Chapter 10

Voluntary Schools 1870–1902

So long as freedom of conscience is maintained, and reasonable
public control secured, the younger generation cares not a jot what
particular modicum of religious instruction is combined with secular
education. It has not the slightest wish to starve out the Church or
the Roman Catholic Schools, and really prefers them to go on
supplying a useful alternative to municipal administration.

Sidney Webb, *The Nineteenth Century* (1901)

The religious influences that inspired elementary education in Sheffield
for generations were now overshadowed by the successful introduction
of the School Board, and the emergence of an effective local authority.
The voluntary schools gradually became a disadvantaged and endan-
gered species. In his introduction to the 1902 Elementary Education
Act, Prime Minister Balfour enlarged on the 'deplorable starvation' of
the voluntary schools and the inadequacy of resources to meet the
needs of a comprehensive system of education.[1] Fourteen years earlier,
the Cross Commission highlighted the inequalities endured by the
voluntary schools compared with the Board schools but a minority
report voiced the fears of many Liberal Nonconformists who maintained that rate aid for denominational schools would not only embitter
educational policy but also intensify sectarian rivalries. The inability of
the voluntary schools to match the quality of staff, the standard of
premises, educational resources and the ratio of children to certificated
teachers effectively prevented expansion once the initial spurt had
been completed. By the end of the century, denominational school
authorities were reduced to very minor partners.

Anticipation of the 1870 Act and the ensuing six months' grace
enabled the denominations to build an impressive number of new
schools.

Table 10.1

Voluntary School Expansion in 1870s

All Saints National	1869	Princess Street Wesleyan	1869
Carbrook National	1869	St Silas National	1869
Heeley Wesleyan	1870	St Matthias National	1870
St James's National	1870	St Mary, Walkley Nat.	1871
St Simon's National	1872	St Charles RC	1872
St Joseph's RC	1872	St Barnabas Nat. Alderson Road	1872
St Barnabas Nat. Cecil Road	1874	St Luke's Nat. Garden Street	1874 (rebuilt)
St Catherine's RC	1876	St Marie's RC Edmund Road	1878
St Wilfred's RC	1879		

A return of efficient elementary schools in 1876 shows the actual school provision within the borough, the average attendance and the strength of the voluntary system.[2]

Table 10.2

Efficient elementary schools in the borough of Sheffield, 1876

	Accommodation	No. on roll on 4 February	Average attendance week ending 4 February
National Schools C of E	16,656	16,262	11,151
Board Schools	11,119	11,735	8,544
Wesleyan Schools	4,559	4,359	3,017
Roman Catholic Schools	3,103	2,759	1,725
Lancasterian Schools	1,100	826	574
Surrey Street British Schools	486	520	374
Hollis Endowed School	220	289	192
Sheffield Ragged School	785	758	437
Other Elementary Schools	2,183	1,901	1,534
	40,211	39,409	27,548

On the transfer of authority from the Sheffield School Board to the Sheffield Education Committee in 1903 it is abundantly clear that the Board School provision had outstripped the voluntary system which had extended its accommodation only marginally in the intervening years.

Table 10.3

Efficient elementary schools in the city of Sheffield, 1903[3]

Class of School	Accommodation	Average no. of children on roll October 1902	Average attendance October 1902	Percentage of attendance
Board Schools	47,530	51,027	44,333	86.8
National Schools	19,639	18,593	16,184	87.0
Wesleyan Schools	2,394	2,520	2,139	84.8
Roman Catholic Schools	4,379	3,448	2,808	81.4
Other public elementary institutions and private elementary schools	384	207	195	94.2
	74,326	75,795	65,659	

As soon as the Congregational Church was satisfied with the advantages of the School Board's provision and the non-sectarian nature of religious instruction, it ceased to maintain day schools. In general, Nonconformists were hostile to the dual system and not all Methodists were convinced of its merits. Dissenters of all persuasions were particularly unhappy in the country districts—fearful that their children would continue to be exposed to Anglican doctrine. When the master of Parson Cross School set parts of the catechism for homework, the Methodist families in Birley Carr, Wadsley Bridge and Southey refused to comply. The master referred the matter to Dr Gatty, Vicar of Ecclesfield, who advised him not 'to press the matter too perseveringly'.

Orthodox Wesleyans in the borough preferred the voluntary system and believed the state should interfere no more than was necessary. They argued that they comprised all political shades and it was essential to safeguard their own schools by ensuring at least two Wesleyan representatives were elected to the School Board.[4] On the retirement in 1882 of Skelton Cole and Henry Shera, Principal of Wesley College, no orthodox Wesleyan replacements were elected and the stock of Methodist schools was gradually reduced. Ellesmere Road, Heeley, Red Hill and Princess Street Wesleyan Schools were the only ones open when Sheffield Education Committee took charge in 1903.

The Wesleyan school at Red Hill had a fine reputation under Mr B.D. Davis and in 1870, 96 per cent of the scholars passed in all basic subjects plus grammar. Two years later Davis was appointed first

Superintendent of the School Board. The Brunswick Wesleyan Schools were the largest in the Methodist Connexion and with one exception were the largest in the borough and amongst the the most successful. Mrs Greenup, headmistress of the Infant School, was the first female inspector to be appointed by the School Board with special responsibility for needlework and domestic economy. The schools were opened to public inspection annually when they demonstrated Bible history, mental arithmetic, natural history, drawing and singing. The closure in 1897 enabled the School Board to proceed with its long deferred proposals to build in Pomona Street. Park Wesleyan School encouraged some pupils to extend their education by conducting classes in organic chemistry. Princess Street Wesleyan School was enlarged to admit 700 pupils within five years of being built and became prominent in times of distress.

The Roman Catholics resolutely defended the dual system and argued that 'if education is to be compulsory, denominational schools must be part of any national system'. A Catholic education for Catholic children was their claim. When St Charles's School at Attercliffe opened in 1871 they were directed 'to train the little ones in the way they should go for as the twig was bent so the tree inclined'. Addressing a Catholic gathering in St Vincent's in 1872, Father Givourie emphasized the importance of nurture in the faith before attempting wider educational objectives.[5] 'The uneducated child was to be found in the streets, learning the secrets of sin and drinking the poisonous waters of bad example. You must give the child a thorough Catholic education. After that you can give them whatever kind of education you like.' Such public sentiments led many observers to question the quality of the secular education provided in the Catholic schools.

Numerically strengthened by Irish immigration, the Catholics deployed their schools as mission churches. Through the generosity of Sheffield's principal landowner, the Duke of Norfolk, St Catherine's School was built in Burngreave in 1876. A replacement boys' school to replace the antiquated premises on Surrey Street was built on Edmund Road in 1878, and St Wilfred's School on Shoreham Street was opened in 1879 for the rapidly growing districts of Sharrow, Heeley and Highfields. The Catholic Poor Schools Committee supported each project but St Marie's had to promise £1,000 towards the Edmund Road schools before the Duke would fulfil his promise 'to find the rest'. In 1885 St Joseph's Howard Hill was classified as a public elementary school and was rebuilt in 1889. Once the schools were open, maintenance became a parochial responsibility.

In general, the Catholic body were suspicious of the School Board and ensured that their candidate was elected by plumping their votes on a single nominee. Whilst liberally supporting their own schools and loyally paying their rates, they jealously guarded their interests. In 1872 they pressed the Board of Guardians to remove Catholic orphans from the workhouse to the Catholic institution at Leeds. Because it would involve them in maintenance the Guardians were not prepared to accede but did eventually allow Catholic orphans to attend St Catherine's on Sundays. Moreover, the clergy were permitted to give religious instruction and minister to them whenever they wished. Similarly, when Father Burke was assigned pastoral supervision of Catholic boys in the Truant School they enlisted Home Office support before the begrudging approval of the School Board was given.

In 1884, a representative meeting of the Catholic church met 'to vindicate and defend the rights and interests of voluntary schools and the maintenance of religious liberty and equality in the question of national education'. The following year Cardinal Manning, Archbishop of Westminster and periodic visitor to Sheffield, emerged as champion of the voluntary schools. He warned against allowing children to become state-controlled and exorted Voluntaryists 'to rise up and say they did not want board schools for their children'.[6] In the ensuing debates within the Cross Commission, of which Manning was a prominent member, the Voluntaryists promoted a favourable majority report recommending rate support and increased resources for all voluntary schools. The minority, led by Lyluph Stanley of the London School Board, opposed any such move. Marginal assistance was advanced by the Voluntary Aid Act after 1897 but the promise of rate aid was deferred until the Balfour Act recognized the injustices in 1902.

The most influential source of elementary education in 1870 was the Church of England. In addition to the 31 National Schools there were seven endowed schools nominally Anglican. When the School Board began to record attendance in efficient elementary schools in 1872, 58 per cent were in Church schools compared with 16 per cent in Wesleyan schools and 12 per cent in Catholic schools. British, endowed and private schools accounted for almost 11 per cent with 3 per cent in the temporary Board schools.

The Vicar of St Paul's, Revd J.E. Blakeney, later Vicar of Sheffield, Archdeacon, and vice-chairman of the School Board, anticipated the competition of rate-aided schools and prepared for a greater proportion

Figure 27. St Joseph's Roman Catholic School, Howard Hill, opened in 1872.

Figure 28. Statue of Blessed Virgin Mary and Infant Christ, St Marie's School, Edmund Road, 1878.

of lay involvement in the general management of parochial schools. At the Church Conference in October 1869, Blakeney proposed the formation of a parochial church council (PCC) in every parish—fifty years before they became compulsory.[7] Within a month St Mary's,

Bramall Lane, had formed a council, as had St Paul's and the Parish Church. In each case the Church Councils resolved to supervise all the education in the parish in National, Infant and Sunday schools. Consequently, the laity became aware of the financial strains of school upkeep.

In April 1870, St Mary's PCC called the attention of the Church Conference 'to the importance of providing primary education for the large and increasing population of Lower Heeley, Mount Pleasant and Highfields'. Negotiations were already in hand for procuring suitable sites and they asked for financial support. The outcome was the erection of schools in Napier Street (St Matthias), Alderson Road and Cecil Road (St Barnabas).

Because the opportunity to teach children unfettered by the local authority 'may never recur again' the Church Conference of 1870 focused entirely on education and urged application for building grants.[8] Some measure of the undertaking and financial contribution can be gathered from the resolution of St Mary's PCC to extend the Hermitage Street School which entailed arching over the River Porter to enlarge the playground. Henry Wilson was approached as it was necessary to purchase a portion of the river. To raise the remaining sum of £1,500, seat holders were canvassed, circulars were distributed and Sunday school teachers, district visitors and PCC members were enlisted to collect donations. Within six months, the structural improvements were made and over £1,000 was promised.[9]

To the east of the Borough, Sir John Brown, having built All Saints, Brightside (John Brown's Church) advocated the building of a day school for 1,200 children. His gigantic Atlas Works already housed a densely overcrowded Sunday school. He predicted that the school would offer continuing education and encouraged his workforce to contribute voluntarily and by so doing reduce the rate burden on the borough. His challenge stimulated the formation of works' committees in every department. The foremost suggestion was the contribution of a day's pay monthly over a twelve-month period. Brown offered a seven-day working week for those who preferred to give their labour rather than their earnings.[10]

All Saints' School, Brightside, was built in the Gothic style, a herald of the School Board's architectural designs, and described in 1872 as 'one of the handsomest and most complete buildings in Sheffield'. 'Admirably lit by gas', the school was built for 300 boys, 300 girls and 300 infants at an overall cost of £5,500. Ventilation received considerable attention and an 'excellent' playground was provided to the rear of the school. The school being set in a predominantly working-class neighbourhood, the trustees underlined the fact that religious instruction was vital to the well-being of the school but parents who conscientiously objected could withdraw their children when it was time-tabled.

In contrast to the wide-scale publicity and fund-raising of St Mary's and All Saints, the modest school at St Mary's, Walkley, opened quietly in 1871. The money had been raised almost entirely by the exertions of the incumbent, Revd Thomas Smith. At the same time, St Silas's more than doubled its school accommodation. The premises built in 1869 became an infant school and the boys' and girls' departments used the new extensions for 900 pupils. The school was built on the initiative of the Vicar, Revd C.S. Wright. His proposals for raising the funds were initially met by 'shrugged shoulders' and he was told it was 'out of the question'. Set amidst a very poor population the congregation was given the task of raising between £1,700 and £1,800. Archbishop Thomson, well loved by many of the working classes in Sheffield, enthusiastically encouraged these parochial activities and condemned the notion of a school purely as a means of social control—'an outdoor nursery where children are kept in good order'. He saw schools as places where the young could be trained to recognize their duties based on a knowledge of religion. 'When they are so taught they are likely to become good, useful and happy men and women.'

The first Anglican clergyman elected to the School Board was the popular Canon Blakeney, in 1876. When elected vice-chairman three years later, the independent, H.J. Wilson—who opposed all questions of denominationalism being raised in the Board—commended Blakeney 'as one who sought the advancement of the education of the poor children of the town'.[11] Significantly, at the time of Blakeney's election, Revd Samuel Earnshaw—'not so much a clergyman as a professor of education'—failed to get elected and came bottom of the poll.

All proposals for new Board schools and extensions were closely scrutinized by denominational representatives. When the scheme to extend Springfield was mooted, it was pointed out that there was surplus accommodation in St Jude's, Eldon Street; St Silas's, Hodgson Street; St Matthew's, Carver Street and St Paul's. Opposition to the proposals concentrated on the argument that it was the Board's duty to see the schools were filled before asking ratepayers for more money—

nevertheless the motion to enlarge Springfield was carried.

Voluntary school income hinged on grants, school fees and subscriptions. Government grants varied from year to year depending on school rolls, average attendance, examination passes, building standards, etc. The quality of the school intake materially affected the number of children able to attempt both basic and additional subjects. Where school managers were compelled to employ only pupil-teachers or less qualified staff in order to balance the books, the grant-earning capacity was reduced even further. In 1881 the Parish Church School was in deficit and the Church Council was asked to devise plans to meet the deficiency. An increased deficit the following year prompted the resolution to set aside two Sundays when all the collections could be put to erasing the debt. In 1887 the council were informed that the debt would reach £350 before the government grant was received.

Examples of the financial strain are legion and in November 1883 the Church Schools Aid Society was formed, 'not only to save the schools from impending ruin but also to make them more efficient'. Archdeacon Blakeney was clearly anxious to make the Church schools as impregnable as Board schools and had no desire to hand them over.

> Firstly the schools have been put under guardianship of the National Church and for us to give up that trust would be a dereliction of duty.
>
> Secondly it would inflict very great hardship upon ratepayers who are already carrying a burden which many can scarcely bear. It would involve an increased outlay of money as 15000 places would have to be provided for the children should we be obliged to hand over to the Board.
>
> Thirdly so long as there are schools connected with the Church, Christian teaching is secured. So long as the Board Schools retain their scriptural teaching let us wish them well—they may not always do so, but at the same time let us make our schools so strong that nothing whatever shall be able to shake them or oblige us to abandon them—we only want £1000 per year to carry on the work.[12]

By 1885 the Society had promoted 'increased vigour on the part of the managers'. Better qualified staff were appointed, apparatus and textbooks were procured and an overall improvement in the methods of teaching was discernible. HMI Blakiston congratulated them 'on the wonderful success achieved by their self denying efforts and the

liberality by which the Church Day Schools affiliated to the Association
have been raised to a state of thorough efficiency which forms a
surprising contrast to their condition four years ago'. Between 1884
and 1886 the Association raised £15,000 from voluntary sources.[13]

Voluntary school budgets were effectively capped in 1891 when the
Education Act abolished all fees in schools charging less than 10
shillings per year. Free education had been discussed informally for
years but not until 1885 did the School Board move a formal resolution
in its favour. It was opposed by all the denominational representatives
who voiced their opposition again in 1890. However, in 1891 the
Board viewed 'with satisfaction the principle of free education as
involved in the Government Bill' and voted unanimously in favour.
The Act introduced a fee grant of 10 shillings per child in average
attendance. The Board and the Roman Catholics abolished all fees in
elementary schools immediately. Churchmen and Wesleyans resolved to
retain their schools but were not prepared to adopt a uniform scale.
Out of the 67 departments affiliated to the Church Day School
Association: 39 schools became wholly free; 3 schools became partly
free; in 13 the fees did not exceed 1d; in 11 the fees did not exceed 2d;
and in 1 the fee did not exceed 3d.[14]

Infants at St Stephen's were charged 1d where previously they had
paid 3d. The managers of St Paul's retained a fee of one penny but
assured parents that children who could not afford it would be admitted
free. At Carbrook the Vicar explained to parents how the school had
been self-supporting and subscriptions raised only to fund improvements. Because 15 shillings per year had been received from children in
the upper school they would have to raise £60 annually to enable all
children above Standard 1 to pay the reduced fee of one penny. He was
convinced that most parents would prefer to pay something.[15]

The effect of the abolition and reduction in fees was most marked in
the town centre. In the suburbs it was mixed, particularly with older
children. The Parish Church School recorded a 'phenomenal'
attendance in the first week and a slight falling off afterwards. St Luke's
Garden Street recorded a marked improvement whereas Shiregreen
National School entered the fact that 'Free education not causing
children in upper classes to attend much better'. In Carbrook, the
modified scale attracted pupils previously attending Board schools
which were totally free—lending weight to the notion 'if its free its
worth nowt'. Parson Cross reported a significant improvement and

WALKLEY ST. MARY'S
NATIONAL SCHOOLS.

Owing to our acceptance of the Government Grant, under the New Education Act, we are enabled to

REDUCE THE FEES

In Standard I	....	.... from 4d. to **1d.** per week.
,, II	....	.... from 4d. to **2d.** ,,
,, III	....	.... from 5d. to **2d.** ,,
,, IV	....	.... from 5d. to **2d.** ,,
,, V	....	.... from 5d. to **3d.** ,,
,, VI	....	.... from 6d. to **3d.** ,,
,, VII	....	.... from 6d. to **3d.** ,,

so that from

September 1st, 1891,

the following Fees will be charged:

ALL INFANTS FREE.

STANDARD I	....	....	....	1d. per week.
STANDARDS II, III, IV	....	....		2d. ,,
,, V, VI, VII	....	....		3d. ,,

These charges will be necessary to keep the Schools in efficient working order.

THOMAS SMITH,
TREASURER & CORRESPONDENT.

J. WRIGLEY, PRINTER, 14, CAMPO LANE, SHEFFIELD.

Figure 29a. Printed notices advising church school parents of the reduction or total abolition of school fees in 1891. **A**. Walkley St Mary's School.

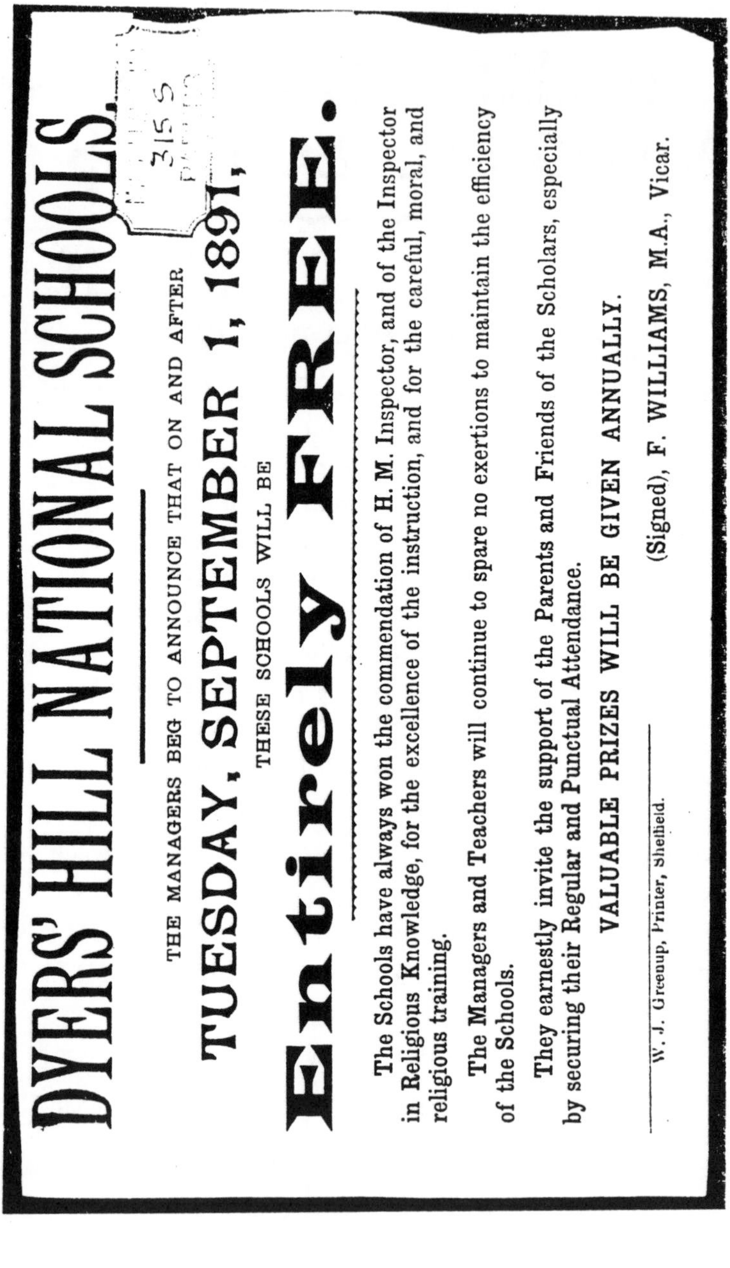

DYERS' HILL NATIONAL SCHOOLS.

THE MANAGERS BEG TO ANNOUNCE THAT ON AND AFTER

TUESDAY, SEPTEMBER 1, 1891,

THESE SCHOOLS WILL BE

Entirely FREE.

The Schools have always won the commendation of H. M. Inspector, and of the Inspector in Religious Knowledge, for the excellence of the instruction, and for the careful, moral, and religious training.

The Managers and Teachers will continue to spare no exertions to maintain the efficiency of the Schools.

They earnestly invite the support of the Parents and Friends of the Scholars, especially by securing their Regular and Punctual Attendance.

VALUABLE PRIZES WILL BE GIVEN ANNUALLY.

(Signed), F. WILLIAMS, M.A., Vicar.

W. J. Greenup, Printer, Shetheld.

Figure 29b. Dyers' Hill National School, Sheffield Park.

an increase in the number of children prepared to stay on till 14. In addition there was an influx of very young children.

> 11th September 1891. Several children under 3 years of age have been to school. Mothers wish to send them to school to be taken care of now that they can do so without cost. Have refused admission to all under 3 years.

The annual threat of fines on schools defaulting in administration, building regulations or inadequate staffing accentuates the inequalities experienced by the voluntary schools compared with Board schools. Between 1883 and 1891, £1,400 was deducted from Church schools and £357 was deducted in 1892 solely on the grounds that government grants exceeded all other income.[16] In 1882 twenty-five schools were penalized for that reason alone. Such niggardly considerations induced schools to limit the curriculum, weaken school staff numbers and neglect repairs and maintenance. In his evidence to the Cross Commission Revd J. Gilmore asserted that all his schools worked very hard to get an Excellent Merit Grant.[17] 'We did our very best, but we only got "Good", in two of our schools we were fined by the Education Department £10. Had we been fortunate enough to get "Excellent" we should have been fined something like £44.' Alfred Wilson gave St Mary's National School £100 in 1889 to ensure it was not penalized.

Grant reductions were intended as a measure to improve standards and efficiency but in practice they had the opposite effect. Unsatisfactory pupil-teacher examination results merited a fine of £10. Insufficient teaching staff reduced the grant at Crosspool National by £20. Falsification of registers could endanger the grant altogether and in 1886 the master at St Mary's was dismissed for serious inaccuracies of registration. Clerks were employed by the authorities to examine registers well into the twentieth century.

Progressive legislation hastened the closure of the older voluntary schools such as Carver Street and Lancasterian (1882). The provision of separate cloakrooms, the partitioning of teaching space, conversion of privies and ash pits and improvements in ventilation inevitably taxed the resources of school managers. A crisis was reached in 1893 when it was calculated that £6,000 was required to bring all the affiliated schools up to Education Department standards. In their appeal for funds the Church Schools Aid Society re-emphasized the scale of rate burden on the city if the Church schools closed—roughly

£25,000, equal to an increase of 6d in the pound.

When Archdeacon Blakeney reviewed the past ten years in 1894, he underlined the marked improvement in attendance in the Church schools.[18] Ten years earlier the average attendance was 8,940 earning £6,249 in government grants. Currently the average attendance stood at 12,821—an increase of 40 per cent—and the grants had doubled to £12,401. 'Within those ten years over £30,000 had been spent on structural alterations and the extension of affiliated schools.' In an attempt to counter criticism and meet government standards a buildings inspector was employed but it was still an uphill task when managers were either negligent or indifferent.

Keeping the schools clean and tidy was the overburdened head-teacher's responsibility for much of the century and accounts in part for the fines incurred for offensive toilets, noisome yards, 'indecent words' scribbled on filthy windows, broken window cords, dirty floors, etc. Where schools were used for parochial purposes, caretakers were employed but their pay compared badly with School Board employees. St Mary's advertised for a caretaker in 1894 and offered 16 shillings per week plus a house rent-free, gas and coals. In addition to the normal sweeping, cleaning and dusting the fires had to be lit each day and the classrooms and stairs had to be washed in soft soap at least once per month.[19]

As the gap widened between the Board and voluntary schools, the School Board recognized the financial strain of the managers and were apprehensive of the additional burden likely to fall on ratepayers if the voluntary system collapsed. In May 1895 the Board resolved to petition Parliament, praying that:

> In the interests of education and economy as well as justice and reli-
> gious freedom, the voluntary schools are entitled to largely increased
> assistance out of public monies and that the present law be amended
> ·in this direction.[20]

The following year the government proposed a bill offering rate aid for all the voluntary schools. Opposed by Liberals and Nonconformists, the Bill was withdrawn. With their expectations dashed the voluntary schools united to form the National Association of Voluntary Schools. Their aim was to protect their interests, defend their rights and promote the welfare of the schools and their teachers.[21] A Sheffield branch was formed in 1897. It resolved 'that no plan for giving aid to voluntary schools can be accepted as satisfactory and final which does not place them on a similar financial basis to the Board's schools'. Membership of the branch was registered as 268. The Association insured an element of administrative unity never before achieved but before the end of the century suspicions emerged of the denominational hierarchy who had secured increased control.[22]

A modified Voluntary Schools Act was passed towards the end of 1897 which abolished the 17s 6d limit on grants—a bone of contention for years. Schools were relieved from paying rates and a grant of 5 shillings per head to be paid through the Association was introduced. This allowed the voluntary system to limp along a little longer. Schools were enabled to increase teaching staff and resources providing efficiency was improved and local financial support was not weakened. To illustrate how schools utilized the grant, Carbrook National School apportioned their allocation as shown in Table 10.4.

Table 10.4

Carbrook National School grant allocation, 1897

	£	s	d
Thoroughly cleansing school	55	10	0
New desks	17	2	3
Increase of salaries	58	0	0
Improvement of staff	67	0	0
Additional school readers	8	14	3
Establishment of school library	5	9	9

plus additional apparatus, enlargement of the museum and various aids to pupil-teacher instruction.

In 1898, the Association received a circular from the Secretary of the Education Department in which G.W. Kekewich reviewed the implementation of the scheme.[23] He considered that the coordination of the voluntary schools was to the benefit of everyone as the interests of the schools had been widened and quickened. No longer isolated, each voluntary school became less exclusively the concern of the parish and more generally recognized as an integral part of the elementary school system. Kekewich focused on the decline in voluntary support and he warned schools to be on their guard against unwarrantable expenditure, the improvident use of existing school funds and 'the adoption of too ambitious a curricula'. Clearly the voluntary system was an administrative nightmare and the need for a more unified whole was a significant factor in ensuring that the 1902 Education Act reached the Statute Book.

On the enactment of Balfour's Education Bill, the Sheffield Education Committee accepted responsibility for the maintenance costs, salaries, etc. of all voluntary schools within the city and the Aid grant to those schools ceased. In February 1903 the Sheffield branch of the Association withdrew from the national body and the Church schools in Sheffield formed their own Federation of Voluntary Schools.

Under the 1902 Act, voluntary schools were designated non-provided because the premises were not provided by the local education authority (LEA). Six managers were nominated, four of whom were appointed in accordance with the trust deed (foundation managers) and two appointed by the LEA. Balfour's Bill enabled the foundation managers to preserve the denominational nature of a school and the local authority managers to keep a check on innovations by over-zealous clergy and convey to the authority any shortcomings in educational provision.

Notes

1. Quoted in W. Van Der Eyken (ed.), *Education, the Child and Society* (1973), p. 79.

2. Bingham, *Sheffield School Board*, p. 69.

3. Bingham, *Sheffield School Board*, p. 87.

4. *SI* (5 November 1879).

5. *SI* (19 July 1871; 14 May 1872; 26 June 1878). See also Hadfield, *A History of St. Marie's*, p. 162.

6. Armytage, *Four Hundred Years*, p. 155.

7. *SI* (16 October 1869); *Sheffield Times* (16 October 1869).

8. *SI* (4 November 1870).

9. St Mary's PCC Minutes (5 April 1871; 23 May 1871).

10. *SI* (28 November 1870; 31 May 1871; 27 January 1872).

11. *SI* (5 December 1879).

12. W. Odom, *Church Notes* (18 July 1884), 1, SCL.

13. Odom, *Church Notes* (25 May 1887). From 1869 the Church Burgesses contributed about £400 annually to the voluntary schools that applied for financial assistance.

14. Odom, *Church Notes* (30 July 1891).

15. C. Parsons, *Schools in an Urban Community* (1978), pp. 28-29.

16. Odom, *Church Notes* (3 June 1892).

17. *Report of the Royal Commission on the Elementary Education Acts (Cross Report)*, 1887, 2, p. 717.

18.   Odom, *Church Notes* (15 June 1894). The Lancasterian School was reopened by the School Board in 1896.

19.   Compare Bingham, *Sheffield School Board*, p. 38.

20.   Bingham, *Sheffield School Board*, p. 172.

21.   National Association of Voluntary Teachers Minute Book, 2 (1897–1909), SCA.

22.   Compare E.J.T. Brennan (ed.), *Education for National Efficiency: The Contribution of Sidney and Beatrice Webb* (1975), p. 90.

23.   St Mary's National School Managers' Minute Book (January 1898).

Chapter 11

Expanding the Curriculum 1870–1902

Commiserate the hapless Board School child, shut out from dreamland and poetry, and prematurely hardened and vulgarised by the pressure of codes and formularies. He spends his years as a tale that is not told.

John Ruskin (1876)

Infant Method

It is argued that the development of infant education during the School Board era made 'the most distinctive contribution to educational science'.[1] By the end of the century almost all infants were to be found sitting at dual desks in their own classrooms rather than huddled together at the end of the schoolroom. The old formal methods 'abstract and verbal' were gradually discarded and replaced by more progressive methods that used actual objects and genuine materials.

Nevertheless, it was still possible to find toddlers sitting on hard wooden seats with a desk in front of them and little to lean their backs against. Told to fold their arms they would sit still and listen before repeating in a singsong voice 'Letter A, Letter B, Letter C', or 'Number 1, Number 2, Number 3', as the teacher directed. Schools were still hampered by their obsession with uniformity and order.[2] Threading a bodkin or needle drill could take up to 20 minutes. Boredom might be relieved by the occasional bout of marching. Playtime was often curtailed by inclement weather or the length of time it took to marshal a hundred 'babies' into the playground and back again. The practicalities of dressing all the youngsters before sending them out was too often not really worth the effort.

In the beginning the School Board considered that in infant schools, 'reading, writing and arithmetic, with special attention to singing and such physical exercises as were practical' was sufficient.[3] However, in 1875, Charles Doncaster was sent to Liverpool to investigate the

Figure 30. Mixed infants in dual desks photographed in Duchess Road School, 1906. It was hard not to fidget when plate photography took so long.

Figure 31. A contrasting photograph of mixed infants at Carbrook School in 1908. Arthur Mayes, left hand side of the class in front of the teacher, later drowned in the canal aged 5.

kindergarten methods being tried in the city.[4] His enthusiastic accounts encouraged the Board to adopt the system and find a competent Froebel teacher as soon as possible. Friedrich Froebel's philosophy had been taken up by the Home and Colonial Society in the mid-1850s but few teachers trained by the Society filtered into Sheffield before 1875. The ideas and concepts fostered by the Froebelian movement formed the roots for the reinterpretation of early learning. Occupations and activities were devised but the positive influence of play was not yet recognized.

A kindergarten class was set up in Springfield Board School in 1876 which attracted a great deal of interest. Lectures and demonstrations were arranged for teachers in both Board and Voluntary schools but the School Board was unwilling to prepare 'lady teachers' for the Froebel Certificate as it still carried middle-class overtones. By the mid-1880s, kindergarten occupations were on most infant timetables but the spontaneity had faded and it degenerated into a subject rather than a principle to pervade the whole school. Activities such as brick building, paper folding, sewing and knitting plus stick laying by forming shapes, letters, etc. were complemented by a series of drills—music drills, needlework drills, position-for-writing drills—which were regularly inspected.

As teachers attempted to awaken the interest of young children in the world about them, the variety of gallery lessons broadened to embrace a whole range of topics from domestic pets and wild animals to natural phenomena. Object lessons advanced alongside the movement for improved pupil-teacher training and more effective lesson preparation. The reality of the situation in 1885 was underlined by HMI Blakiston when he observed a fourth-year pupil-teacher in Park Infant School 'set to give an object lesson to 104 children seated in the great gallery on shoemaking without either blackboard or anything to illustrate the lesson with'. Park Infant School had grouped its topics as follows:

Domestic:	furniture, chair, sofa, clothing, bricklayer, postman, etc.
Animal:	parts of the human body, camel, tiger, ostrich, whale, etc.
Vegetable/plant:	trees, plants, grasses, sugar, rubber, etc.
Natural phenomena:	sun, moon, seasons, day, night, clouds, wind, etc.

The most vital of all subjects—the teaching of reading—made the least progress. The alphabetic method, using alphabetic names of letters before pronouncing the words, was a method sanctified by tradition. Ingenuity and a real understanding of the problem was lacking. In June 1878 the Board arranged for two infant teachers to spend time in Leeds watching demonstrations of the phonic system. Influenced by reports that 'at least 12 months of the time now occupied by instruction' could be saved and 'that many children of 5 years of age could read fluently and effectively and they soon had a good pronunciation and sounded their "h's" correctly', the Board resolved to introduce Robinson's Phonic System.

As the teachers became conversant with the method through in-service training in Darnall and Pyebank, the system gradually spread, but not until 1883 was Netherthorpe allowed to introduce it. The system demanded that the books given to the children were printed in new characters in order to indicate the sounds of vowels and consonants. When these were mastered, the child was put back to ordinary print. Twelve months later Blakiston carped at the overall progress and reported 'a temporary falling off in the reading' generally.

Evidence of overwork, inadequate staffing and insufficient books led to the total abolition of the system in 1887. The Board's inspector was asked to report on the subject where it was still taught and how it was affecting the health of the teachers. He confirmed disturbing accounts of work-related stress and it was decided that the 'phonic system of teaching shall be entirely discontinued in the schools of the Board'.

The phonic method did not die, however. In 1893 the managers of St Paul's Infants consented to the introduction of the method and other schools persisted with a combination of phonic and 'look and say' methods with older children from the mid-1880s. Emphasis was placed on recognizing words as a whole and not by decoding every letter. The dictum 'repeat without ceasing' was inherent in every classroom.

Not until 1895 was a uniform system of handwriting adopted throughout the Board schools. HMI drew the attention of the School Board to the introduction of approved copybooks. Styles that 'dazzled the eye' and were difficult to read were condemned. The Board agreed that 'it was desirable to secure continuity from the infants' departments upwards' and asked headteachers to confer and promote a style based on the approved list which included *Arnold's Copy Books, Chambers' Copy Books* (Government Hand) and *Cusack's Copy Books*, 1 to 7.

Standard Practice

Before the School Board issued curriculum guidance to the elementary schools, the course of instruction pursued in four voluntary schools was examined, namely: St Peter's (Parish Church) and Holy Trinity (National), Brunswick (Wesleyan) and the Lancasterian Schools. In October 1871 the following guidelines were circulated:

> In Boys' and Girls' Schools; Reading and explanation of the Bible, Reading from graduated lesson books, Writing, Arithmetic, English Grammar, Geography, History, Vocal Music, Drawing and Drill. In Girls' schools only, plain needlework and cutting out.

Shortly afterwards the Board issued a list of textbooks and educational equipment 'from which selection *shall* be made'. This policy was modified as teachers became anxious to use the most up-to-date and improved books and resources. The initial list included maps, atlases and diagrams, drawing models, and for each school a *Chambers' Etymological Dictionary*.

The comprehensive curriculum outlined above was an objective to be aimed at rather than a description of the situation. Progress was gradual and patchy. During the first ten years, instruction in the Board schools was confined largely to the Bible and the three Rs. Once the teachers came to terms with the host of undisciplined pupils herded into large boisterous classes, the curriculum broadened considerably. Influenced by such educational thinkers as T.H. Huxley, Matthew Arnold, Herbert Spencer and John Ruskin, the Education Department issued their Code of 1871, and opportunities for a more liberal approach to the curriculum were opened up. A grant of 3 shillings became available for each pupil who went beyond the three Rs to pass in two specific subjects. Foreign languages and applied science were permitted where schools were able to form Standards 4, 5 and 6. The long-established voluntary schools reaped the most benefit because compulsion kept the children in school longer and higher standards were achievable.

In 1875 the Education Department introduced 'class' subjects—grammar, geography, history and plain needlework for girls—for which an additional grant was made. Only two subjects could be taken and to qualify for grant they must be taken throughout the whole school. A 'good' pass in any two 'class' subjects earned 4 shillings per head, a 'fair' pass earned 2 shillings. Specific subjects were raised to 4 shillings but the grant for the three Rs was reduced to 3 shillings. The focus of instruction was clearly shifting towards a broader education. Unfortunately, it led to more cramming, memorization and rote learning—payment by results in a different guise.

English and English literature were optional until 'class' subjects were rearranged in 1882. Grammar and literature were then integrated into the English syllabus and became obligatory. Because recitation was now demanded in every school as a condition of grant, the verses to be learnt were entered in the logbook annually from 1884 onwards.

Table 11.1

Poetry in the Classroom

	Park Board School, 1884	*Carbrook National School, 1888*
Standard 1	'The Blackbird'—Tennyson	'The Village Blacksmith'—Longfellow
Standard 2	'The Brook'—Tennyson	'Cassabianca'—Mrs Hemans
Standard 3	'Wreck of the Hesperus'—Longfellow	'Inchcape Rock'—Southey
Standard 4	'Burial of Sir John Moore'—Wolfe	'Burial of Sir John Moore'—Wolfe
	'Hohenlinden'—Campbell	'Battle of the Baltic'—Campbell
	'Destruction of Sennacherib'—Byron	
Standard 5 and 6	Hubert and Arthur (*King John*)—Shakespeare	Selections from the *Merchant of Venice*—Shakespeare

Singing never lost its popularity as a welcome change from dull routine. Singing from the modulator sung to note names and the widespread use of tonic sol-fa to improve voice, ear, and sight-reading advanced as pianos and harmoniums became accessible. The Education Department stipulated that 'songs should be by some recognised composer' but national airs and patriotic songs retained their place in most schools. Percussion instruments were bought and percussion bands evolved. Drum and fife bands proved very popular in the voluntary schools.

Elementary drawing emerged as an essential component of popular education. Convinced of its practical usefulness in the preparation of boys for the Sheffield trades, drawing was taught in all the Board's boys' schools and in five girls' schools in 1882. Voluntary schools continued to present boys in the upper standards for the grant earning examinations of the Department of Science and Art. Freehand drawing was tackled with reasonable success but geometrical drawing, model and perspective, often proved beyond the reach of the majority. It is interesting to find that at the time the Cross Commission (1885–88) considered it advisable for all boys to be taught drawing, HMI advised some of the Board schools in the poorer districts such as Park to drop it 'so that more time may be devoted to elementary subjects'.

Because the School Board attached great importance to the teaching of drawing they complained to the Education Department in 1886 that teachers and managers would be disinclined to teach the subject under the conditions set out in the New Code. Revd James Gilmore, chairman of the Board, went further.[5] In his evidence before the Cross Commission he told them 'it does not pay at the present time to teach drawing'. Nonetheless, the schools persevered with freehand and geometrical drawing and when the Code of 1890 made it compulsory for boys, simple geometrical drawing was set alongside object lessons as 'suitable occupations' for all children.

Proposals to introduce practical cookery in the Board's girls' schools in 1875 were opposed by Revd H.R. Sandford HMI on the grounds that, of the girls in six of the Board's largest schools, only 161 out of 2,066 (8 per cent) had passed beyond Standard 4. He argued that the Board should confine its attention to elementary teaching as much as possible and not allow special subjects like cookery to occupy the time of teachers. Undeterred, the School Board appointed Mrs Greenup, headteacher of Brunswick Wesleyan Girls' School, as superintendent of needlework at £120 per annum and arranged for her to attend the National School of Cookery at South Kensington. She was to give special attention to bread making, the preparation of suitable economical dishes and other household work in addition to her inspection of needlework.

Cookery lessons were organized on an area basis for fifth and sixth Standard girls in Attercliffe, Park, Lowfield, Springfield, Crookesmoor, Walkley and Pyebank schools. Two-hour lessons were arranged fortnightly for most of the girls but Springfield and Netherthorpe girls were allowed to attend a class each week. They were taught how to provide dinner appropriate for 'the homes of the artisan class'—nourishing, tasty and inexpensive. The basic text book adopted, *Health in the House*, was recommended by the South Kensington Cookery School.

In February 1877 a reporter from the *Sheffield Independent* accompanied Mundella and J.F. Moss on a visit to Crookesmoor where Mrs

Greenup was taking a class of 48 girls with note books in hands.[6] She demonstrated how to make hash by boiling the bones from a cold joint and how to thicken, flavour and colour the gravy. She emphasized the old adage 'waste not want not' and then rehearsed the work of previous lessons on soup making, cooking cow heels and Yorkshire puddings. It was pointed out that the girls might not actually go out to work but it was likely they would be required to mind the house, prepare the food and make the home happy and comfortable. The reinforcement of Victorian values was clearly an integral part of domestic economy and was seen as an essential preparation for a girl's future role in society as mother and housewife.

Opportunities for girls to take part in cookery were severely limited. There was a dearth of qualified teachers and facilities were restricted. Under the Code of 1883 all girls over the age of twelve were entitled to practical cookery but the Board found it impossible to arrange this for all the 2,049 girls eligible, and it was confined to Standard 5 and above. Converted classrooms in eight more schools were fitted up with inexpensive gas stoves and cooking utensils but the grants for cookery were jeopardized because many senior girls left before the end of the school year or failed to make the necessary attendances. After 1890, the subject developed under the name of domestic economy when the Board scheduled the science demonstrator to visit each school fortnightly and give a fifty-minute illustrated lesson/demonstration for the girls in the fifth and higher Standards.

Nevertheless, many teachers were still making do in converted classrooms with trailing gas tubing feeding the stoves and inadequate equipment in 1902. Normal classes were disrupted to accommodate girls from other schools and occasionally time was wasted 'thawing out the gas meter'. However, hygiene, housewifery and cookery emerged as essential components of every girl's education. When inspectors raised the question of laundry classes in the better resourced centres the Board offered to popularize the activity but felt the time spent on laundry work impinged on more important aspects of the curriculum.

Suggestions that physical exercise should enter the curriculum were canvassed widely in the 1860s but not until the Code of 1871 was military drill recognized as advantageous to the health and formation of character of the country's youth. Statistics of physical debility emanating from the army and navy recruiting offices were alarming.[7] Even so, many disputed that sports and games would remedy the situation even if practicable. However, advocates of the Prussian system of education pressed their case with the result that 'attendance at drill under a competent instructor for not more than two hours per week and twenty weeks in the year may be counted as school attendance'.

Robert Lakenham, late master gunner in the Royal Artillery, was appointed by the School Board in 1875 to be the drill instructor at a salary of 25 shillings per week. He was provided with a plain suit rather than a uniform. Seven years later the number of instructors was increased so that one of them could visit every Board school once per fortnight. Class teachers were expected to learn the drills and practice them on alternate weeks. They were also expected to co-operate with the instructor in maintaining discipline but some classes proved a handful even for drill masters.

> October 1877, Springfield Boys' Board School.
> Drill master complained of restlessness of Standard II at drill and has refused to drill them again. He admits receiving them in order and I pointed out it was his responsibility to maintain order while the children were under his charge.

Not content with regimenting physical exercise in the playground, the School Board was anxious to see 'a little more smartness when moving about school'. Eventually, Swedish drill and dumb-bell exercises were introduced. There is clearer evidence of girls taking drill as a regular activity after the publication of the Cross Report. By that time most schools organized a few minutes of exercise daily, not only to rouse a languid class or quieten a restless one but in the firm belief that true education includes both mental and physical development.

Military drill increased in popularity in the larger voluntary schools. Ex-policemen and soldiers home on leave were enlisted to enliven the manoeuvres and routine. At St Paul's, drill was used 'to encourage attendance on Friday afternoons'. In the Parish Church School, Scholars' Brigades were formed on the lines of the Boys' Brigade in 1892. Each boy paid 6d for his cap and he received his belt free. The Boys' Brigade at St Mary's was provided with muskets and the managers had to allocate storage space for them. Normally, the drills were timetabled during playtime. Muskets in the Board Schools were mooted but the Board was not prepared to allow them.

Swimming was encouraged once the Health Committee granted swimming time at Corporation Street and Attercliffe baths in 1881. Bramall Lane baths became available in 1885. Halfpenny tickets were issued for morning sessions between 7.30 and 9.30 a.m. providing

Figure 32. Waiting for the command 'Heels—raise!'. Unidentified girls' physical training, early 1900s.

pupils were accompanied by a teacher. Free admission between 3.30 and 4.30 p.m. became possible towards the end of the century on condition that a competent teacher was in charge.

Enthusiasm for inter-school cricket was long-standing in the voluntary schools. In the 1880s, boys from St Paul's and the Parish Church schools were taken regularly to Norfolk Park on Friday evenings. Football after school emerged in the 1880s and the Parish Church School entered teams for the Clegg Shield annually from 1889. Representative matches between neighbouring school boards were arranged from 1895 onwards. As with swimming, all games and sports depended on the initiative and enthusiasm of individual teachers with little financial support from either local or central sources. Sports days were promoted by individual headteachers and in 1890 a centrally organized athletics meeting was arranged at Bramall Lane 'to encourage physical training' and raise funds for the Firs Hill Teachers' Orphanage.

The inclusion of science in the elementary school curriculum was slow to develop. By 1870 science classes were held in most of the Adult Institutes as well as in the evening schools connected with Neepsend and St Paul's National Schools. Once the School Board established its own night schools, science classes were organized in consultation with the Science and Art Department. With the opening of the Higher Grade Central School (1880), applied science was seen as an essential component of the day school curriculum but this enabled only the 'selected and deserving' pupils to benefit. For the most part, elementary science was confined to specific 'object lessons' except where a gifted or enthusiastic teacher was encouraged to experiment with inorganic chemistry as in Park Board School. Elementary botany was allowed to replace English as a class subject in Heeley Bank School.

In response to a question from Sir Henry Roscoe, a member of the Royal Commission on Technical Instruction in 1883, the Board agreed that 'the extension of science teaching in elementary schools was very desirable, provided that thorough and efficient instruction in the ordinary subjects be not interfered with'. However, it took another six years before a determined effort was made to introduce the subject throughout the Borough. The experience of peripatetic science demonstrators in Nottingham, Birmingham and Liverpool were closely studied. In each of these cities a central laboratory was set up where the apparatus was stored and experiments prepared. Heads and responsible class teachers were expected to observe the demonstrations, rehearse the salient points and test the children afterwards.

E.J. Bedford, chief science demonstrator in Nottingham, was appointed in June 1889 on a salary of £250 per annum. An assistant was engaged together with two youths to act as porters and trundle the apparatus around. Crofts Board School was equipped as the central laboratory. In general, experimental lessons in mechanics and physics were reserved for the boys whereas the girls concentrated on the chemistry of air and water with a bias towards biology.

In order to compete, St Matthias National School introduced the subject in the upper Standards and the Parish Church School appointed a specialist science teacher who tackled expansion, contraction and evaporation with Standards 3 and 4, and experiments on the composition of water and the atmosphere, valves and ventilation with the older children. An after-school activity club was also organized. A central class was arranged for nearby Church schools, and science classes were formed in Carbrook and Neepsend National schools. Not until after 1900 was the School Board able to offer the services of the demonstrator to the voluntary schools, permitting them to 'buy in' at the rate of $1^1/_2$d per head per lesson.

Because elementary science required laboratories, suitable furniture and equipment, plus a nucleus of qualified teachers, the subject was largely confined to the older scholars before the turn of the century. In addition, there remained a popularly held belief 'that much of the work was too advanced for children under the age of 14'. On the other hand, the educative value of a training in observation and reasoning was now clearly recognized and theories of discovery learning emerged in the development of object lessons and the organization of visits to parks and museums.

The question of manual instruction was raised in 1890. Some head-teachers were anxious to offer it to their senior boys but not until a subcommittee had visited workshops in London and Liverpool and received a recommendation from William Ripper was it sanctioned in the Board Schools. Ripper, one-time head of Walkley Board School and teacher of science at the Central School, now Professor responsible for teacher-training at the Technical School, reported enthusiastically about the 'hand and eye' training he had seen in London. He developed a scheme of work built on progressive kindergarten activities which he believed 'would lead systematically to the technical education' taught in the Central School and provide 'an ideal preparation for the future artisan'.

Ripper discouraged all suggestions of adopting the Swedish Sloyd system which in his view sacrificed creativity in pursuit of technique. Instead of the laborious exercises in the use of the knife to make simple wooden models, he promoted the idea of handicraft centres for the teaching of woodwork for boys in Standards 6 and 7. Workshops in Duchess Road, Huntsman's Gardens and Crookesmoor, together with the Teachers' Centre in Holly Street, were equipped with the aid of local manufacturers but the limitations of the initiative had to be stressed to allay the fears of the Joiners' Amalgamated Union.

Teaching the Scriptures

Religious teaching in the voluntary schools was taken for granted and rarely figured in the list of subjects the school claimed to teach. Portions of the Bible formed an essential part together with the cate-chism and prayer book collects in the Church schools. The recitation of Scripture, hymns and prayers were common to all the denominational schools except the Catholic schools where a greater emphasis was placed on the sacraments and Catholic doctrine.

The place of religious instruction in the Board schools was agreed from the outset. Within three months of taking office the School Board—an essentially religious body—unanimously approved the reading of the Bible accompanied by an explanation. A crucial change to the 1870 Act which ruled that 'no denominational religious instruc-tion would be allowed in board schools' enabled the members to accept the provision without prolonged debate. The additional timetable conscience clause which prescribed that religious instruction could only be given during the first or last periods of the school day was inserted to ensure no one missed intrinsic secular education. The conscience clause became a condition of grant aid that affected every elementary school. It permitted children to be released from religious teaching if parents so desired, and prevented the clause from being invalidated by spreading the teaching over the school day.

Members of the National Education League led by H.J. Wilson were suspicious of all state interference in the realms of religion and opposed any explanation of the Scriptures but their hostility was short-lived. In order better to inform the debate, Robert Leader sent a journalist to investigate how religious instruction was being imparted. His graphic report on Broomhill School in November 1873 was illuminating if slightly overdrawn.

Figure 33. Manual instruction. The boys of All Saints' School, Ellesmere Road, 'display their prize winning woodwork skills' in the C. of E. Educational Institute, 1904. The institute in St James' Street was leased to the Education Committee in 1903 and equipped as a handicraft centre for boys in Standards 6 and 7.

Hardly had the clock struck nine when the voices of the children in the playground hushed...the voice of the master can only be heard. In simple military movements the children entered in decent order 'Right turn. March!' They marched upstairs like an army of minia-tures. Every one to his place without noise or confusion. Some seated themselves at desks, others stood in rows or half circles mindful always to place their toes upon a chalk line marked on the floor for that purpose.

Every one in his place, Master blows a shrill whistle and in an instant silence is so perfect that one almost forgets he is in the presence of a hundred boys full of life etc. The door is now shut and then comes the request 'Hold up your hands and close your eyes'. Whilst all are in this attitude of prayer the master commences 'Our Father, which art in Heaven' and the children say it as it appeared to me, very reverently the prayer...

This over the master offered a few brief prayers for guidance and blessing, for encouragement and support. On this occasion they were selected from the beautiful collects of the Church of England but that this should not cause a wrong impression to go abroad, I ought to say that it is his custom to offer extemporaneous prayers so that even in this matter of supplication with thanksgiving there may not be the slightest tinge of denominationalism. Then came a simple little hymn, such a hymn that children can understand and which too is a child's prayer.

It commenced thus:-
> Through the dangers of the night
> Preserved O Lord by Thee
> Again we hail the cheerful light
> Again we bow the knee.

> Preserve us Lord throughout the day
> And guide us by Thy arm
> For they are safe and only they
> Whom Thou dost keep from harm.

The children sang with much feeling—little hands clasped and eyes on the master—thoughts winging away to realms above etc. Hymn closed almost too soon—but the time-table doesn't allow much time for religious teaching. The smallest children—those who cannot read and who are too young to understand the Bible teaching were now sent into a classroom—the others were ordered to stand up while two little fellows handed a Bible to each of them. 'We'll read,' said the master, 'some verses in the 5th Chapter of St. Matthew beginning at the 13th. verse'. The Bibles were opened, leaves were turned and in a minute every eye was on the verse, each not knowing whether he might be called on to read it. One was selected and he read and so on to the end of the verse. Then came the master's examination—clear, short and precise.

He explained that the chapter was called 'the Sermon on the Mount'—preached on the side of a mountain. They were likened unto salt. Questions followed on the value of salt. Then a boy read the next verse. 'The light of the world' was explained, followed by more questions on the light under a bushel etc. When the explanations were concluded, the verses previously read by boys separately were read by the whole school—the lesson came to a close. The school door was re-opened—a few boys who were too late were admitted and the ordinary work of the school commenced. The whole time occupied in prayer singing and reading was not more than half an hour.[8]

Anxious to safeguard the subject, the School Board required their inspector to examine each school regularly. The Board was convinced that this important area of the curriculum should be supervised, 'otherwise work was less likely to be efficiently done'. A syllabus of biblical knowledge which embraced both Old and New Testaments was approved in November 1874[9] and in June 1875 Skelton Cole stressed that 'children would receive Biblical instruction but not religious instruction, as under that term almost any kind of nonsense might be taught'.[10]

The examinations could be observed and reporters were impressed that 'their knowledge was not confined to a mere gabble of names and places but most of the answers bore the impress of individual thought'.[11] In the higher Standards each child received a card containing five questions on the lives of Jonah and Christ and was given an hour to write his or her answers. The Board was satisfied that the subject was 'being thoroughly attended to without sectarian bias or the least infringement of the Education Act'. On the retirement of Inspector Davis in 1885, local clergy were invited to undertake the role of honorary examiners. The overall tenor of their reports was consistently appreciative of the teaching and the attitude of the children.

Reporting in June 1890 the Revd George Barlow wrote:

After three years experience as Honorary Examiner I must confess to a strengthened admiration of the system of Biblical Instruction adopted by the Board. The working syllabus is excellently arranged

SHEFFIELD SCHOOL BOARD.

Proposed Course of Instruction in Biblical Knowledge (for Scholars).

	OLD TESTAMENT.	NEW TESTAMENT.
FOR INFANTS.	Adam and Eve. Cain and Abel. Joseph and his Brethren, and David and Goliath	The Birth and Early Life of Our Lord, and the Lord's Prayer.
STANDARD I.	The Patriarchs: Abraham, Isaac, Jacob, Joseph, and Moses, and Ten Commandments.	An Outline of the Life of our Lord, and the Parables of the Good Samaritan and the Prodigal Son.
STANDARDS II & III.	The Kings: Saul, David, and Solomon, with a frequent repetition of the Commandments.	More particular knowledge of the Life, Mission, and Death of Our Lord, with exact knowledge of Miracles at Cana, Nain, Bethany, and Capernaum.
STANDARDS IV. V. VI.	The Prophets: Elijah, Elisha, Daniel, and Jonah, with a short account of the Tabernacle and its Service.	The principal events in the lives of St. Peter and St. Paul.

Offices of the Sheffield School Board,
Fitzalan Rooms, December, 1874.

Figure 34. Sheffield School Board syllabus of Biblical Knowledge, 1874.

as to the variety and interest of topics, as to the passages selected for committal to memory and is graduated according to standards so as to impart a valuable amount of scriptural knowledge throughout the school course. The moral influence of such knowledge upon the school is incalculable especially upon a class of children who, as I have ascertained *go to no Sunday School,* have *no home religious training,* and whose knowledge of the Bible while young is that gained in your schools.

The scholars show a keen interest in the scripture lesson and I have it on the testimony of several teachers that the beneficial influence of the scripture teaching is an appreciable help to them in maintaining order and in raising the moral tone of the school.

The Bible retained its importance as the primary source book throughout the century. Referred to in 1846 as the 'classics of the poor' and reinforced by T.H. Huxley in 1870 when he said 'the mass of the people should not be deprived of the one great literature which is open to them', the compilers of the *Handbook of Suggestions for Teachers* confirmed the Bible as a seminal influence on children's understanding and their use of English.[12]

Criticism of the syllabus emerged towards the end of the century. Easier narratives were offered to the infants and the missionary journeys of St Paul were incorporated into the work with older children. Headteachers campaigned for inspection rather than examination but the Board refused to budge on the issue. Reports were issued annually and a from a cross-section of schools examined in 1893, 129 classes were graded 'excellent', 106 'very good', 18 'good' and only 4 'very fair'. Any suggestion of denominationalism was reported, as in Springfield when a teacher implied that 'we must be born again by Baptism' or similarly the infants at Whitely Wood who were discovered praying for their 'God fathers and God mothers'. Clearly, the quality of instruction overall was sound, as Revd S.E. Keeble confirmed in 1895, 'In every school without exception I found a high standard of excellence. The moral tone of the teaching and the schools was high— indeed may be said without exaggeration, Christian'.

Nevertheless, under the pressure of an expanding curriculum there was a tendency to omit the occasional scripture lesson and a circular was reissued reminding teachers of the penalties for breaching the regulations. Procedures were also revised for the marking of registers and the final closing of doors. From January 1896 the school door was closed at 9 a.m. School was opened by a hymn and a prayer, after which the early attendances were marked. Doors were then reopened, late attendances marked and registers closed. Scripture lessons lasted from 9.10 a.m. until 9.45 a.m. except for the infants who only had fifteen minutes. Secular instruction finished ten minutes before the final bell to allow the day to be closed with a hymn and a prayer.

The voluntary schools enjoyed a little more flexibility to enable clergy or visitors to give the occasional scripture lesson but the demands of the secular curriculum lay just as heavily on them as in the Board schools. Diocesan Inspectors were afforded the same measure of fear and respect as HMI and the master of St Paul's described the form of their examination in the upper Standards:

> Besides the usual viva voce subjects the children have to write the following from memory
>
> A1   What did your God parents promise for you at Baptism?
> 2   What do we keep in mind at Easter and Lent?
> 3   Write a short account of St Peter's visions.
>
> B1   What were you made at Baptism?
> 2   What do we keep in mind at Whitsuntide and Epiphany?
> 3   Write an account of the Conversion of St Paul.

The withdrawal of children from religious instruction on grounds of conscience in the voluntary schools was rare. In 1902, the Sheffield Association of Voluntary Teachers distributed a questionnaire to discover its extent. From the response of 27 schools, only two children were excused all religious teaching and 162 were withdrawn from part, 158 of them being Jewish. The 'religious difficulty' does not appear to have caused any real problem for the people of Sheffield and confirms the opinion of observers elsewhere.[13]

Character formation and moral training, though often allied to religious instruction, tended to be more dogmatic. Preaching in St Mark's, Broomhill, in 1893, the bishop of Beverley maintained that 'the formation of the character is the most important part of education and the only true and sure foundation on which to attempt to build up the character is faith in God and a knowledge of His good and holy law'.[14] Not everyone shared his outlook and some consciences were offended by reading Christian scriptures, yet there were those like Huxley who admitted to being 'perplexed to know what practical measures the religious feeling, which is the essential basis of conduct, is to be kept without the use of the Bible'. Whilst strenuously advocating the secularization of public elementary education, the Cross

Commission declared most emphatically that 'they regarded religion as the true basis of education'. The pre-eminence of character training was fostered by the Code of 1904 by reinforcing the concept that 'the purpose of the Public Elementary School' was to form and strengthen the character.

Insistence on cleanliness became mandatory. In 1885 the Education Department affirmed that 'children may be refused admission for neglect of personal cleanliness and managers may insist on freedom from filth or infection'. Dishonesty undermined the character and was sinful. Thrift was inculcated by the Board from 1876, and in 1882 Skelton Cole spelt out its value to the well-being of the population, whilst admitting that 'the carrying out of penny banks was not included in the ordinary duties of the school teacher, many of whom most cheerfully volunteer to give the necessary time to encouraging the children to cultivate habits of forethought and frugality'.[15] The importance of thrift was endorsed when the Education Department decided that the operating of penny banks should be taken into account when assessing the 'Merit' grant which had been introduced in 1882. Governed by rigid timetables, punctuality and good timekeeping was precious to the Victorians and inculcated at every opportunity.

Temperance was much more controversial and was not given the prominence Nonconformity would have liked. Throughout the nineteenth century, observers criticized the drinking in ale shops and public houses as the staple pastime of Sheffield's working classes. Yet not until the Band of Hope assembled propaganda against intemperance and the evils of drink was education recognized as a key to the problem. The Band of Hope galas were an institution in Sheffield, and decorated drays and tableaux organized by the Nonconformist Sunday schools campaigning for total abstinence processed through the town. The School Board sympathized with the Union's motives but were irritated by their interference with school attendance.

In 1889 the National Temperance League targeted pupil-teachers, but when it was proposed that scientific lectures should be given on the pernicious effects of alcohol the Board only permitted free use of school rooms as an out-of-school activity. Eventually, the Board allowed the distribution of a temperance book and permission for one reading lesson per fortnight reinforced by twice-yearly examinations in Standard 5 upwards. Not until 1901 was the Board persuaded to support a Bill prohibiting the sale of intoxicating liquor to children below the age of 16.

When tracing the expansion of the curriculum, we must be mindful not to exaggerate its effect. HMIs retained their oversight and the School Board imposed the textbooks. The voluntary schools were even more limited by the economics of school management. The conservative nature of schools and the mixed quality of staff precluded wide curriculum development. Religious teaching 'when given with knowledge and sincerity' was seen as the major factor in training mind, personality and character,[16] but elementary education by definition was designed for the labouring poor and directed at eradicating illiteracy and disseminating useful knowledge. 'The three Rs and the standard subjects offered the main criteria for giving grant and were (still) recognised as the ultimate and final essentials in elementary schools.'[17]

Notes

1. G.A.N. Lowndes, *The Silent Social Revolution* (1937), p. 38.
2. See K. Bathurst, 'The Need for National Nurseries' (1905) in Van Der Eyken, *Education, the Child and Society*, pp. 119f.
3. Bingham, *Sheffield School Board*, p. 117.
4. *SI* (28 May 1875).
5. *Cross Report*, 1887, 2, p. 773.
6. *SI* (2 February 1877). See also *SI* (17 January 1879).
7. P.C. McIntosh, *Physical Education in England since 1800* (1852), p. 104.
8. *SI* (6 November 1873).
9. For complete syllabus of biblical knowledge for pupils and pupil teachers see Bingham, *Sheffield School Board*, p. 162.
10. *SI* (1 June 1875).
11. *SI* (7 May 1875).
12. See Lawson and Silver, *Social History*, p. 271; C. Bibby (ed.), *T.H. Huxley on Education* (1971), p. 25; Board of Education, *Handbook of Suggestions for Teachers* (1927), p. 68.
13. See J.S. Hurt, *Elementary Schooling and the Working Classes* (1979), p. 174. A large proportion of Jewish children attended the Parish Church School in the 1890s. In 1894 there were 80 on the roll. Many of Russian origin were unable to speak English.
14. Odom, *Church Notes* (1894), 1.
15. S. Cole, *Sheffield School Board Statement* (1882).
16. Board of Education, *Handbook of Suggestions*, pp. 20f.
17. E.J.R. Eaglesham, *The Foundations of 20th Century Education in England* (1967), p. 12.

Chapter 12

Towards More Effective Teaching 1870–1902

> Having got our children to school, the supremely important
> question remains: What is the quality of the education there given
> to them? On this point no materials exist for any confident answer.
> Since the abolition of the individual examination of the
> Government inspectors, no common measure has been applied to all
> the schools, and there is no statistical evidence to appeal to.
>
> Sidney Webb, *Nineteenth Century* (1903)

The quality of elementary education in the last quarter of the nineteenth century was transformed under the Board's guiding hand.
Contrary to the views of many contemporary commentators, the
proficiency of the headteachers in Sheffield's major voluntary schools in
the 1870s is undeniable but their assistants were 'mere boys and girls'—
pupil-teachers aged between 13 and 18. The competence and
qualifications of the teachers was at the heart of the matter and one of
the earliest decisions of the Board was to employ a larger number of
certificated staff than was possible in the voluntary sector, restricting the
number of pupil-teachers in relation to qualified assistants to two to
one.

The majority of certificated teachers qualified 'on the job' as pupil-
teachers and then by examination as an 'acting teacher'. Fewer than 50
per cent of male teachers were college-trained and the opportunities
for girls were even more limited. Only 32 per cent of female teachers
nationwide were college-trained in 1914.[1] Twenty-seven per cent
qualified 'on the job' and 41 per cent were either ex-pupil-teachers or
unqualified 'supplementary' assistants 'Art 68s'—women over the age
of 18, vaccinated against smallpox and recognized by HMI
as 'employed during the whole of the school hours in the general
instruction of the scholars and in teaching needlework'.

In their attempts to secure 'the best possible teachers' the training
colleges were regularly visited in order to select the most able

Figure 35. The teaching staff at St Mary's C.E. School, Walkley c. 1890. Many pupil teachers were barely older than the children they were expected to teach.

candidates. The Board emphasized the value of the two-year training courses for 'those who wished to reach the highest ranks of the profession' but warned parents that they were unable to retain every pupil-teacher apprenticed. Even so, the shortage of adult assistants was so critical in 1884 that advertisements for ex-pupil-teachers were placed in four local and scholastic papers in August and September and in nine newspapers circulating in Lincoln, Hull, Grimsby, Huddersfield, Leeds, Derby and Doncaster. The net result was ten applications of which hardly any proved suitable.

The preliminary tests for pupil-teachers embraced grammar, dictation, geography and arithmetic. Before completing their apprenticeship they were examined in biblical knowledge, grammar and composition, arithmetic plus Euclid, algebra and mensuration, English history, geography, domestic economy for the girls and school method. Furnished with progress reports over the four years, the Board was enabled to select the most competent. Nevertheless, not every headteacher was qualified to instruct their pupils in every subject to the standard required and the variability of pupil-teacher training was a recurring theme throughout the period.

Educated almost entirely within the elementary school system, pupils who attended the Board's Central School and St Matthias National School—which drew from a very wide area—had a distinct advantage over their peers. A variety of in-service training courses—early morning and evening—were inaugurated in 1881 which led eventually to the creation of a pupil-teachers' centre in the Central School in 1887. Day release for pupil-teachers was not approved until 1895. Four years later the purpose-built Pupil Teachers' Centre was opened in Holly Street. Shortly afterwards Catholic pupil-teachers were transferred to the RC Centre in Cavendish Street.

Because the Church of England still monopolized the teacher-training colleges, Nonconformist and Catholic students experienced great difficulty gaining admission. Not until day training colleges attached to university colleges were established was the problem mitigated. Largely as an outcome of the Cross Enquiry, pressure mounted locally for the creation of a day training college in Sheffield. A college attached to Firth College became a reality in 1890 and Duchess Road Board School was chosen for school practice. The municipal day training college in Sheffield did not open until 1905.

The Code of 1896 did determine three years' apprenticeship for pupil-teachers who successfully completed their first year's examination

Figure 36. The teaching staff at Hunters' Bar Board School, late 1890s.
By the end of the century more teachers had been to college and were a little more mature.

papers, but pay scales were still derisory—£25 per annum for boys and £17 10s per annum for girls at the age of 17. This system was denounced by Sidney Webb in 1903 as 'a combination of child labour and soul-destroying intellectual drudgery unworthy of a civilized nation'.[2] The dearth of male candidates and the volume of criticism led the Board of Education to revolutionize the system. In future all teachers were to receive instruction in a college or pupil-teachers' centre or spend at least two years in secondary education. No longer would the nation's teachers be drawn entirely from the elementary schools. By 1907 this transition was well under way.

Despite the disadvantage of arduous training arrangements, a School Board appointment offered security and a social status that compensated for comparatively poor pay. The certificated male assistant averaged about £90 per annum in 1870 which increased to £100 by the turn of the century. Teaching for women was much more appealing though salaries were hardly attractive. Female assistants earned about £60 a year whilst the certificated female could rise to £80.[3] When Maud Maxfield and Jonathan Taylor campaigned for the abolition of sex differentiation in salary negotiations in 1901 they could gather little support. Nevertheless, a career structure emerged as the more successful teachers mastered the demands of higher standard work.

Teacher Appraisal

The key to effective elementary education for those responsible for assessing the efficiency of the system was evaluation. Before 1862 inspection was the sole criterion. The master was observed while he examined the pupils and a statement as to the level of his competence was written on his parchment. In his evidence before the Newcastle Commission, HMI Watkins itemized the factors he used to judge the school's character and ethos:

> I am influenced by what I call the tone of the school, its general character which is rather the effect of the discipline than the discipline itself. Also how far the children apply their religious teaching to their own circumstances in life. There is also an entry made on the state of the school and the apparent bearing of the master on it.[4]

In the wake of the Revised Code (1862) school inspections gave way to a combination of assessment and examination. Subjective evaluations were replaced by objective assessment. National performance targets were set in the three Rs and when 'class' subjects were introduced, attainment targets in English, geography and elementary science were formulated.

On taking office, the School Board appointed B.D. Davis as its first superintendent. By 1874, having shed some of his initial responsibilities, he described the nature of his role as the Board's inspector. Focusing on the classroom techniques of the staff, he assessed the proportion of pupils likely to pass their examinations and gauged the effectiveness of the discipline by observation and the quantity of entries in the punishment book.

> I am required to visit all the Board Schools of the town at least once a week; and my report of their organization, discipline, registration and general system of book-keeping has to be laid on the table at each of the meetings of your committee...In all my visits I endeavour not merely to collect facts upon which to found a report but to make these visits of use to the scholars and pupil teachers...As the schools are too numerous to admit of my spending but a short time in each department...every week I take in order a few to which I devote considerably more time and attention than to the others. By this arrangement I am enabled from time to time not only to test the attainments of the scholars, but to form a pretty correct estimate of the skill and diligence of the teachers.

In the drive for more effective schools and the assurance of a higher quality of education, the Education Department introduced the Merit grant in 1882.[5] The merit award was based on a three-dimensional assessment: (a) organization and discipline; (b) intelligence employed in the instruction; and (c) the general quality of the work especially in 'class' subjects. The suitability of instruction and the appropriateness of the various kindergarten occupations was the yardstick applied in the infant schools. Schools were classified as 'fair', 'good' and 'excellent'. Merit tables were devised and each school's position in the league was scrutinized. Sheffield School Board accepted nothing less than 'good'.

> If a school be reported upon by H.M.I. as not entitled to the Good Merit Grant the work of the Head Teacher of such school for the year of service current at the time of such inspection *will not be regarded as satisfactory*...

Voluntary school managers were required to indicate in their annual report to the Education Department the standard of conduct, character and attention to duty of the teaching staff. Failure to exercise proper supervision imperilled the grant. Nevertheless, their oversight was never as effective as the Board's professional approach.

Monitoring teacher performance before the advent of the classroom was informal and relatively simple for the headteacher. When the central hall design was developed in the 1880s the Board was convinced the plan would enable every head 'to have his eye constantly on anyone of the classes around him'. On the retirement of B.D. Davies in 1885 performance appraisal of assistant staff was formally delegated to headteachers. They were empowered 'to note defective methods and unintelligent teaching either by assistants or pupil teachers and should when necessary give direct teaching'. In order to monitor classroom work more closely the Board directed that there should be criticism lessons 'regularly given by every member of the staff in the presence of the Headteacher' whose notes should be open to the inspector of the Board.

The art of lesson preparation derived new impetus and in order to frame constructive criticism, record books were issued with attendant guidelines:

(a) Record the matter and method of the lesson fully.
(b) Assess the manner and language of the delivery.
(c) Gauge the effectiveness of the discipline and class management.
(d) Identify the use or lack of illustrations and resources.

The scheme of appraisal was refined in 1890 when headteachers were asked to make an annual assessment on every teacher, reporting under the following headings: name, training, punctuality, industry and attitude, maintenance of discipline, ability as a teacher, general conduct and remarks.

The maintenance of discipline was synonymous with the preservation of good order and sound class control for much of the nineteenth century. What HMI Watkins referred to as the tone of the school in 1859 was interpreted as the overall effect of the discipline. The Code of 1876 signalled a wider interpretation.

> Managers and Teachers will be expected to satisfy the Inspector that all responsible care is taken in the ordinary management of the schools, to bring up the children in habits of punctuality, of good manners and language, of cleanliness and neatness, and also to impress upon the children the importance of cheerful obedience to duty, of consideration and respect for others and of honour and thankfulness in word and action.[6]

This hidden curriculum underpinned the ethos of the good school, but faced with hundreds of unschooled children compelled to attend and assisted largely by teenage apprentices, many headteachers achieved the impossible by a combination of professional competence and the time-worn rod.

Rewards and Punishments

Many of the rewards and punishments employed in the monitorial schools were discarded but corporal punishment was officially endorsed. One of the earliest resolutions of the School Board in 1871 authorized its use but confined the infliction of physical punishment to headteachers only.

> No corporal punishment be administered in the schools of the Board except by the headteacher who shall be required to record every instance of its infliction and the cause there of and report the same quarterly to the Board.

The Management Committee Minutes over the first 15 years are sprinkled with cases of excessive caning and the infringement of rules by assistant teachers barely older than the pupils themselves. School logbooks are permeated with warnings given by headteachers to pupil-teachers and assistants wrestling with the problems of discipline.

Newspapers were ever ready to report flagrant offences that led to the magistrate's court. One seven-year-old was flogged unmercifully for 'blotting his copy book'. Another youngster, when threatened with being kept in at dinner time for shoddy work, burst into tears and refused to go to the head. On hearing the commotion, the head came over, gave him three strokes then carried him to his desk and caned his backside again. The stipendiary dismissed the case but asserted that the punishment was more severe than necessary and that to cane a pupil as young as seven was not desirable. In general the magistrates were inclined to support education's representatives of law and order.

An inquest on a Board school girl in 1878 obliged the School Board to review its regulation. A ten-year-old had asked to go to the closet. On being refused the child's insolent retort earned her a slap across the face and having her ears clipped. It was alleged that the girl became subject to convulsive fits as a direct cause and later died. No action was taken against the school but the Authority, alive to its responsibility, advised all headteachers to be more vigilant and required that, however slight, no corporal punishment should be administered until a record of the offence and the nature of the punishment had been entered in the punishment book.

Comparable rules were imposed in the major voluntary schools. Financial penalties were incurred for any breach of the policy by pupil-teachers and, as in the Board schools, gross violation rendered all assistants liable to instant dismissal. These procedures were not universal, however, and led to complaints by Board school headteachers in 1883. They argued that when HMI assessed the school for the Merit grant they were disadvantaged compared with their counterparts in denominational schools because of the Board's insistence that every case, however slight, should be recorded.

Over the years, teacher associations campaigned for a relaxation of the rules but without success. In 1877 the National Union of Elementary Teachers in Sheffield opposed the abolition of corporal punishment on the grounds that it would endanger the fabric of education. 'Cases will continually arise requiring the rod and...on general grounds it would be unwise to banish it from the schools.' In 1883 the senior mistress at Duchess Road was allowed to administer corporal punishment to the girls instead of the headmaster but even in 1890, when senior masters were appointed in the larger and 'more difficult' schools, no delegation of powers was authorized.

When the School Board issued a punishment book to each teacher, certificated assistants were optimistic that they might be allowed to punish for minor offences such as disobedience or carelessness but the Board reaffirmed its view that 'corporal punishment was a debasing influence and not as a rule the best means of enforcing discipline'. The Board returned to the subject of physical punishment in 1891 and declared that 'cases of excessive corporal punishment by headteachers are too frequent—a sign of lack of self control or refusal to observe the regulations'.

A combined deputation of heads and assistants bearded the Board in 1896 requesting modification of the regulations. They argued that the delegation of powers for class offences would suppress the improper forms of punishment everyone knew were happening. Pupils were aware that assistant teachers could not use the cane and were baiting them accordingly. Their conditions of service were becoming increasingly 'harassing and vexatious and with some would be almost intolerable'. The Committee refused to reverse their decision. 'They are of the opinion the present regulation is essentially necessary for the proper protection of the children for whom they are responsible and they rely upon the teaching staff for its faithful observance.'

Assumptions that physical punishment was 'the rule' in Victorian schools are quite clearly very wide of the mark. What is clear is that it was widely used but with differing degrees of frequency and it was not the only disciplinary measure employed. Detention after school was frequently imposed for latecoming and indolence. In response to a request the School Management Committee framed the following guidelines:

> The teachers are quite justified in keeping children in for a reasonable time—say half an hour—for being disorderly or saucy; for talking or playing in school and for carelessness in school work especially if wilful or repeated.

> As for swearing, deliberate lying or indecency the Committee thinks these offences should be punished by some mark of disgrace in school or by keeping in on more than one occasion but not for protracted periods.

> Backwardness and dullness cannot in any sense be considered as 'bad conduct' and should not be punished either by keeping in or in any other way whatever.[7]

The voluntary schools were apt to take detention to greater lengths. The master at St John's National School frequently detained children until 7 p.m.—usually for truancy. Expulsions were rare but enforced for irregular attendance, theft and lying. Street children were often excluded for arriving in 'nothing but rags from head to foot' but such exclusions were forbidden after 1885 by a directive from the Education Department.

> Children may reasonably be refused admission for neglect of personal cleanliness and managers may insist on freedom from filth or infectious disorders but must not be refused admission because ill clad or even ragged.

Rewards during the period showed some originality. Park Infant School produced red rosettes for the children who were particularly good. 'They have a wonderful effect in keeping them all very well behaved.' Good marks for regularity, punctuality, cleanliness, industry and attention were widely used. William Ripper instituted the school captain in Walkley Boys' School and presented class medals monthly. Walkley, under Ripper, was recognized as 'one of the best schools in the borough'. Book prizes for good conduct and attendance were awarded by the Board in the 1890s, but towards the end of the century headteachers became increasingly disenchanted with the Board's choice and asked for permission to select more suitable titles. Because bulk-buying was more economical the Board retained its discretion.

A new strategy to raise pupil performance was introduced in 1898. A leaving or Merit Certificate was issued which sought to improve attendance, provide a record of achievement and assist job prospects.

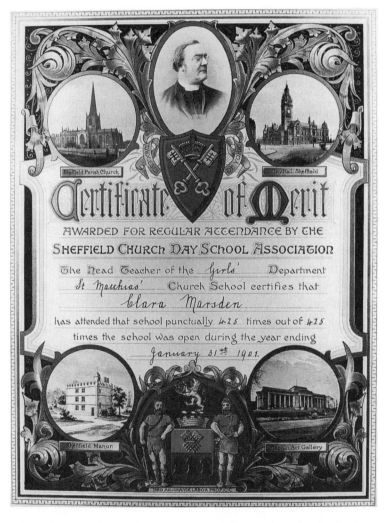

Figure 37a. Certificates of Merit were awarded to pupils in church schools to encourage punctuality and good conduct.

The certificate confirmed the satisfactory conduct and attendance of the scholar and furnished evidence of his or her ability in reading, handwriting, spelling, composition, arithmetic, geography of the British Empire and any other qualifying subject at Standard 6 or 7 level. The following statistics were published in 1900.

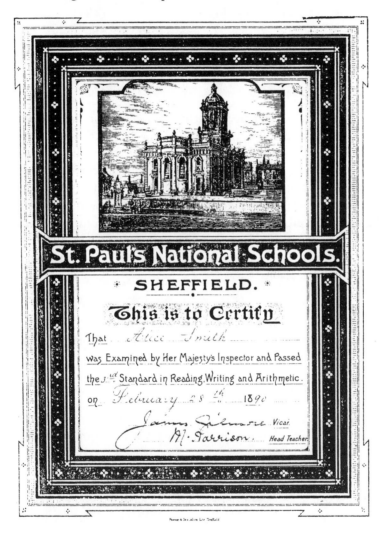

Figure 37b. St Paul's national School Certificate recognised that Alice Smith had successfully completed the examination in the 3Rs at Standard 3 level. These certificates should not be confused with the Merit Certificates introduced in 1898 by the School Board for scholars whose attendance and conduct was satisfactory and had passed an examination in the ordinary subjects of either Standard 6 or 7.

Table 12.1

Merit Certificates[8]

	1899	1900
No. of scholars examined in Standard 6 work	724	821
No. of scholars passed	215	389
Percentage of passes	29.7	47.4
No. of scholars examined in Standard 7 work	185	359
No. of scholars passed	88	219
Percentage of passes	47.5	61

As the content and practice of elementary education did not admit a diversity of teaching styles, traditional approaches were reinforced and experiment discouraged. Nevertheless, with the phasing out of 'payment by results' in 1895, a greater flexibility in curriculum development emerged, its value was enhanced, and the widespread demand for secondary education at the turn of the century was a demonstration of the overall improvement in pupil performance. Continuous teacher assessment unquestionably raised the standards of competence and professionalism of the teachers and its positive effect on the children's education is incalculable.

Notes

1.   Horn, *Victorian and Edwardian School Child*, pp. 165, 183. See also Lowndes, *Silent Social Revolution*, Graph C.

2.   Brennan, *Education for National Efficiency*, p. 114.

3.   See Bingham, *Sheffield School Board*, ch. 4 for details of salary improvements.

4.   *Newcastle Report*, 1861, 6, p. 146.

5.   C. Birchenough, *History of Elementary Education* (1920), pp. 148-49.

6.   *SI* (31 March 1876).

7.   SSB School Management Committee Minutes (13 January 1885), SCA.

8.   SSB School Management Committee Minutes (20 September 1900).

Chapter 13

Extending Ladders 1870–1902

It did seem desirable to us as guardians of elementary education of
this large manufacturing town, to provide for these promising pupils
a somewhat broader basis of general education that would enable
them more intelligently to apply the scientific knowledge they may
have acquired to the manual part of the work which they may hereafter be called upon to perform in the manufactories of this town.
    Skelton Cole, Chairman of the Sheffield School Board (1882)

Elementary education for the masses was the prime objective of the
1870 Education Act. Although most children still left school as early as
possible, the downturn in job opportunities before the age of 13 led to
a growing tendency to stay on at school and attempt more advanced
work. A.J. Mundella opposed any suggestion of an exclusively rudimentary education and submitted to the School Board the advantages
of providing a sound education for the working and poorer middle
classes whereby 'Latin, French and German should be taught and
elementary science and political economy...It would stimulate the children in the elementary schools and induce the parents to retain them in
school as long as possible'.[1]

The creation of a higher grade of elementary school for the more
intelligent and highly motivated was inevitable and in 1873 J.F. Moss
was despatched on a fact-finding tour of Europe. His report on the
German 'Real' and 'Trade' schools which emphasized science and
technical education inspired the Board to consider the erection of a
centrally situated school with an explicit bias towards science.

The Board was convinced it was within its powers 'to encourage
and foster the cultivation of sound scientific knowledge among those
who were hereafter to take active parts in pursuits upon which the
commercial prosperity of the district so largely depended'. A scheme
was devised whereby able children from the elementary schools could

be drafted in and given more advanced teaching. Moreover, the chairman, Sir John Brown, was anxious to resuscitate the practical science classes he promoted when mayor in 1861–62.[2]

Questions of site, finance and design of the Central School delayed its opening until July 15 1880. Proposals to create a link with Mark Firth's college of higher education and the amalgamation of new administrative offices to replace the inadequate accommodation in the Haymarket led to objections over the cost of such a project, but there was no public outcry. Few voices opposed the plan for progressive learning 'fixing not only the first but several successive rungs on the ladder by which children of ability and application may mount to the higher stages of intellectual training'.[3] This re-echoed the observation of T.H. Huxley when he said, 'I conceive it to be our duty to make a ladder from the gutter to the university along which any child may climb'.[4]

Smith Street—later renamed Leopold Street—was chosen as the most appropriate location for this complex which would include an infant school, a junior mixed for Standards 1 to 4, a mixed school for Standards 5 and 6 and a higher grade school. HMI Sandford opposed the site location because of its proximity to a number of Church schools. Some Board members balked at the estimated cost of £25,000 but the motion to proceed was passed on the casting vote of the chairman who assured the Board that they were building not just for the present but 'for all time' and the 'enormous expenditure' was on land unlikely to depreciate in value.

Endorsement of the notion of a central higher grade school came from W.E. Forster in 1874 when he congratulated the Board on conceiving the idea.[5] 'It is trying to carry out for Sheffield what we in parliament have hoped to do by making use of endowments and it may be doing it with more effect.' In in his own constituency of Bradford, schools were being adapted for well-to-do parents who could afford something better than the ordinary Board school whereas Sheffield was aiming to cream off the able from existing elementary schools.[6]

The concept of a ladder to higher education was extended by the creation of entrance scholarships. During 1874, Mark Firth, mayor of Sheffield and vice-chairman of the School Board, proposed a scholarship scheme for selected exceptionally clever boys attending public elementary schools. Together with John Brown and others, Firth offered to fund the exhibitions and the Revd J. Cardwell, principal of the Collegiate School, announced that eight exhibitions would be

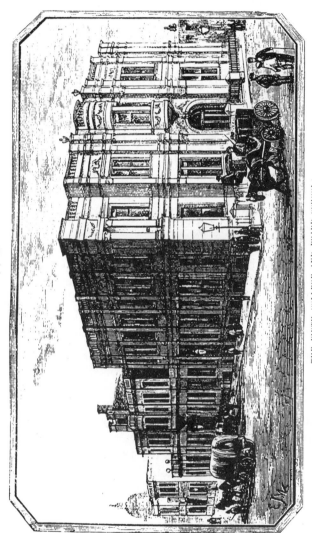

Figure 38. Firth College and School Board Offices 1880. The complex was designed conjointly by T.J. Flockton and F.R. Robson, the architect of the London School Board.

established in the school, awarded by competitive examination, to able youths under 14 years of age. Pupils were to be examined in arithmetic, geography, English composition, Latin accidence, reading, grammar, spelling and dictation, algebra and geometry. In January 1875, 60 scholarship candidates sat the examination. In 1877, 14 exhibitions were awarded and eleven of the successful candidates were educated in the voluntary schools. A concert given by 500 Board School pupils was held in the Albert Hall that year to augment the scholarship fund.

Meanwhile, a testimonial fund was opened in recognition of the invaluable contribution to education of Revd Samuel Earnshaw. School governor and coordinator of the major Church schools in the borough, Earnshaw stimulated the secondary sector when he engineered the introduction of the Cambridge Middle Class Examinations and worked ceaselessly for the extension of higher education. The promoters were hopeful of establishing joint action with the trustees of Mark Firth's university college by providing scholarships for pupils attending any public elementary school and tenable at the secondary schools and ultimately at Firth College itself.[7]

More scholarships became available after 1882 from funds accumulated from the sale of the Lancasterian and Grimesthorpe Endowed schools.[8] The scholarship ladder enabled some to win awards at the Royal School of Mines, the Normal School of Science at South Kensington, the Royal School of Science in Dublin as well as Firth College and the Queen's scholarship for teachers but the number of poor children assisted was small. Most of those benefiting were the offspring of skilled artisans, shopkeepers and tradesmen—a class that merged with the lower middle class.

Delayed by the acquisition of properties in Smith Street, Orchard Lane and Sans Paviour, the Central School, designed to serve upwards of a thousand children by E.R. Robson, architect of the London School Board, eventually opened in July 1880. The infant and junior departments were located on the ground floor and classroom accommodation for 500 senior boys and girls was created upstairs. A science laboratory, cut off from the rest of the school to exclude 'offensive smells', was fitted out for practical experiments, and another room was equipped for cookery and domestic economy. The assembly hall was built into the roof space, large enough to gather the whole school together for the opening and closing of each day, examinations, singing and so on.

Admission to the higher grade school was by examination, initially for those capable of mastering Standard 3 work but later Standard 4 became the accepted entrance qualification. The curriculum for the first year embraced biblical knowledge, English literature, mathematics, Latin, French, mechanics, animal physiology, physical geography, history, botany and domestic economy (for the girls). Assisted by liberal grants from South Kensington for an organized three-year course in science, the school was able to experiment with technical courses bearing on local industry and vocational courses for those preparing to become pupil-teachers.

Although the liberal curriculum developed within the Codal requirements for elementary schools, its gravitation towards science and technology bordered on the work of secondary schools and the Board was warned by the Education Department 'they might at some date find it necessary to place restrictions upon Higher Grade schools in order that no departure may be made from the terms in which the parliamentary grant is made for primary education'. Clearly the government was reacting to the kind of arguments pursued by Dr Shera, principal of Wesley College, who reminded the Board that 'to grasp at secondary education was beyond their function'.[9] As a member of the School Board, Shera was fully aware of the competition posed by the school where fees could not rise above 9d per week.

The Samuelson Commission on technical education (1882–84) was so impressed with the school's practical and experimental work—which ranged from the construction of wooden models and apparatus to demonstrate the use of levers, pulleys and cranes to the mechanics of roof, arch and bridge making—that they recommended the creation of more 'Higher Elementary Schools like those in Sheffield and Manchester' for advanced pupils in the primary school willing to be kept at school to the age of 14 or 15.[10]

Conscious of the concern of local industry to compete with European and American rivals, co-operation was sought with employers and manufacturers who might provide tools and fit out the proposed workshops. In order to convert the ground floor into a technical school, the infants and junior-aged children were transferred to Carver Street in 1885. Ten years later a new technical block adjoining the Central School was erected to house 'chemical and physical laboratories, machine drawing room, lecture and demonstration rooms, workshops for wood and iron, laundry &c'.

The Technical Instruction Act of 1889 authorized local councils to spend the product of a penny rate on technical and manual instruction. The tax on spirits in 1890—the whisky money grant—was also diverted to county and borough councils to supplement technical and scientific education. The combined legislation freed the School Board from all ambiguity as to its legitimacy in managing an organized science school and enabled it to apply to the Town Council for extra funding for ex-Standard children—those above Standard 7 level who could no longer earn Education Department grants.

Little time was lost in forming a Technical Instruction Committee as an agency of the Town Council, and Sir Henry Stephenson was appointed chairman. Prohibited from subsidizing the teaching of elementary school pupils in the Standards, the object of the Committee was to secure 'the supply of technical instruction out of the rates', ensuring that 'evening school classes were within the reach of the ordinary artisan'. The lion's share of these funds was channelled into the Technical School and Firth University College, the Grammar School, the School of Art, the Church Institute and the School Board's evening classes. Smaller grants were made for the manual instruction of teachers and the Blind Institute where money was allocated for the purchase of pianos and the tools for tuning them. The total income of the Committee from 'the whisky money' and local rates increased over the years from £4,534 in 1891 to £11,002 in 1904 when the Committee, having provided the City Council with its first involvement in Secondary and Technical education, was merged into the new Local Education Authority.[11]

Day schooling at the Central School was now free, all charges being abolished in November 1891, but not before persistent lobbying had convinced the Board that doing so would bring the school within the reach of all classes. Despite consistently achieving 'excellent' awards and lavish praise for the biblical instruction, mathematics, practical physics, chemistry and handicrafts, defects in the arts subjects did emerge—partly owing to the variability of pupil attainments on admission. Unevenness in the standard of English language and the lack of geographical understanding were particularly noticeable. History teaching appeared to be variable but the most persistent curricular weakness was in language training, especially in French.

In the 1890s the school embarked on commercial courses. German, bookkeeping, shorthand, commercial correspondence and similar subjects were added to the curriculum for those pupils staying on beyond Standard 7 and at night school. In response to questions raised by the Chamber of Commerce in 1892, the Committee reported 'thoroughly efficient teaching in all the essential branches of knowledge required to fit young people for business careers'. Moreover, those aiming for the teaching profession were able to prepare for every subject demanded by examination. The Committee was entirely

Figure 39. The Central School, 1879. The Central Higher Grade School creamed off some of the most able pupils in the elementary school sector

satisfied that the measures proposed would secure for Sheffield 'a nearer approximation to the ideal educational ladder from the infant school to college and university or the teaching profession on one side and to the technical school, the manufactory or commercial enterprise on the other'.

The school was described as 'the finest thing of its kind in the country' by the Royal Commission on Secondary Education in 1895[12] and Sheffield School Board applied to the newly created Board of Education (1899) for the recognition of the Central School as a higher elementary school under the Minute of 1900. Syllabuses, curriculum and timetables were revised and modified in order to earn the higher rate of grant eligible to schools offering a four-year course for pupils aged between ten and 15. When the School Board requested discretion on this item because it jeopardized the education of pupil-teacher candidates and others aspiring to enter the technical branch of the University College, the Board of Education sanctioned the science courses but rejected the commercial and literary branches. The commercial courses were then switched to Saturday mornings and evening classes. The effect of this cut-back was drastically to reduce the school roll from 1,146 in 1901 to 943 in 1902, yet that entailed classes being taught regularly in the assembly hall and lecture rooms.

The promise that the Central School would provide the productive skills essential for local industry was never quite fulfilled.[13] More pupils entered the commercial world as clerks or professional assistants than as artisans and industrial workers. Nevertheless, late-Victorian Sheffield recognized the school's inestimable value in meeting the needs of those striving to enter business or manufacturing employment. The promotion of technical subjects had clearly encroached upon the realms of secondary education which was distinguished largely by the social backgrounds of the pupils—'the higher ranks and the liberal professions where the home life may be expected to supplement and strengthen school instruction'.[14] That debate carried on into the twentieth century but the 1902 Education Act opened the door for schools 'other than elementary' and the stage was set for the conversion of the Central School and the Pupil Teachers' Centre into recognizable secondary schools.

Figure 40. A class of Central School boys c. 1900. To the left of the group is the headmaster J.W. Illiffe. The science master J.M. Brown is on the right and the French master J.F. Fah is half hidden towards the back.

Notes

1. Quoted in Bingham, *Sheffield School Board*, p. 178.
2. *SI* (27 April 1861).
3. *SI* (10 January 1874).
4. Birchenough, *History of Elementary Education*, p. 131.
5. *SI* (19 August 1874).
6. See J. Roach, *Secondary Education in England 1870–1902* (1991), pp. 90-101.
7. *SI* (24 December 1874; 15 January 1875; 22 April 1876; 29 January 1877).
8. *Endowed Charities* (Sheffield), pp. 264f., 317f.
9. *SI* (8 January 1879).
10. Quoted in HMSO, *The Education of the Adolescent (Hadow Report)* (1927), p. 20. See also Roach, *Secondary Education*, p. 98.
11. SSB School Management Committee Minutes (14 November 1889), SCA; Bingham, *Sheffield School Board*, pp. 314-19.
12. Quoted in W.H.G. Armytage, 'The Emergent Concept in the System of Education', in Pollard and Holmes, *Economic and Social History*, p. 267.
13. Roach, *Secondary Education*, p. 114.
14. *PP* 1906, *Report on the Consultative Committee upon Questions Affecting Higher Elementary Schools*, pp. 22-23, quoted in Van Der Eyken, *Education, the Child and Society*, p. 138.

Chapter 14

Special Needs and Social Concern 1870–1902

The defective and abnormal child has stimulated the best kind of teachers to make studies that are resulting in improved methods. It is now the turn of the starveling to enter the arena and it is pretty certain that his little person will be the centre of even greater reform.

Margaret McMillan, *London's Children: How Not to Feed Them* (1909)

Industrial expansion in the second half of the nineteenth century attracted an enormous growth in population and created wealth and poverty in equal measure. Five per cent of the population were assisted by parochial relief midway through the century and Sheffield Union was still supporting 4 per cent in 1873.[1] The squalor of those living in the heart of the town was exacerbated even further by the atmospheric pollution and insanitary conditions that encased them. A survey undertaken by *The Builder* in 1861 reported:

Of all the towns surveyed, Sheffield in all matters relating to sanitary appliances is behind them all. The three rivers sluggishly flowing through the town are made the conduits of all imaginable filth. They are polluted with dirt, dust, dung and carrion, the embankments are ragged and ruined, here and there overhung with privies: and often the site of ash and offal heaps…The trades engender some ills but a far more fearful source of trouble is harboured in every alley and street and we might say every house. This immense concourse of people live, eat, drink and sleep in a space crammed with cesspits full of their own ordure, and when the contents of their heaped up ash and offal middins are retained within sight and scent of their dwellings Sheffield is as devoid of the decencies of civilisation as it was in the Dark Ages.[2]

Apart from the workhouse provision, hospital accommodation was totally inadequate to cope with virulent cases of infection and disease.

Infant mortality was abnormally high and still averaged 197 per thousand births between 1885 and 1904. The Children's Hospital was eventually opened in 1876 in the face of determined opposition and the municipal fever hospitals, Winter Street (1884) and Lodge Moor (1888) struggled to stem the tide of widespread epidemics towards the end of the century.[3]

Employment for married women and widows was negligible. After childbirth the majority of mothers were at home to care for their families. Sadly, many of the underclass married very young and having worked in the more unhealthy trades were physically incapable of producing vigorous, healthy children. Many died when young whilst others succumbed to the scourge of smallpox, tuberculosis and scarlet fever leaving them weak, blind, deaf, and mentally or physically handicapped.

Smallpox was particularly virulent in 1863, and the Town Council implemented the 1853 Vaccination Act which required all infants to be vaccinated. Opposition to compulsory vaccination was led by Isaac Ironside. Having successfully inoculated his first three children himself but failed with the fourth he argued that the benefits were slight compared with the army of 'Jenner quacks, spies and informers' who would lay information.[4] A new Vaccination Act in 1867 reinforced earlier legislation and one of the first items on the School Board agenda was the recommendation that managers of each school be empowered to examine the arms of every child on admission to ascertain whether or not the child had been vaccinated. Offenders were reported to the Board and by the 1880s it was estimated that over 85 per cent of all children were immunized.

Handicapped Children ·

Deaf–mute children were the first group of handicapped children catered for by the Board. Private schools for the deaf and mute existed in the 1860s but when Joseph Farrer offered to transfer his school in Gloucester Street to the Board it was rejected. A Roman Catholic school for the deaf was established in Woodhouse by the Misses Edwards where they employed a Belgian teacher of embroidery. In addition to the day pupils, seven children were resident in 1871 but only one came from Sheffield. In the census of that year 15 deaf children and 9 mute children were recorded in the borough.

Although the School Board recognized the need for central provision, a free school was not opened until 1879. The Division Street rooms of the Adult Deaf and Dumb Association were made available for a morning school six days a week under the direction of George Stephenson. By the end of the year 25 boys and girls were registered. The Quaker industrialist, Charles Doncaster, took a particular interest in their progress and examined the older pupils in lip-reading, signs and finger language.[5] In 1882, Skelton Cole reported '30 children on roll, the arithmetic was good and their copybook writing was both clean and neat'.

In the absence of any state provision for handicapped pupils, the School Board drew attention to this deficiency by asking the Cross Commission to consider state aid for the elementary education of the deaf in 1886. Because the ratio of pupils to teachers was necessarily high the costs were correspondingly greater than for ordinary classes and most of the pupils were from poor backgrounds, 'unable to help themselves'.

Parental pressure, supported by the Deaf and Dumb Association, led to full-time day schooling. Premises in Charles Street were acquired in 1887 and the master's salary was increased from £50 per annum to £100 and an unqualified assistant was also employed. Once the 1893 Education (Blind and Deaf) Act was on the statute-book HMI took an active interest in the school and objected to the 'make shift' premises. They urged the need for two qualified teachers, improved resources and expressed dissatisfaction with the oral system adopted with the younger children 'who mixed too freely on Sundays and at playtime on weekdays with children taught by signs'.

The day classes were transferred to the Orchard Lane wing of the Central School where 45 children attended regularly. The more severely handicapped with limited mental capacity were found boarding places in the Yorkshire Institute for the Deaf in Doncaster, Boston Spa (Catholic) and the Jewish Home for the Deaf. Not until 1922 was the Sheffield School for the Deaf established in Ringinglow Road.

The periodic spread of contagious diseases inevitably left some blind or partially sighted. Few children were born blind. According to the census of 1881 only 11 out of the 143 blind inhabitants were born blind.[6] Most of them lost their sight through illness or industrial accident. Whereas industrial training for blind adults was already in operation, concern for the education of blind children did not surface until 1873. When the Sheffield Board of Guardians sent a subscription to the Yorkshire School for the Blind in York, the Local Government Board opposed the contribution but encouraged them to send blind pupils to the school and pay for their maintenance.[7] Meanwhile, the Secretary of the Blind Institute raised the issue with the School Board having identified 25 school-age blind children in the borough.

In 1875 the bequest of Daniel Holy for the endowment of a residential Blind School was released and a site in Manchester Road was chosen. Supported by donations, subscriptions, school fees and the sale of handmade goods, Tapton Mount Residential School for the Blind was opened in 1879 to accommodate 80 pupils. By 1887, 52 boys and girls were in residence.[8]

Children over the age of seven were admitted 'who were blind or only just able to see light, not deficient in intellect, must have been vaccinated against or have had small pox and must not be subject to fits'. Fees for those under twelve years were £7 per annum, and £10 for older children. Pupils from outside the borough were charged a more economic rate of £10 and £12 respectively. Education for blind children in the workhouse was finally realized.

The curriculum emphasized musical activities and, in 1882, 22 children were learning to play the piano. Handicrafts were fundamental. Girls were trained to cane chairs, taught sewing and knitting, while basketwork proved popular with the boys. Instruction in the Braille system of reading and printing was given, together with some unsuccessful experiments in the form of raised lettering. Once the gymnasium was fitted out, the physical exercises combined with a well-balanced diet significantly improved the children's well-being.

Whilst approving the use of spectacles for those in day school with defective vision, the Board saw no need for separate provision for the blind when they were so adequately catered for at Tapton Mount. In a memorial to the Royal Commission in 1888 it was stressed that 'an institute carried on exclusively for the care of the blind would involve more difficulties than are encountered in dealing with deaf and dumb children'. Under the 1893 Education (Blind and Deaf) Act, the Board applied for the school to be certified by the Department and the expenditure on education, board and lodging for up to 70 blind scholars was duly recognized.

Not until the last decade of the nineteenth century was any attempt made to segregate the educationally subnormal, physically handicapped, delicate or epileptic into special classes. Normally they remained in the lower Standards, a burden to their teachers and classmates, and a strain on the grant-earning capacity of the school. Compared with the clearly definable category of the deaf and blind, the Board believed that those with a medical condition required special treatment outside their legitimate province and should be the responsibility of private philanthropy. When asked by the Guardians to arrange for the education of children in the Childrens' Homes Hospital in 1895, the Board restated that 'they had no power to provide for the instruction of children elsewhere than in a public elementary school within the meaning of the Elementary Education Acts'.

Nationwide pressure culminating in the 1899 Education (Defective and Epileptic) Act empowered school boards to provide special accommodation for such handicapped children. In 1900 the School Board's inspector was directed to investigate the problem so far as Sheffield was concerned and report on extreme cases 'who ought not to be taught along with other children on account of weak intellect &c'. The outcome was the formation of a special class for mentally impaired children in the recently erected Pomona Street Board School. Under the superintendence of a newly appointed subcommittee, parents of handicapped pupils were invited to bring the children to a medical examination where it was considered that 17 of them could benefit from specialist teaching.

The Board's scheme to experiment with special classes within the confines of ordinary schools posed peculiar problems; not the least was the difficulty of transporting children day by day to their units. Suitably qualified teachers were scarce and ordinary classrooms were only approved as an interim measure. The provision of permanent buildings at the dawn of special education was not thought practicable but the need for a medical officer to oversee the specific nature of the programme was acknowledged. Two special units were organized in 1900. The Pomona Street class opened in June with 13 children. Vacant land adjoining the school was fenced and levelled so that gardening could be taken as a manual occupation. A more permanent centre was opened in Newhall in October with 29 on roll. Boys were instructed in woodwork and girls in cookery. In the first year 38 children were classified as suitable but the severely mentally handicapped and 'congenital idiots' were regarded as ineducable and recommended for institutional training.

HMI took a very sympathetic look at the Newhall situation and identified the disadvantages of trying to teach two classes in an unpartitioned room, especially when tackling reading. The teachers also had to contend with street noise as well as the uproar in the junior boys' playground. To compensate they suggested that 'proper arrangements ought to be made for giving the teachers a reasonable interval of rest between morning and afternoon for the work is hard'. Approval was also granted for a further 30 handicapped children to be taught in the Lancasterian School providing that 'the small ventilating window from the neighbouring slaughter house which overlooks the playground is removed'. The Medical Officer of Health defended the situation on the grounds that the slaughter of pigs was clean, free from effluvia, and the acquisition of a public abbatoir was imminent. The stench in fact derived from the tempering of steel in fish oils at an adjacent steel works.

In 1901, Dr Caley, the School Board's medical officer, was elated to discover that, after twelve months of specialist teaching, some pupils were able to return to mainstream schools having made educational progress beyond his expectations. It was also becoming clearer that the educationally subnormal were a very wide category and that extreme cases could not be catered for by every local authority. Severe physical handicaps proved less of a problem. Only two cases of children requiring invalid chairs or appliances were reported.

The integration of handicapped children in the conventional classroom was now thought detrimental to the education of all, particularly in manual subjects where they demanded the teacher's whole attention and distracted the rest of the class. HMI were not impressed when visiting mixed cookery lessons locally and the School Board resolved to acquire sites at Highfields and Springvale and convey the youngsters to the centres. Even so, real progress was limited until the passing of the Education (Administrative Provisions) Act in 1907 and the setting-up of the School Medical Service a year later. Handicapped children living outside the city boundary were even less fortunate. The West Riding Education Authority which absorbed the Handsworth and Ecclesfield School Boards funded the boarding-out of the severely handicapped but overall their special services were totally inadequate for years.[9]

Provision for the Under Fives
Middle-class children spent a lot of time playing in the nursery but evidence of public initiatives for working-class children is confined to London and Manchester.[10] However, day nurseries did open elsewhere and one was established in St Philip's Road in 1873 for mothers 'obliged to go out to work'. Admission was later extended to the offspring of 'dissolute and drunken husbands'. The crèche was opened by a group of ladies, headed by Mrs R.E. Leader, who charged 3d per day. Like similar voluntary action it had to be self-supporting. Between

12 and 18 toddlers, from one month old to five years, 'kept happy and healthy by kind nurses, good food and treatment', attended daily.

In February 1877, Mundella and Moss were most impressed on their visit to the nursery; 'cleanliness everywhere apparent, the watchfulness and care exhibited gave very much satisfaction'. The toddlers were supplied with milk, a midday meal, 'looked after and amused'.[11] In 1892 the day nursery was rehoused in Edward Street (Beet Street) and opened by the Countess of Wharncliffe and the patron, Lady Edmund Talbot. Admission charges were reduced to 2d per day. A century later the day nursery still serves the needs of the neighbourhood but local authorities were unable to provide nursery services until 1918.

The infant school movement of the 1830s publicized the economic advantages of schools freeing parents of young children to carry on working but they failed to capture wide support. As the School Board extended school provision, parents were invited to send their infants to school as soon as they could toddle 'not that they might learn mere book lessons but be taught order and obedience and then they would get on much better'.[12] Three-year-olds could not be refused admission and 'babies' classes proliferated. With the demise of the dame schools it was reckoned that 40 per cent of infants between the ages of three and five attended elementary schools at the end of the century.[13] The percentage of infants under five showed a marked increase after the abolition of school fees in 1891 but proportionately decreased in the first decade of the twentieth century. The table below indicates the number of children under five attending board schools, matched I suspect by a similar proportion in the voluntary sector.

Table 14.1

Infants aged between 3 and 7 in Sheffield Board schools, 1890–1900

Year	Infants under 5	Percentage of infants under 5	Infants between 5 and 7
1890	1,910	24.5	5,875
1895	2,486	25.2	7,381
1900	3,814	36.7	6,583

Child Welfare

The humanitarian impulses that inspired the Society for Bettering the Condition of the Poor and the introduction of soup-kitchens at the turn of the nineteenth century invariably re-emerged when times were hard. Feeding the poorest children was at the heart of the Ragged

School's success and in December 1869 the managers of St Paul's schools arranged to provide dinners for their starvelings. Again in 1878, 200 children were fed daily with a bowl of soup and a chunk of bread. Princess Street Wesleyan School did the same, and in March, Holy Trinity, Wicker, reported that 2,024 children had received meals in the past fortnight.[14]

Wretchedness that year exceeded all previous experience and a relief committee set up by the Mayor raised over £12,000 which included donations from the Prince and Princess of Wales, the Duke and Duchess of Norfolk, and Florence Nightingale. A considerable number of school fees were remitted and the headteacher of the Parish Church School recorded that the school board officer called on 12 December 1878 'with a list of six and half foolscap pages of names of children belonging to the Crofts Board School exempted from paying school fees'. The list represented but a small proportion of those in distress, and parochial relief schemes were organized in St Stephen's, St George's, Attercliffe and Carbrook schools. In All Saints parish, children from Grimesthorpe, Carlisle Street East, Newhall and Brightside were fed daily by the Scripture Readers and Town Missioners.

A children's refuge was organized for the town-centre street children. Five hundred children who regularly wandered the streets, sold newspapers, matches or toys, were gathered together three times a week. In February 1881 the *Sheffield Independent* reported that the organizing committee doubled the number of tickets to a thousand and that, since January, 11,966 children consumed 140 gallons of soup, 345 gallons of cocoa, 2,420 loaves of bread (4,840 lbs) and 1,210 buns. 240 café tickets were issued 'owing to the breakdown of a chimney' at an average cost of $1^{1}/_{2}$d.[15]

The voluntary schools resumed their role as social agencies late in 1884. Between 156 and 609 penny dinners were provided daily in the Charles Street Mission Rooms for children in the Parish Church School and St Paul's. Archdeacon Blakeney augmented the provision, and soup was provided by the Mayor's relief committee in other selected schools. School fees were reduced to one penny which created an influx of infants attracted by a combination of cheaper schooling and free school meals.

At the same time, the School Board set up a committee to oversee the provision of penny dinners in the Board schools. A basement in the Crofts Board School was the first to be nominated. Duchess Road, Huntsman's Gardens, Burgoyne Road and Park were added to the list.

When the head of Burgoyne Road asked permission to use the cookery apparatus twice per week for the poorest children, the experiment had to be abandoned 'because it interfered with the ordinary work of the school'. In March 1886, Park Board School provided penny and halfpenny dinners and 40 free meals to their own scholars and children from Park National Schools. The service ceased in April when the demand diminished. In February 1890, Crofts Board School was again allowed to serve halfpenny dinners, supplied by the caretaker and supervised by the teachers.[16]

Whereas the School Board's powers to organize school meals were restricted until 1906 there were no such constraints on voluntary action and the scale of provision was considerably extended in the 1890s. Milk breakfasts twice per week were introduced in the Parish Church School in 1892 plus free dinners for the needy. The free tickets issued by St Paul's and the Parish Church schools improved attendance significantly as they were only offered to regular attenders. The meals were subsidized from funds collected by the Church of England Society for Waifs and Strays and the National Society for the Prevention of Cruelty to Children. One headteacher observed that 'the recipients are more regular, more attentive, brighter in themselves and show a greater aptitude for mastering the subjects taught'. Breakfasts were also provided at Red Hill Wesleyan School and on Sunday mornings in the Montgomery Hall by the Sunday School Union.

One outcome of the colliers' riot in Broughton Lane and ensuing lock-out in September 1893 was the provision of breakfasts of cocoa, bread and butter daily including Saturdays and Sundays, and soup dinners at Carbrook National School from September through to spring. The head of St Paul's commented that 'the present distress appears to be bringing many families in this district on the verge of starvation—the children are undergoing untold miseries'. From 1895 the serving of breakfast, dinner and tea became a daily occurrence in most of the town-centre voluntary schools. The meals were organized and supervised by the staff from funds donated by managers and friends. In May 1899 Emmerson Bainbridge MP donated dinners for the Parish Church School because 'the destitution of the parish is appalling'. When HMI visited St Luke's in 1901 they commented that 'The children are from very poor homes and some are palpably in want of food'.

Inadequate clothing was another cause for concern. Speaking at a Church Conference in May 1869, Revd J.B. Draper, Vicar of All

Figure 41. Soup for the poor outside No. 9 Tannery Street, Woodhouse. Children and adults were fed daily when times were hard.

Saints, said, 'The want of clothing is a far greater cause of absence from school than most people recognise. A provision of clothing would have to be made if a compulsory system is to work satisfactorily for the children of decent parents would not otherwise associate with them'.[17]

Child welfare in the nineteenth century was invariably the mission of charity and voluntary service. Before 1876, the Ragged School was the most obvious recipient of clothing and footwear. Though initially allotted as rewards, the distribution of petticoats, trousers and clogs became a regular undertaking. Clogs were generously given by the employees of Cammell's Cyclops Works and many other gifts went unreported. Both School Board and voluntary school managers recoiled from admitting the ill-clad street children outside the benefit of Poor Law supervision. In 1877 the School Board conceded that such children should be educated with ordinary scholars but took the view that the provision of sufficient clothing 'seems rather to call for effort in the direction of a charity organization than for interference at the expense of the School Board fund of the Borough'.

The following year the Revd J.B. Draper reiterated his plea for clothing.

> One great need in this destitute district besides that of food is clothes. Many of the women and children are most scantily and indecently clad—few have a single article beyond what they now wear. Many children are bare footed. Parcels of boots and cast off clothing will be thankfully received by the clergy or dissenting ministers in the distressed districts.[18]

During the 1880s the School Board reported that gifts of suits of clothing for poor children had been received from wealthy donors. Clothing and boots were also distributed in the voluntary schools where meals were prepared. A concerted effort was made in the 1890s. In co-operation with the voluntary sector, the School Board permitted simultaneous collections for children's charities. In 1895 the Poor Children's Clothing Fund enabled welfare officers to distribute boots, clogs and garments on a much wider scale. Two years later the School Children's Clothing Guild was allowed the use of a room by the Board for the collection and parcelling of items. The Guild was able to allocate 1,416 garments, 500 pairs of boots, 200 pairs of clogs and 300 pairs of stockings. The Sheffield Voluntary Schools Clothing Guild established in 1903 performed a similar function for the Voluntary schools but over the years both organizations targeted the schools of greatest disadvantage, yet some parents still found it difficult to accept charity.

Notes

1.   *SI* (20 September 1856; 16 October 1873).

2.   *SI* (28 September 1861: 7 October 1861).

3.   *The Sheffield Hospitals*, Local History Leaflet 7 (1959), SCL.

4.   *SI* (12 March 1863; 1 July 1863; 12 April 1866; 16 August 1867).

5.   *SI* (15 July 1880). For the deaf and mute in Handsworth see Hadfield, *A History of St. Marie's*, p. 146.

6.   M.P. Dunn, *For the Love of Children* (1989), p. 23.

7.   *SI* (6 March 1873; 14 November 1873).

8.   *Endowed Charities* (Sheffield), pp. 292f.; Dunn, *For the Love of Children*, p. 25. For more detailed study of the blind school, see B. Bournat, 'The History of Tapton Mount, Broomhill, Sheffield 1879–1947' (unpublished MEd thesis, Sheffield University 1982–83).

9.   P.H. Gosden and P.R. Sharp, *The Development of an Education Service: The West Riding* (1978), p. 138.

10.   N. Whitbread, *The Evolution of the Nursery Infant School* (1972), pp. 44-45.

11.   *SI* (12 October 1875; 2 February 1877).

12.   *SI* (4 March 1873).

13.   Whitbread, *The Nursery Infant School*, p. 144.

14.   *SI* (5 March 1878; 9 March 1878; 15 March 1878).

15.   *SI* (3 March 1881; 25 March 1881). Emmerson Bainbridge erected a home for Waifs and Strays in Norfolk Street in memory of his wife Effie in 1894.

16.   Bingham, *Sheffield School Board*, pp. 237-39.

17.   *SI* (25 May 1869).

18.   *SI* (23 November 1878).

Chapter 15

Evening Schools and Classes 1870–1902

The most trying and dangerous part of boys' and girls' lives is *JUST WHEN THEY LEAVE SCHOOL* and are constantly tempted to idleness and vice. Good habits formed at this period last for a lifetime.

EVENING CLASSES are working at Lowfield, Huntsman's Gardens, Pye Bank, Philadelphia, Springfield and the Central Schools and the teachers will welcome all scholars however backward they might be. No one need despair of learning.

By this means *BOYS AND GIRLS ARE KEPT HEALTHILY EMPLOYED* in ways that will make them able to *EARN BETTER WAGES* and everyone of any age can *MAKE UP FOR LOST TIME*.

Address to Parents, Sheffield School Board (October 1886)

Evening schools in 1886 were still considered an extension of elementary education and limited to pupils between the ages of 12 and 21 by the Code of 1876. The number of young people seeking basic instruction at night had declined and the School Board welcomed the campaign by the Trades Council and Improved Evening Schools Association to revitalize the classes in 1885.[1] They proposed to improve attendance by influencing their parents and employers, recommended the introduction of musical entertainment and magic lanterns to illustrate lectures and offered to provide competent teachers for classes in designing, modelling, carving and drawing, and so on. Headteachers were encouraged to promote the advantages of continuing education but the Board was still constrained by regulations that stipulated basic subject qualification before grant aid could be given; for instance, a girl wishing to take laundry or cookery must also have passed Standard 6.

Faced with the fact that less than one in 40 girls advanced beyond Standard 4 in 1870, prospective members of the first School Board were in no doubt about the need to extend instruction once schooldays were over. Mayor Thomas Moore declared his intentions quite clearly—'to carry out the compulsory clauses of the 1870 Act, providing night schools for those children whose assistance was needed to the support of the families to which they belonged'.[2]

At that time, elementary evening classes in basic subjects were available in every adult educational institute and in all the larger voluntary schools throughout the borough. Science and other 'useful subjects' were mainly concentrated in the town centre. The Ragged School evening classes were long-standing as was the North Church Street Adult Educational Institute, where for twenty years, intelligent working-class members devoted most of their Sundays to instructing young men 'of their own class' in rudimentary education.

The Friends' First-Day School (1845) opened new premises in 1871 and extended its evening provision. By 1876 there were 285 members in 20 elementary classes for men and seven for women. Ten years later there were over a thousand members but attendance at the thrice-weekly night school declined and it was eventually discontinued. The Methodist-inspired Christian and Educational Institute on Surrey Street developed into one of the town's more successful evening schools. It stemmed from the 'lamentable deficiency' in elementary education of its senior Bible class members and in the 1860s and 1870s broadened its curriculum considerably. In 1875 it presented 130 15- to 18-year-olds for examination. The elementary classes of the Church Institute continued to attract the highest government grants for the night schools of Sheffield.[3]

Many of the widespread Christian Institutes maintained their religious influence on their students by offering non-vocational subjects such as music, elocution and sport in addition to the three Rs and biblical instruction. The more energetic and gifted voluntary school masters, anxious to supplement their income, held evening classes and were very critical of the age limits imposed by the Department which confined grant aid to the 12 to 18 age-group until 1876.

In October 1871 the School Board recommended the establishment of evening schools but waited until Newhall and Philadelphia were open in 1873 before beginning operations. Initially the classes opened four evenings per week and teachers were paid £2 per month for each twice-weekly two-hour session, plus an additional shilling for every scholar attending regularly. HMI Sandford pressed for the extension of night school provision and quarterly examinations, but when the Board opened night schools in Broomhill, Netherthorpe, Park and Carbrook in September 1874 the student response was patchy and Broomhill soon closed. Teachers' salaries were eventually readjusted to embrace the government grant, student fees, plus free use of gas, books, apparatus and schoolroom. When the Nunnery Colliery applied to rent rooms in the Park temporary Board school for the elementary education and skill training of their workforce, the Board whilst sympathetic were obliged to refuse permission for activities outside their jurisdiction. Evening classes for girls and young women were strictly single-sex and conducted only by females. They were organized to begin and end a quarter of an hour earlier than male classes in order to discourage improper behaviour.

During the first ten years of the Board's administration, Netherthorpe evening school proved to be one of the most successful. In 1876, 104 scholars were examined: 64 were presented in reading and with one exception all passed. 60 passed in handwriting and 52 were successful in arithmetic. HMI commented, 'In this school there is life and vigour, the Master has shown a great amount of patient labour and is really instructing and improving his scholars'. At the close of 1876, nine effective schools were in operation—The Crofts, Walkley, Springfield, Pyebank, Fulwood, Grimesthorpe, Newhall, Park, Carbrook and Netherthorpe, with 773 students on roll.

In an attempt to stimulate further education in and beyond the town of Sheffield the South Yorkshire Association for Promoting Education in Evening Schools was formed.[4] Inspired by HMI Sandford and chaired by Lord Wharncliffe, prizes were awarded for achievement and merit but the initiative ceased when Sandford departed. Meanwhile Sheffield School Board was proud to reveal that 59 per cent of scholars in evening classes were studying the fourth to seventh Standards and only 41 per cent were being taught in the more elementary grades. A demand for special subjects such as geography, grammar, English history and other useful subjects embraced in the new Code emerged, but they could not be fully met without the Department's support which was not forthcoming.

When the School Board established evening classes in the new Central School they were clearly extending the boundaries of elementary education. The curriculum was far in advance of anything attempted in the district evening schools. The professed aim was 'to supply a link between the classes and the classes at Firth College' and was seen as an integral rung on Sheffield's educational ladder. William

Ripper, the science master at the Central School, was appointed organizing master for the evening school. Science and art classes were established immediately and language classes in French, German and Latin were started. The Higher Evening department included machine drawing and construction, mathematics, animal physiology, physiography, magnetism and chemistry. Fees were fixed at 6d per week or 5 shillings per quarter.

The enforcement of the rule that every scholar must take an examination in the basic subjects in order to attain grant aid for additional subjects accounted for the falling-off in attendance in the district schools—a decline that was mirrored nationally. In 1882 only six local authority night schools were in operation: the Central School, Carbrook, Springfield, Langsett Road, Lowfield and Darnall. Reporting on the contraction, Skelton Cole had mixed feelings because in his view 'there were indications that the purely elementary element of evening school work was being superseded by something better. It was not always easy to make them attractive to young people who have been all day hard at work in other ways.'[5]

Attempts to make the evening schools more popular and attractive from 1885 onwards set the School Board on a collision course with the local government auditors. Magic lanterns and slides purchased to reinforce geography teaching were questioned by ratepayers who argued that the expenditure of £7 11s 9d on such apparatus was unreasonable and should not be allowed. 'The subject should be taught orally and through books without resorting to visual aids.' Fortunately for education, the Education Department ruled the expenditure admissible. Nevertheless, school boards had little power to exercise discretion over the fiscal parameters of elementary education.

By 1890 the slide presentation of lessons in geography, history and elementary science—permitted only on Monday evenings—improved the .attendance at many schools, especially in Sharrow. HMI commented that 'if all schools were as popular and attractive there would soon be a larger increase in the number of young folks willing and eager to devote their evenings to worthy pursuits'. Shorthand classes and laundry work at Sharrow contributed to the school's success. At Gleadless Road School, physical exercises proved popular. Sergeant Major Moss was appointed drill instructor at one guinea per school per term. Boxing, which had been encouraged, was now discontinued. As the evening continuation schools continued to expand they branched out on a wide scale of commercial subjects: bookkeeping, commercial correspondence, shorthand (all stages), commercial French, German and Spanish, arithmetic, geography and typewriting.

The resurgence of interest in the schools created its own problems. An unruly element was attracted to some classes. At Huntsman's Gardens the police were employed on patrol duty to preserve the peace at closing-time when gangs of lads bent on mischief provoked the more serious scholars. In May 1887 HMI commented, 'The rough boys attracted to these evening meetings have sorely taxed the powers of the teachers especially in the upper divisions to maintain even moderate order. Their attainments in elementary subjects are as good as could be expected under these circumstances.' The master at Broomhill was faced with casual indifference. 'He would have done better had he from the first repressed frivolity and allowed those only to continue in attendance who clearly desired to improve themselves.' As more schools opened in the 1890s more teachers were employed but the proportion of weak and inexperienced staff also increased and caused the School Board considerable disquiet.

In 1892 all elementary classes became free both for adolescents and adults. The additional costs were met from subsidies by the Town Council empowered by the Local Taxation Act of 1890. The increased funding enabled the School Board to extend its practical work for both sexes, provide better scientific and technical apparatus and offer free studentships in the science and art classes.

The Education Department's long-awaited revision of evening school conditions in 1893, plus the abolition of fees for the basic subjects, injected new life into the Board's evening schools and the intake of students expanded sixfold in as many years. Average attendance in 1891 was only 725. Enrolment more than doubled in 1892 to 1,787 and by 1897, 9,069 students were on roll. By this time most of the voluntary sector institutes had folded. The People's College closed in 1879 on the opening of Firth College. The Mechanics' Institute was dissolved in 1890 and the adolescent students were absorbed into the Board's evening schools. The resources of the Institute enabled twelve exhibitions to be offered at Firth College and when the trustees closed their books the balance provided scholarships 'tenable only by persons of the artisan and labouring classes' at the University College in 1897. The Church Institute continued to enrol between 1,500 and 1,600 students annually to the end of the century but with the introduction of the 1902 Education Act it was considered something of an anachronism and closed in 1903.

The revisions of 1893 endorsed the Cross Commission recommendation that evening continuation schools need no longer confine themselves to elementary education as a condition of grant aid. Students who had passed Standard 5 were excused further examination in the three Rs. All under 21 years could be recognized for grant, and capitation was to be calculated on the basis of hours of instruction rather than the average attendance. This alleviated the problem of scholars arriving straight from work after long shop hours, overtime and so on forfeiting their attendance mark if a few minutes late. Examination by HMI was replaced by inspection.

Free from the more restrictive evening school codes HMI proposed the segregation of adolescents from adults in order to attract men who were likely to be inhibited by the presence of youths more recently educated. The upturn in recruitment of older women highlighted the need for separate consideration. Adequate and less exposed toilet facilities were necessary. All females were required to use separate staircases to prevent them passing unscreened male 'offices'. Dark playgrounds were hazards to be avoided.

The withdrawal of grant aid for millinery, fancy needlework, paper and leatherwork in 1896 provoked an outcry. The Board had no option but to levy higher fees for those taking more than two subjects in order to recoup the costs of buckram, wire, cotton, needles, muslin and other materials. It was no longer practical to take single subjects and recreative 'women's subjects' were clearly threatened. The substantial increase in subjects ineligible for grant compelled the School Board to apply to the City Council in 1898 for more financial assistance from the 'whisky money' and Technical Instruction Act funds. Additional income came via the scholarship scheme devised by Sir Frederick Thorpe Mappin. The scheme enabled the Board to send young working men free of charge to the Central School science and art classes and to the Technical School promoted by Mappin, the eminent scientist Henry Clifton Sorby, Sir Henry Stephenson and others in 1886.

At the start of the twentieth century, local authority evening schools were held in 15 Board schools and in another six voluntary schools. Inevitably, enrolments fluctuated from year to year and some classes were of short duration. Opening hours were adjusted to accommodate females from 7 to 9 p.m. and males from 7.30 to 9.30 p.m. three evenings per week. Although elementary classes were free to regular students a returnable deposit was imposed at the beginning of each session.

Fears that expenditure on technical and vocational courses would be severely restricted if the Cockerton Judgment of 1900, which censured the London School Board for financing post-elementary education from the rates, was not immediately reversed or rectified led to a petition in 1901. The School Board argued vigorously that 'the development of evening continuation schools were essential to a national system of education in order that full advantage may be derived from the education already acquired in the day schools...Interference with the work therein carried on would be a national calamity.'

Amending legislation and the 1902 Education Act enabled the newly created Education Committee to undertake an objective analysis of evening-school provision in the City.[6] Released from the constraint 'that the principal part of the education given must be elementary' the Local Authority was free to lift much of the work above elementary school level. Even so, the schools continued to attract adolescents rather than adults—many of whom enrolled on leaving school and rapidly disappeared. The difficulty lay in stimulating others to return after an interval of years to relearn what they had forgotten.

Spanning the School Board era but dedicated to the higher education of the middle classes and the more intelligent artisans was the University Extension Movement. The movement stemmed from the deep concern for girls' secondary education and the training of women teachers. In 1867, the North of England Council for Promoting the Higher Education of Women invited the young James Stuart, Fellow of Trinity College, Cambridge, to give a series of lectures in five northern towns and cities including Sheffield.[7]

The women's movement attracted the attention of those involved in promoting wider educational opportunities and the foundation of provincial colleges. By 1873 the Extension Movement was recognized by the University of Cambridge and in May 1874 Sheffield School Board considered the practicality of bringing University Extension courses to the town but decided that the proposition was outside its terms of reference. At a meeting in December, presided over by Mark Firth, the Revd Samuel Earnshaw outlined how the University was prepared to place 'its resources at the disposal of the towns in the country bringing the advantages of University education to the very doors of the people'.[8]

The first University Extension lectures, given by Cambridge lecturers, were delivered in January 1875. Literature, history and English grammar attracted the largest audiences, followed by physical and economic science. Trade union interest was sharpened and such groups as the Scissor Grinders' Union paid the fees for all their members between the ages of 18 and 21 to attend the classes on political economy.[9] Pupil-teachers profited from the more liberal studies and the courses for women enjoyed enormous success. In the first three years 3,566 student tickets were sold—an annual average that exceeded the People's College and the Mechanics' Institute attendances together even in their most flourishing years.[10]

The singular success of the University Extension Movement aroused wider interest in the development of Firth College which opened in 1879. The professed aim of the college 'was the promotion of the moral, social and intellectual elevation of the masses as well as the middle and upper classes of the town'.[11] The decision to concentrate on advanced teaching diverged somewhat from the Extension lecture programme except for the evening classes in chemistry which developed on University Extension lines. The introduction of popular lectures in the main hall on Saturday nights—monthly at first but later fortnightly—appealed to regular audiences of between two and four hundred.

One elementary school boy whose career was fashioned by evening study at Firth College was John Alfred Green. A pupil at Parson Cross School, he was admitted as a candidate for pupil-teacher apprenticeship aged $13^1/_2$ in Langsett Road Board School in 1886. Given sole responsibility for Standards 4 to 6 in his third year, he went on to qualify for Borough Road Training College. Within a month of his first teaching appointment at Park Board School he was released to take up a post as Junior Tutor at Borough Road before eventually becoming Professor of Education at University College, Bangor, and returning to Sheffield in 1905 as the first Professor of Education at the University.

Pressured by the Trades Council for the progressive advance of evening classes and bolstered by newspaper agitation, Extension Courses in Firth College were resuscitated in 1887. In addition to the classes arranged in college, lectures were given in various parts of the borough—fostering further the demand for women's education. In working-class districts such as Attercliffe, Brightside and Heeley, free lectures were organized and subsidized by the Town Council.[12] In a letter to the *Sheffield Independent* ten years later Dr Arthur Hall, later Professor of Medicine at Sheffield University, wrote:

We all know how the middle and upper classes have benefitted intellectually from the presence of Firth College amongst us, but perhaps there are many who do not realise what a great work is being done by the College amongst the poorer classes, largely by the free Extension lectures delivered in the less well-to-do parts of Sheffield. Managers of our large works could I think tell us how greatly the working men appreciate these free lectures given at their very doors; the numbers that attend them and their desire for more, are however sufficient evidence.[13]

The Technical and Medical Schools combined with Firth College to create University College in 1897. Between 1897 and 1904, evening classes increased from 800 to more than 1,300 per year—the Technical School drawing the majority. The evening classes were clearly successful in attracting skilled artisans, clerks and tradesmen, and there was a growing demand for Saturday classes by elementary school teachers, but the less skilled were largely untouched. Whilst the University Extension Movement had 'an air of respectability about it' the intellectual direction had shifted from the clergy-dominated courses in the People's College and the Christian Educational Institutes to the professional academic specialists who were to staff the provincial universities, such as Sheffield which received its charter in 1905.

By the end of the nineteenth century the range of opportunities for young adults to extend their elementary education was both varied and accessible. Increasing co-operation between industry, the evening schools and the Extension Movement had brought some of the working classes to the threshold of higher education. What was required was the coordination of the various avenues into a progressive educational system, not only to fulfil the dreams of its architects but also to satisfy the demands of the twentieth century.

Notes

1.   SSB School Management Minutes (24 July 1885), SCA.
2.   *SI* (28 November 1870).
3.   J.H. Barber, *Sheffield Friends Adult School, An Account of the First Ten Years* (1885); J.A. Woodcock, *Surrey Street United Methodist Church, One Hundred Years* (1931); W. Odom, *Fifty Years of Church Life* (1917); *Sheffield Red Books* (1870–1903); Bingham, *Sheffield School Board*, p. 224.
4.   *SI* (7 June 1878).
5.   S. Cole, *Sheffield School Board Statement* (1882).

6.   M.E. Sadler, *Report on Secondary and Higher Education*, Sheffield Education Committee (1903).

7.   J.F.C. Harrison, *Learning and Living* (1961), pp. 221-35.

8.   A.W. Chapman, *The Story of a Modern University: A History of the University of Sheffield* (1955), p. 14. See also *SI* (4 December 1874; 11 December 1874).

9.   *SI* (6 March 1875).

10.   *Development of Adult Education in Sheffield*, Sheffield Social Survey Committee (1932).

11.   Chapman, *Modern University*, pp. 14f.; W.M. Hicks, *Local Colleges and the Higher Education of the People* (1886).

12.   Chapman, *Modern University*, pp. 86f.; Hicks, *Local Colleges*.

13.   Chapman, *Modern University*, pp. 99-100.

Conclusion

The wealth of documentary evidence available for the study of elementary education has inevitably led to an emphasis on the development of formal schooling and obscured informal methods of learning and the countless number of teachers 'who came forward to supply that demand for education for which there existed no adequate public provision'. Informal learning was the tradition of centuries, long before any child saw the inside of a schoolroom. As society developed, fitting the child 'for the work of life' evolved as the overriding purpose of education. Parents, relatives, friends and neighbours were all made use of in the search for basic literacy. Self-instruction features in many working-class autobiographies of the eighteenth and nineteenth centuries[1] and, from 1800 onwards, a combination of Sunday schools, evening classes and improvement societies sustained the cultural development of the people alongside the amalgam of public and private sector schooling.

By the same token, working-class private school teachers have been dismissed as mere 'baby minders' and peripheral to any serious discussion on education. Yet each and every one contributed to the rise of popular literacy. The 65 per cent male literacy rate achieved in 1760, in the total absence of a centralized public policy and only a handful of endowed schools, reinforces the notion that the popular demand for literacy before 1800 was met largely by the private school market.

The monitorial schools offered a solution to the illiteracy of the burgeoning township but for many parents the daily journey for their children was a step too far. For others the mechanistic ordering of little ones marshalled into barn-like vaults could not compare with the cosy if chaotic informal surroundings of the dame or common day school where 25 or 30 youngsters could share the individual attention of a caring adult.

As formal education groped its way forward from the province of religion to that of utility, it responded in turn to local initiative, private philanthropy, evangelism, social unrest, the fear of democracy and the commercial and industrial needs of society. Charitable schooling for the lower classes, deemed sufficient for the market town in 1818, was totally inadequate for the steel metropolis in 1867.

With the expansion of the National school network, every effort was made to wean the children away from the private sector. The voluntary schools toned down their insistence on religious and moral indoctrination and superimposed the importance of basic literacy. By that time observers believed the Wesleyan schools were becoming more acceptable to the working classes and the popularity of the Nonconformist Sunday schools tends to support that impression.[2]

Whilst many employers looked to the public schools for their work-force—not only for their recognizable educational standards but for their inculcation of obedience, diligence, cleanliness and subservience—there were others such as the ironmaster Thomas Booth who stated quite categorically:

> I encourage private or small schools in preference to large public establishments where education is carried out on the Lancasterian plan for reasons which it would be superfluous in me here to state.[3]

The blanket condemnation of working-class private schools by nineteenth century educationalists who recognized formal public schooling as 'the only legitimate channel of education' has been accepted without question by many historians until recently.[4] Yet their sustained approval fed by 'currents of alternative culture' was an implicit rejection of formal public schooling.

Although the 1870 Education Act disregarded the private sector, many teachers charging less than 9d a week feared their eventual closure. In response to a female correspondent in December 1870 Robert Leader confirmed their fears:

> The class by whom she has been supported is the class that will be most affected by the Elementary Education Act. The schools will be in direct competition. These schools will have the benefit of rate or parliamentary aid. She will have only school pence—the competition will be most unequal. The Act 'indirectly' puts an end to such schools by making their existence an impossibility...Old fashioned dame schools will collapse if and where the boards enforce attendance.[5]

But their decline was far from immediate. The School Board's authority did not extend to private school provision. Its duty was simply to determine the extent of school deficiencies and ascertain the number of gaps to be filled. Where teachers of private schools refused to allow inspection or the examination of scholars, neglected to complete the essential forms or were merely overlooked, such schools were not considered to be offering efficient elementary education. When the forms were completed the Inspector of Returns accompanied by school board officials visited the schools to satisfy themselves they were satisfactory as to instruction and premises. If endorsed, and few could measure up to the standards of state-subsidized schools, they were placed on a list of schools recognized as efficient.

In the course of 1871 Inspector Fitzmaurice reported that 19 elementary adventure schools had 'given up'.[6] Out of 86 schools placed on Schedule D of the first statistical enquiry, only 18 were ratified as efficient, the rest were 'struck off'. Requests for compensation by destitute teachers were raised but their pleas went unheeded and clearly the Board sought their demise. 'Many of them are still being carried on and their pernicious influences can only be expected to cease when the compulsory powers of the Board are thoroughly exercised throughout the district.' However, the right of parents to select whichever school they chose—providing it was considered efficient—was recognized and the Board conceded that in some localities further accommodation would be met 'either by the establishment of new private adventure schools or other public elementary schools apart from the agency of the Board'.

Many local authorities admitted that their attempts to enforce school attendance were obstructed by working-class private schools who refused to keep adequate registers and allowed children to come and go as they pleased. In November 1874, Hull School Board enlisted Sheffield's support for a memorial to the Education Department requesting the compulsory inspection of private schools and a redefinition of the word 'efficient' so that interpretation was not left to the magistrate's discretion.[7] In the main, magistrates stoutly defended parental choice and some argued that dame schools were efficient for the class of children attending them. J.F. Moss declared that 'it was no easy matter to convince a bench of magistrates that a school conducted by a fairly educated person might be in many respects miserably inefficient—many deplorably incompetent. The temptation to buy "a rod and turn pedagogue" when other means of gaining a livelihood have failed should be effectively removed'.[8]

Despite the pressure of school attendance officers to break down popular support for the private schools by exploiting the confused legal position, driving the youngsters into the public domain by harassment, warnings, threats and fines, it had only limited success. In an article on Sims Croft in 1876 a journalist wrote:

> In another court was a small house in which an old lady was 'keeping school'. The schoolroom was a very small apartment which contained a very large number of children who were all in as clean a condition as was consistent with their having been washed once since birth. The cubic feet of air to each child could be about five or less and the amount of elementary education given to each was even smaller in proportion. But the old lady does not profess to give them education, she merely took them off their mothers' hands for a few hours of the day and crammed them into a fever breeding atmosphere from which if they escaped it would be a miracle.[9]

Such conditions of squalor and deprivation were totally unacceptable to the authorities but not dissimilar to those in the homes described in the series of reports on the Crofts in inner Sheffield.[10] Clearly, that school environment was irretrievably wretched yet HMI Kennedy regarded comparable schools as more appropriate for 'the many poor children of the "residuum" who could hardly be received with advantage among the decent and tidy scholars of the public elementary schools'.[11]

The outcome of communications between Hull and 200 other boards was a deputation of seven MPs including Mundella and Roebuck from Sheffield who met Lord Sandon in 1875. The compulsory inspection of private working-class schools was rejected on the grounds of cost-effectiveness. There was a fear that parental choice would be eroded and more livelihoods destroyed. However, a measure inserted into the 1876 Education Act undermined the existing establishments.

By introducing the term 'certified efficient school' the Act effectively determined the future of the working-class private schools. Moreover, no child under ten could be employed legally without a certificate of proficiency in the three Rs to Standard 4 level or evidence of at least 250 attendances annually over the past five years—commonly known as the dunce's certificate. Some time elapsed before the Act could be fully implemented but in 1877 it was reported that in addition to the 56 private schools already closed there were another 47 which could not be certified as efficient though they were affording 'fairly efficient instruction'. Eight schools with 882 children on roll were said to be eligible for a certificate of recognition.[12]

Nevertheless, differences of opinion between the Board's officials and the magistrates persisted over what the professionals described as 'efficient' and 'unacceptable'. The Sheffield-based HMI Sandford observed in 1879 'that a school may be very bad and not yet bad enough for a bench of magistrates to ignore its existence and treat the children who attend it as if they were attending no school at all'.[13] While some parents considered that private schools were 'more genteel' than the ones the common children went to, schools like the one in Sims Croft were gradually eliminated.

Outside the borough, headteachers faced with gross overcrowding were prepared for infants to be accommodated in neighbouring private schools. Before Hillsborough Board School was built, Benjamin Chatterton, head of Parson Cross, reluctantly agreed that Mrs Ashforth could accept little ones up to the age of eight in her dame school in the Wesleyan schoolroom at Wadsley Bridge. Seven years later, in 1885, Ecclesfield School Board recorded six private adventure schools in the district—two in Ecclesfield, three in Hillsborough (including Mrs Ashforth's) and one in Thorpe. The school attendance officer was very dubious about the parents' motives, believing that they were simply evading their responsibilities.[14]

The lifeblood of the working-class private school finally drained away with the abolition of school fees in 1891. They could no longer compete with free education in the well-resourced rate-aided schools. Park Infant and Park National Schools both received pupils from Mr Griffiths' long-standing school held in Talbot Street Methodist Chapel without complaint. The head of Carbrook National School was not so fortunate. Having accepted 12 boys from Miss Carden's school in 1891, 21 girls were admitted in 1892. He noted: 'The girls are exceedingly backward. All have been placed in the preparatory class which is now too big.'[15]

White's *Commercial Directory* for Sheffield (1889) listed 89 private schools in the borough. Nine years later only 36 appeared. Middle-class private schools, untouched by elementary school regulations, continued to flourish until the 1930s. They appealed to those parents prepared to pay between 2 shillings per week and 4 guineas per quarter for a 'better class' of school than the ordinary public schools. State intervention in the middle-class private school sector 'was rejected as an infringement of liberal freedom'.[16]

Although the loyalty of the working classes was gradually transferred to the more democratically controlled Board Schools,[17] school enrolment continued to outdistance school attendance. Even so, examination results in the school board era indicate that the gap between pupils able to read and write was narrowing and the proportion able to count and do basic arithmetic was reaching parity with those able to read and write.[18]

The basic index of literacy based on marriage signature marks reveals a dramatic increase over the period, particularly for young women. Due to the accessibility of state-subsidized schools for much of the country and the evident success of the compulsory schooling legislation, the Registrar General discontinued presenting the percentage of marks by registration district in 1885 and concentrated solely on counties. By 1887 only 91 in 1,000 males and 106 in 1,000 females were unable to sign the register. He spotlighted the acceleration of female literacy since the passing of the 1870 Education Act and pointed out that although males maintained their superiority in the manufacturing counties, 'in the agricultural counties the women are the better educated sex'. By 1890, the male literacy rate in the West Riding stood at 92.7 per cent and female literacy was 89.7 per cent compared with a national average of 92.8 per cent and 91.7 per cent respectively. At the turn of the century approximately 95 per cent could sign the marriage registers.[19]

With the evolution of an educational framework, the source of a system recognizably like the current one emerged. More public schools were built in the School Board era than the sum total of earlier centuries. The length of school life for the mass of the population doubled. Educational standards were raised significantly and the principles of professionalism set. Together with the rapid expansion of the public sector came a marked improvement in educational attainments. From the norm of Standard 2 in 1870 it leapt to Standard 5 by 1900 with an escalating proportion reaching Standards 6 and 7. By 1902 average attendances topped 65,000 from a base of 17,821 in 1872. Enrolments had reached 75,795. The Central School anticipated today's Secondary Technical College by moore than a century and evening schools penetrated the realms of further and higher education.

For thirty years, elected members promoted the education of an emerging city unhampered by extra municipal considerations. Elected 'to supply and maintain public elementary schools where the need existed' they fulfilled their brief with little pain and much admiration.[20] Costs were met in part by fees until 1891, partly by government grants, and the deficit was found by ratepayers. Critics of school boards, led by Sir John Gorst, Vice President of the Committee in Council for

Education, were jealous of their privilege to spend divorced from other civic responsibilities, particularly when they encroached into secondary and higher education. The need to integrate the voluntary sector into a unified system was also recognized.

Throughout the nineteenth century the uncoordinated voluntary schools had developed as social, religious and educational agencies alongside the poorer sections of the community. Divided as to the extent of state aid and intervention, they joined forces in pressing for the recognition of their service, not only over the recent past but over the centuries 'in training up the people in honesty and godly learning'. Significantly, by the end of the century there was a marked contraction of the authority of the Church in a territory once conceived to be within its legitimate charge.

What transpired from the ensuing parliamentary debates was the proposal for a single education administration in each district with powers to coordinate all educational provision. Difficulties did arise over the question of the smaller local authorities but Sheffield with a population of 409,070, having recently absorbed Norton and parts of Ecclesfield, was set to become a major educational influence.

The effect of Balfour's Education Act of 1902 was to replace the democratically elected School Board with the nominated City of Sheffield Education Committee. J.F. Moss, 'the Father of Education in Sheffield', was appointed Secretary of the Committee and little time was lost in unifying the City's educational provision. The unequal competition experienced by the voluntary schools was transmuted by the Act. It gave them equal status within the system and secured their existence. The broad aspects of child health and welfare were addressed, evening school courses were overhauled, and secondary education—so long perceived as a vehicle with a different ethos, an education for a distinctive walk in life—was critically examined.[21]

Now that pupil-teachers were no longer admitted under the age of 16, the narrow objective of only training elementary pupils for teaching in elementary schools was outdated and the Pupil Teachers' Centre was converted into a broadly based secondary school with a shift towards a more academic and literary curriculum. The acknowledged inadequacy of teacher training was met by establishing a municipal Day Training College for Teachers in Collegiate Crescent (1905).

The long-held assumption that elementary education alone was appropriate for the working classes was in the process of reinterpretation, yet the Board of Education remained convinced that

Figure 42. Sheffield Education Committee had to meet the needs of an ever-growing child population. A. Hammerton Street Council School, Darnall, was one of three new schools opened in 1904

B. Children and teachers assembled in the new school hall at Hummerton Street, 1904.

whatever the standard reached 'the education they received should be the kind of education likely to make them efficient members of the class to which they belong'.[22] Compulsory schooling had eradicated the tinge of charity and affirmed education as a birthright and an essential preparation for the work of life. But the schoolchild's prospects changed little. The odds against a child from a public elementary school obtaining free secondary education were still rated at 40 to one in 1914.[23]

The problem of children leaving school early was not resolved until the Education Act of 1918 fixed the school-leaving age at 14 and abolished all exemptions. In the years leading to the First World War it was still possible to take the Merit Certificate in Standard 6 at 12-plus and leave immediately afterwards. In fact many were withdrawn from school once the statutory age was reached and few went beyond 13. In 1911 it was estimated that 40 per cent of all children had left by that age and only 7 per cent in secondary schools stayed on to the age of 15.[24] Nevertheless, the boundaries of childhood had been pushed back, illiteracy virtually eliminated and full-time labour effectively checked. For the poorer sort impatient to leave, the transition from childhood to the adult world of work promised release from the 'tyranny of school', a measure of independence, a new status in life and a genuine opportunity to contribute to the family's survival.

Notes

1. Mitch, *Rise of Popular Literacy*, pp. 136-38; J. Burnett, *Destiny Obscure: Autobiographies of Childhood, Education and Family from the 1820s to the 1920s* (1982).

2. P. Gardner, 'Our Schools, Their Schools', *History of Education*, 20.3 (1991), p. 170n.

3. Quoted in D. Smith, *Conflict and Compromise 1830–1914* (1982), p. 128.

4. Gardner, *Lost Elementary Schools*, pp. 1-3.

5. *SI* (3 December 1870).

6. *SI* (15 December 1871).

7. Gardner, *Lost Elementary Schools*, p. 200; Bingham, *Sheffield School Board*, p. 65.

8. *SI* (7 October 1874).

9. *SI* (6 January 1876).

10. *SI* (4 January 1876; 13 January 1876; 20 January 1876; 3 February 1876).

11. Gardner, *Lost Elementary Schools*, p. 90.

12. *SI* (13 June 1877).

13. *SI* (23 August 1879).

14. Mercer, *School at Parson Crosse*, p. 68; D. Postles, 'The First Years of the Ecclesfield School Board 1882–88', Essays in Local History, SCL, p. 7.

15. Parsons, *Schools in an Urban Community*, p. 7.

16. Gardner, *Lost Elementary Schools*, p. 189.

17. Gardner, 'Our Schools, Their Schools', p. 168.

18. Bingham, *Sheffield School Board*, pp. 149f.

19. *Registrar General's Annual Reports* (1887, 1890); Mitch, *Rise of Popular Literacy*, p. xxvi.

20. See Bingham, *Sheffield School Board*, for a detailed account of the elected members.

21. Sadler, *Report on Secondary and Higher Education*.

22. Quoted in Van Der Eyken, *Education, the Child and Society*, p. 127.

23. Lowndes, *The Silent Social Revolution*, p. 113.

24. See Board of Education, 'Final Report of the Departmental Committee on Juvenile Education after the War' (1917) in Van Der Eyken, *Education, the Child and Society*, pp. 206-12.

Bibliography

Given the nature of elementary schooling before the onset of compulsory education there is no single source of material. The archives of the York Diocesan Registry at the Porthwick Institute of Historical Research provide invaluable evidence of the spread of schools and schoolmasters between 1560 and 1800. Also of prime importance are the Minutes and Reports of the Committee of Privy Council on Education from 1839 onwards and the parliamentary reports on Education and Child Employment in the Library of Sheffield University.

Local newspapers and directories are particularly informative on private schools, adult institutions, libraries and accounts of important meetings and conferences. Sheffield City Library has a comprehensive collection of local directories and newspapers together with annual reports of schools and societies, the Reports of the Charity Commissioners for 1828 and 1897 and a full set of Sheffield School Board Minutes. Preserved in the Sheffield Archives are countless manuscript records of Sunday Schools, Vestry minutes, parish registers, apprenticeship indentures and school log books containing more valuable information.

Primary Material

Newspapers: Selection of eighteenth and nineteenth century local newspapers in the Local Studies section of the Sheffield City Library.

Sheffield Public Advertiser	1760–1787
Sheffield Register	1787–1794
Sheffield Courant	1793–1797 1827–1834
Sheffield Iris	1794–1835
Sheffield Mercury	1807–1826
Sheffield Independent	1819 onwards
Sheffield Daily Telegraph	1855 onwards

Minutes of the Sheffield School Board 1870–1903.
Boys' Charity School Annual Reports.
Girls' Charity School Annual Reports.
Lancasterian School, Sheffield Annual Reports 1817–1824.
Sheffield District National Society Annual Reports 1815, 1820–1826.
Society for Bettering the Condition of the Poor, Sheffield Annual Reports 1815–1818.
Sheffield Sunday School Union Annual Reports 1813–.
Sheffield Wesleyan Methodist District School Society Minute Book 1838–1845.
Red Hill Wesleyan Sunday School Annual Reports 1818–.

Parliamentary Papers

Abstract of the Answers and Returns made Pursuant to Act 55 Geo III C42 for procuring Returns relative to the Expense and Maintenance of the Poor in England, 1818, vol. XIX.

Digest of Returns to Circulars from Committee of the State of Schools and means of Parochial Instruction, 1819, vol. IX pt II.

Abstract of the Answers and Returns made Pursuant to an Address of the House of Commons, 1835, vol. XLIII.

Report of Committee on the best means of Providing Useful Education for the Poorer Classes, 1837–1838, vol. VII.

Minutes and Reports of the Committee of Privy Council on Education, 1839–1872.

Report of the Royal Commission on the State of Education in England (Newcastle Report), 1861, 5, vol. XXI.

Report of the Schools' Inquiry Commission (Taunton Report), 1868, 9, vol. XXVIII pt VIII.

Report of the Royal Commission on the Elementary Education Acts (Cross Report), 1887, 2, vol. XXIX.

First Report of Commissioners for Inquiring into the Employment and Conditions of Children in Mines, 1842, vols. XV, XVI.

Second Report of Commissioners for Inquiring into the Employment and Condition of Children in Trades and Manufactures, 1843, vols. XIII, XIV.

Fourth Report, Children's Employment Commission, 1865, vol. XX.

Census of Great Britain: Reports and Tables on Education in England and Wales (Education Census 1851), 1852–53, vol. XC.

Reports of Commission concerning Charities: 18th Report, 1828, vol. XX *19th Report*, 1828, vol. XI, *21st Report*, 1829, vol. VIII.

Report of Commission Concerning Charities
    City of Sheffield, 1897, vol. LXVII pt III.
    Yorkshire, West Riding, 1897, vol. LXVII pt III.

Secondary Material

Local History—General

Armytage, W.H.G., *A.J. Mundella: The Liberal Background to the Labour Movement* (London, 1951).

Bell, A.B., *Peeps into the Past* (Sheffield, 1909).

Binfield, J.C. et al. (eds.), *The History of the City of Sheffield 1843–1993* (Sheffield, 1993).

Caulton, T.J. (ed.), *Children of the Industrial Revolution in Sheffield* (Sheffield, 1985).

Eastwood, J., *History of Ecclesfield* (London, 1862).

Evinson, D., *The Lord's House: A History of Sheffield's Roman Catholic Buildings 1570–1990* (Sheffield, 1991).

Flett, J., *The Story of the Workhouse and the Hospital at Nether Edge* (Sheffield, 1984).

Freemantle, W.T., *Bibliography of Sheffield and Vicinity* (Sheffield, 1911).

Gatty, A., *A Life at One Living* (London, 1884).

Graham, J.T., *History of Wesleyan Methodism in Sheffield Park* (Sheffield, 1914).

Hadfield, C., *A History of St Marie's Mission and Church, Norfolk Row* (Sheffield, 1889).

Harrison, J., *Survey of the Manor of Sheffield 1637* (Worksop, 1908).

Hawksworth, G.F.B., *The Central Congregational Church in Sheffield* (Sheffield, 1971).

Hey, D.G., *The Village of Ecclesfield* (Huddersfield, 1967).

—*The Rural Metalworkers of the Sheffield Region* (Leicester, 1972).

—'Sheffield on the Eve of the Industrial Revolution', *Transactions of the Hunter Archaeological Society* 14 (1987).

—'The Pattern of Nonconformity in South Yorkshire 1660–1851', *Northern History* 8 (1973).

Holland, C.C., *Inquiry into the Moral, Social and Intellectual Condition of the Industrial Classes* (Sheffield, 1839).

—*Vital Statistics of Sheffield* (Sheffield, 1843).

Hunter, J., *Hallamshire: History and Topography of the Parish of Sheffield* (ed. A. Gatty; London, 1875).

Kilham, H., *Memoirs of Hannah Kilham* (London, 1837).

Leader, J.D., *Records of the Burgery of Sheffield* (Sheffield, 1897).

Leader, R.E., *Sheffield in the Eighteenth Century* (Sheffield, 1901).

—*History of the Company of Cutlers in Hallamshire* (Sheffield, 1905/6).

Linton, D.L., (ed.), *Sheffield and its Region: A Scientific and Historical Survey* (Sheffield, 1956).

Lloyd, G.I.H., *The Cutler Trades: An Historical Essay in the Economics of Small Scale Production* (London, 1913).

Longden, H., *The Life of Henry Longden* (Sheffield, 1813).

Manning, J.E., *History of Upper Chapel* (Sheffield, 1900).

Odom, W., *Fifty Years of Sheffield Church Life 1866–1916* (London, 1917).

—*Hallamshire Worthies: Characteristics and Work of Notable Sheffield Men and Women* (Sheffield, 1926).

Ollard, S.L., and P.C. Walker, 'Archbishop Herring's Visitation Returns 1743', *Yorkshire Archaeological Society* Vols. 71, 72, 75 (1928–1931).

Pawson and Brailsford, *Illustrated Guide to Sheffield and Neighbourhood* (Sheffield, 1862; reprint, 1971).

Pollard, S., *A History of Labour in Sheffield* (Liverpool, 1959).

Pollard S., and C. Holmes, *Essays in the Economic and Social History of South Yorkshire* (Barnsley S.Y.C.C., 1976).

Postles, D., 'An Early Modern Town; Sheffield in the Sixteenth Century', *Transactions of the Hunter Archaeological Society* 12 (1983).

Pybus, S., *'Damned Bad Place, Sheffield': An Anthology of Writing about Sheffield through the Ages* (Sheffield, 1994).

Sheffield City Libraries, *The City Libraries of Sheffield 1856–1956* (Sheffield, 1956).

Transactions of the National Association for the Promotion of Social Sciences (1865).

Thomas, A., *The History of the Parishes and Churches in the Deanery of Handsworth* (Sheffield, 1932).

Walton, M., *Sheffield: Its Story and its Achievements* (Sheffield, 1968).

Wickham, E.R., *Church and People in an Industrial City* (Lutterworth, 1957).

Local History—Educational

Austen, T., 'Notes on Milk Street Academy and its Founder', *Transactions of the Hunter Archaeological Society* 7 (1957).

Bernard, T., *Account of Free School for Boys, Sheffield* (London, 1812).

Bingham, J.H., *Education under the Local Authority in Sheffield: The Sheffield School Board* (Sheffield, 1949).

Board, M.J., 'A History of the Private Adventure Schools in Sheffield' (MA Sheffield, 1959).

Bournat, B., 'The History of Tapton Mount, Broomhill, Sheffield 1879–1947' (MEd Sheffield, 1982/3).

Chapman, A.H., *The Story of a Modern University: A History of the University of Sheffield* (Oxford, 1955).

Cooper, D., 'A History of Education in the Civil Parish of Ecclesfield 1830–1970' (MA Sheffield, 1972).

Dunn, M.P., *For the Love of Children* (Sheffield, 1989).

Eltringham, G.J., 'Lancasterian Schools in Sheffield', *Transactions of the Hunter Archaeological Society* 5 (1943).

Goodwin, E., *Address to Parents, Masters and Poor Children relative to Sunday Schools* (Sheffield, 1786).

—*The Poor Girls' Primer: For the Use of the Charity School in Sheffield* (Sheffield, 1787).

Hicks, W.M., *Local Colleges and Higher Education for the People* (Sheffield, 1886).

Innocent and Brown, *Illustrations of Public Elementary Schools* (Sheffield, 1874).

Moore Smith, G.C., 'The Sheffield Grammar School', *Transactions of the Hunter Archaeological Society* 4 (1937).

—*The Story of the People's College Sheffield 1842–1878* (Sheffield, 1912).

Mercer, V.M., 'The Contrasting Patterns of School Provision in three South Yorkshire Parishes—Ecclesfield, Rotherham and Sheffield 1480–1833' (MA Sheffield, 1978).

—*The School at Parson Crosse 1630–1980* (Sheffield, 1980).

—'William Ronksley (1650–1724) Schoolmaster, Writer and Philanthropist', *Transactions of the Hunter Archaeological Society* 14 (1987).

—'The Hollis Educational Trust: A Nonconformist Contribution to Elementary Education', *Transactions of the Hunter Archaeological Society* 12 (1983).

Noblett, W.A., 'Printing and the Book Trade in Sheffield in the latter half of the Eighteenth Century' (MA 1974, Sheffield).

Parsons, C., *Schools in an Urban Community: A Study of Carbrook 1870–1965* (London, 1978).

Sadler, M.E., *Report on Secondary and Higher Education* (Sheffield Education Committee, 1903).

Salt, J., 'The Sheffield Hall of Science', *The Vocational Aspects of Secondary and Further Education* (1972).

—'Isaac Ironside 1808–1870: The Motivation of a Radical Educationist', *British Journal of Educational Studies* XIX (1971).

—'Early Sheffield Sunday Schools and their Educational Importance', *Transactions of the Hunter Archaeological Society* 9 (1969).

Wallis, P.J., 'Thomas Smith', *Transactions of the Hunter Archaeological Society* 7 (1957).

Wigfull, J.R., 'An Early Sheffield School', *Transactions of the Hunter Archaeological Society* 3 (1929).

—'Sheffield Grammar School', *Transactions of the Hunter Archaeological Society* 4 (1937).

Other Works

Allen, W.O.B., and E. McClure, *Two Hundred Years: The History of the Society for Promoting Christian Knowledge 1698–1898* (London, 1898).

Armytage, W.H.G., *Four Hundred Years of English Education* (Cambridge, 1964).

Beales, A.C.F., *Education under Penalty* (London: U.L.P., 1963).

Bernard, T., *Education of the Poor* (London, 1809).

Birchenough, C., *History of Elementary Education 1800–1920* (Oxford, 1920).

Bradford Corporation, *Education in Bradford since 1870* (Bradford, 1970).

Burnett, J., *Destiny Obscure: Autobiographies of Childhood, Education and Family from the 1820s to the 1920s* (Harmondsworth, 1984).

—*Useful Toil: Autobiographies of Working People from the 1820s to the 1920s* (Harmondsworth, 1984).

Brennan, E.J.T. (ed.), *Education for National Efficiency: The Contribution of Sidney and Beatrice Webb* (London, 1975).

Clarke Lowther, W.E., *A History of S.P.C.K.* (London, 1959).

Curtis, S.J., *History of Education in Great Britain* (London, 1950).

Dickens, A.G., *The English Reformation* (London, 1967).

Dunlop, O.J., and R.D. Denman, *English Apprenticeship and Child Labour* (London, 1912).

Eaglesham, E., *The Foundations of Twentieth Century Education* (London, 1967).

Gardner, P., *The Lost Elementary Schools of Victorian England* (Beckenham, 1984).

—' "Our Schools: Their Schools": The case of Eliza Duckworth and John Stevenson', *History of Education* 20.3 (1991).

Gordon, P., *The Victorian School Manager* (London, 1974).

Gosden, P.H., and P.R. Sharp, *The Development of an Education Service: The West Riding* (Oxford, 1978).

Harrison, J.F.C., *Learning and Living 1790–1960: A Study in the History of the English Adult Education Movement* (London, 1961).

Harvey Darton, F.J., *Children's Books in England* (Cambridge, 1958).

Hill, C., *Society and Puritanism in Pre-Revolutionary England* (Panther, 1969).

—*Reformation to Industrial Revolution* (Harmondsworth 1969).

Hoole, C., *A New Discovery of the Old Art of Teaching School* (Scholar Press reprint 1973).

Horn, P., *The Victorian Country Child* (Gloucester, 1985).

—*The Victorian and Edwardian Schoolchild* (Gloucester, 1989).

Hughes-Hallet, P. (ed.), *Childhood* (London: Collins, 1988).

Hurt, J., *Elementary Schooling and the Working Classes 1860–1918* (London, 1979).

Johnson, M., *Derbyshire Village Schools in the Nineteenth Century* (Newton Abbot, 1970).

Jones, M.G., *The Charity School Movement* (Cambridge 1938).

Jordan, W.K., *Charities of Rural England* (London 1961).

Laqueur, T.W., *Religion and Respectability: Sunday Schools and Working Class Culture 1780–1850* (Yale, 1976).

Lawson, J., *Medieval Education and the Reformation* (London, 1967).

Lawson, J., and H. Silver, *A Social History of Education in England* (London, 1973).

Lowndes, G.A.N., *The Silent Social Revolution* (Oxford, 1937).

Maclure, J.S., *Educational Documents: England and Wales 1816–1963* (London, 1965).

McCann, P. (ed.), *Popular Education and Socialization in the Nineteenth Century* (London, 1977).

Marchant, R.A., *Puritans and the Church Courts in the Diocese of York 1560–1642* (London, 1960).

Matthews, H.F., *Methodism and the Education of the People 1791–1851* (London, 1949)

Mitch, D.F., *The Rise of Popular Literacy in Victorian England* (Philadelphia, 1992).

Norman, E.R., *Church and Society in England 1770–1970* (Oxford 1976).

Owen, D., *English Philanthropy 1660–1960* (London, 1969).

Pinchbeck, I., and M. Hewitt, *Children in English Society from Tudor Times to the Eighteenth Century* (London, 1969).

Purvis, J.S., *Educational Records* (York, 1959).

Read, D., *Press and People 1790–1850* (London, 1961).

Roach, J., *Secondary Education in England 1870–1902* (London, 1991).

Ronksley, W., *The Child's Weeks-work* (London, 1712).

Sanderson, M., 'Literacy and Social Mobility in the Industrial Revolution in England', *Past and Present* 56 (1972).

—*Education, Economic Change and Society in England 1780–1870* (London, 1983).

Sangster, P., *Pity my Simplicity: The Evangelical Revival and the Religious Education of Children 1738–1800* (London, 1963).

Seaborne, M., *The English School; Its Architecture and Organization 1370–1870* (London, 1971).

Silver, H., *The Concept of Popular Education: A study of ideas and social movements in the early nineteenth century* (London, 1965).

Simon, J., *Education and Society in Tudor England* (Cambridge, 1966).

—'Was there a Charity School Movement?', in B. Simon (ed.), *Education in Leicestershire 1540–1940* (Leicester, 1968).

—*The Social Origins of English Education* (London, 1970).

Stephens, W.B., *Education, Literacy and Society: The geography of diversity in provincial England 1830–1870* (Manchester, 1987).

Sturt, M., *The Education of the People* (London, 1967).

Sylvester, D.W., *Educational Documents 800–1816* (London, 1970).

Thompson, E.P., *The Making of the English Working Class* (Harmondsworth, 1968).

Van Der Eyken, W. (ed.), *Education, The Child and Society: A Documentary History 1900–1973* (Harmondsworth, 1973).

Walvin, J., *A Child's World: A Social History of English Childhood 1800–1914* (Harmondsworth, 1982).

Wardle, D., *English Popular Education 1780–1970* (Cambridge, 1970).

—*Education and Society in Nineteenth Century Nottingham* (Cambridge, 1971).

Watson, F., *The English Grammar Schools to 1660* (Cambridge, 1908).

Wearmouth, R.F., *Methodism and the Working Class Movements in England 1800–1850* (Epworth, 1937).

West, E.G., *Education and the State* (London, 1970).

—*Education and the Industrial Revolution* (London, 1975).

Whitbread, N., *The Evolution of the Nursery Infant School* (London, 1972).

Index